Urban Women: Life, Love, and Work in the Medieval Low Countries

Urban Women

Life, Love, and Work
in the Medieval Low Countries

Edited by
Jelle Haemers, Andrea Bardyn,
and Chanelle Delameillieure

LEUVEN UNIVERSITY PRESS

English translation copyright © 2025 by Leuven University Press / Universitaire Pers Leuven / Presses Universitaires de Louvain. Minderbroedersstraat 4, B-3000 Leuven (Belgium).

First published in 2019 as *Wijvenwereld: Vrouwen in de middeleeuwse stad* by Uitgeverij Vrijdag, Antwerp (Belgium).

All rights reserved. Except in those cases expressly determined by law, no part of this publication may be multiplied, saved in an automated datafile or made public in any way whatsoever without the express prior written consent of the publishers. All TDM rights (Text and Data Mining) are reserved.

ISBN 978 94 6270 449 7 (Paperback)
e-ISBN 978 94 6166 636 9 (ePDF)
e-ISBN 978 94 6166 637 6 (ePUB)
https://doi.org/10.11116/9789461666369
D/2025/1869/10
NUR: 693
Cover design: Daniel Benneworth-Gray
Cover illustration: Ovide, *Héroïdes*, traduction d'Octavien de Saint-Gelais. Français 875, f. 5v. Bibliothèque nationale de France
Lay-out: Crius Group

Contents

Acknowledgements	7
Introduction. A different history of the medieval city	9
Chapter 1. From girlhood to widowhood: On the rights of women and children *Andrea Bardyn & Jelle Haemers*	23
Chapter 2. Women and marriage: Choice of partner, matrimonial conflicts, and relations *Chanelle Delameillieure*	49
Chapter 3. Industrious women and their life in business *Andrea Bardyn*	73
Chapter 4. Pious women: Beguines and their virtuous lives together *Kim Overlaet*	97
Chapter 5. Working women: women's professional activities in and outside craft guilds *Nena Vandeweerdt & Jelle Haemers*	121
Chapter 6. "Bad women": Violence, crime, and rebellion *Jelle Haemers*	147
Chapter 7. Eros and women: Sexuality, consent, and prostitution *Chanelle Delameillieure & Jelle Haemers*	175
Conclusions. Of "wise women" and "witless men"	205
Primary sources	211
Literature	213
About the authors	231

Acknowledgements

In the Middle Ages, just as today, authors penned prologues and epilogues explaining the reasons for writing a work, or thanking those who had helped produce it. In the prologue to her major work *The City of Ladies* (1404-5), the French author Christine de Pizan tells how one fine evening, while whiling away time in her study, her eyes fell upon a little book by a famous author which roundly criticized women. This scorn spurred her to take up her pen to rectify these unfair comments. For our part – without claiming that the lack of any solid book on the history of women in the library at Leuven University led us to a similar riposte – we have shared Christine's fervour. Admittedly, famous authors have recognized the fascinating history of the women of the southern Low Countries, but we have felt the need to make up for a gap encountered – all too frequently – when researching the lives of the women of yesteryear. For there is no major work on recent discoveries relating to the presence of women in the Middle Ages in general and to their social position in Brabant towns in particular. That is why we, too, have taken up our pens to write our own *City of Ladies*. Though less querulous than Christine de Pizan, we are no less enthusiastic.

Many individuals have supported our enduring enthusiasm and have helped us bring this wonderful project to life. We first thank our publishing house, Leuven University Press, in the persons of Veerle De Laet and Nienke Roelants, for having provided welcome support in publishing the book and in settling many practical questions inherent to such a venture. Iason Jongepier shared his knowledge for compiling the maps. Minne De Boodt, Dominique Delameillieure, and Benjamin Goyvaerts read the manuscript and provided many invaluable comments. We thank various colleagues who responded to our pestering and who, by sharing their scholarship, have lit our way. Our particular thanks go to Brigitte Meijns, Paul Trio, Ben Eersels, Jirki Thibaut, Valerie Vrancken, Ruth Lintermans, Luc De Grauwe, Monique Van Melkebeek, and Walter Prevenier. We are also most grateful to many history students at KU Leuven for having listened with interest to our approach, as well as for the research some of them have conducted on topics relating to the history of women. Their critical questioning and own discoveries have acted as a powerful stimulus in writing this book. At the "Felixarchief" in Antwerp and at the Leuven City Archives, the volunteers who contributed to the "Itinera Nova" project have done a great deal of work making available various sources relating to our study. Our friends, acquaintances, and family have of course been indispensably important in producing this work, probably far more than they realize. We are happy to dedicate it to them.

A final word on the origins of this book: in 2019, we published an overview (in Dutch) of the history of women in late medieval Brabant, entitled *Wijvenwereld. Vrouwen in de middeleeuwse stad* (Vrijdag/Pelckmans). A reworked and supplemented version of this book was published in 2022 as *La femme dans la cité au Moyen Âge* (Racine). Both books aimed to inform the wider public about this fascinating subject. They contained as few footnotes as possible; only quotations or references to primary sources were given a footnote. A list of appropriate literature was only included in the bibliography and arranged by chapter. In this English version, we have kept it that way. The book you are reading now is the translation of the French, reworked version. We are very grateful to Adrian Morfee for translating it; he did a wonderful job. We wanted to publish this book in English to give scholars worldwide an overview of the research that has been done on the history of women in the medieval Low Countries. We hope it will inspire others to continue this research!

The editors, Leuven-Ghent-Antwerp, November 2024

INTRODUCTION

A different history of the medieval city

> People's excellence or inferiority resides in neither their loftiness nor their sex, but in the perfection of their conduct and virtues.
> —Christine de Pizan, 1405.[1]

"So justice has been done", Liesbet must have thought on winning her lawsuit against her husband, Thomas, on Saint Sylvester's Day, 1490, in Leuven. Thomas had been refusing to pay the rent for their house. Liesbet had explained to the judges that for some time her husband had not been living with her but cohabiting "adulterously" with another woman.[2] If she had accused Thomas of living an "indecent life", it was not so much because he was living with another woman, as because he was refusing to fulfil his financial obligations as a husband. In justification, Thomas referred to Liesbet's status as a trader. The law authorized female traders (*coopwijf*, as Liesbet would have called herself) to conduct their business without their husband's involvement, unlike other married women. Liesbet thus had her own income and, Thomas argued, was perfectly capable of paying rent. The aldermen's court did not agree with the arguments advanced by the unfaithful Thomas, however, and obliged him to pay the rent on the spot. Even if the couple were no longer living together, Liesbet and Thomas were still married, and that came with obligations. Additionally, the aldermen explicitly stated that their ruling was issued as an example, to lay down a line of conduct for all inhabitants in Leuven, for they deemed it unacceptable that husbands treat their wives thus. They did not demand that Thomas return to live with his legitimate wife, though that was not what Liesbet had requested, either. She just wanted her husband to pay the rent, and in mentioning Thomas's adultery, she increases her chances for obtaining a favourable verdict.

The judgment issued by the Leuven aldermen's court is remarkable, for it shatters a string of stereotypes about how men and women lived in medieval towns. The Middle Ages are often depicted as a dark time when women had no rights whatsoever. Anyone who so wishes may unearth a wealth of misogynistic examples in medieval literature confirming this cliché. Thus, in the early fourteenth century, the Antwerp town clerk Jan van Boendale stated that "woman is naturally unreliable, stingy, and grasping".[3] His tirade describes them as childish, capricious, and underdeveloped. As confirmed by a few additional texts portraying the women of yesteryear in a similarly unflattering light, it used to be taken for granted that all Jan van Boendale's contemporaries thought as he did. Admittedly, this period of history saw many misogynistic statements. Even Erasmus, the sixteenth-century humanist and "hero of the Renaissance", hewed to a disparaging attitude towards women. While his ideas about the Church's role in society were revolutionary, they were far less so concerning relations between men and women: his opinion was, for instance, that a husband was necessary to control a woman's emotions. It is hardly surprising then that a dark image has often been associated with the Middle Ages, together with a bleak fate for women. In our contemporary popular culture, medieval society is therefore thought of as a violent world dominated by kings, knights, and the clergy, a world in which women played scarcely any role.

Of course, other – more positive – ideas about women also circulated during the Middle Ages, and Jan van Boendale's contemporaries did not hesitate to criticize his writings. One well-known example is the work of Christine de Pizan. This Venetian-born writer published influential works at the fourteenth-century French court about the role of women in the society of her period. In the prologue to her major work – *The City of Ladies*, dating from 1404-5 – Christine tells how one fine evening, while whiling away the time in her study, her eye fell upon a little book in which a famous author roundly criticized women. This scorn spurred her to take up her pen to rectify these unfair comments. To prove that this author was wrong, she fervently portrayed the virtues of women through history, drawing on historical and mythological examples. Christine also explained that while women may be physically weaker than their male counterparts, this condition makes them more likely to privilege peace over war. The epigraph for this introduction reflects this idea: the value of people's acts and thoughts are determined not by their sex, but by their virtues. In one passage, Christine even advises women to trust especially their own knowledge of female nature rather than be swayed by male authors' ignorant and wrongheaded pontifications. These ideas led her to write her works, which she described as "new things born of a woman's mind", adding "new things are pleasing".[4] Yet it must be acknowledged that Christine de Pizan did not

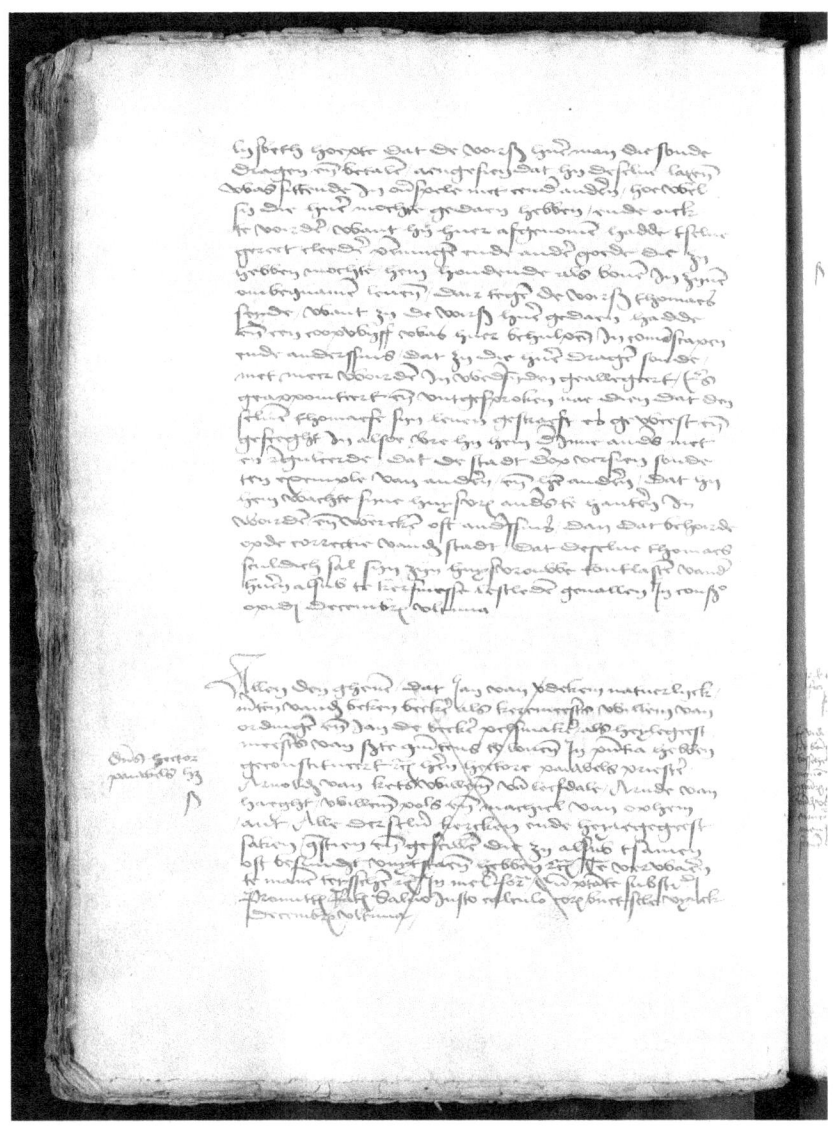

Image of the aldermen's register of Leuven with (at the top of the page) the act in which the aldermen gave their judgement on the case between Liesbet and Thomas, on New Year's Eve 1490 (City Archives Leuven, n° 7384, 270v). https://www.itineranova.be/in/SAL7384/270V%C2%B0/folio

dream up these ideas from scratch. While women only enjoyed limited rights and restricted freedom of movement, it does not mean they lived passively within the walls of their medieval households. Women were more active in public life than we tend to think, as clearly illustrated by the example of Liesbet in Leuven. In this case, Liesbet comes across as an independent woman running a business and successfully defending her rights. Admittedly, the judicial world was a man's world – women having no administrative power – but the judges dispensing justice did not necessarily take decisions hostile to women. Quite the contrary, in fact.

Over the course of the fifteenth century – the period at the heart of this book – writers clashed over the role of women in society. One of the best-known and most popular works of the Middle Ages, the *Roman de la Rose*, is very negative about women. This fourteenth-century literary work reduced them to "roses to be plucked", whose prime function was thus as sexual playthings for men. One of the main authors of this work, Jean de Meung, had compiled many erotic stories for this misogynistic work intended to educate and entertain. It triggered sharp reactions. The French cleric Martin Le Franc, for instance, gave Jean de Meung the nickname *Malebouche* (Evilmouth) in his book *Le Champion des Dames* in which, like Christine de Pizan or like Giovanni Boccaccio in *De claris mulieribus*, Le Franc paid tribute to women's many qualities. He stated that "they surpass men in terms of human knowledge".[5] A miniature illustrating his work shows Malebouche's army besieging a castle inhabited by various women. Writers at the Burgundian court likewise regularly extolled the qualities of women of importance. Duchess Mary of Burgundy, for example, was praised on several occasions for her virtue and the gentleness with which she sought to restore peace in her lands. According to the chronicler Jean Molinet, her daughter Margaret was "clever in science and virtue, gracious and humble, wise as one in a thousand".[6] These authors were of course favourably disposed to their patrons irrespective of sex, but many of the merits attributed to these ladies stemmed, to their mind, from women's loving and benevolent character. The fifteenth century was thus the scene of heated debate about the role and nature of women.

In this book we set out to study these questions and will therefore follow the path taken by Christine de Pizan. Rather than grounding our arguments in literary and intellectual works, written and read mainly by the social elite, we will be drawing on writings about daily life so as to bring out the social role played by medieval women. As yet there is no concise work on recent discoveries about women in the Middle Ages and their social role in towns in the Low Countries. Though less combative than Christine de Pizan, we are just as enthusiastic, and so have decided to write our own *City of Ladies*. By analogy, we have called this book *Urban Women*, given that its protagonists are townswomen. Thus we shall consider, for instance, the exceptional case of Liesbet of Leuven in order to find out to what extent the late medieval Low Countries were a "women's world"? What opportunities were available to them, and how did they seize them? We will look at women's social role in various activities: as wives, traders, businesswomen, craftswomen, benevolent mothers, beguines, investors, and brothelkeepers, without forgetting the odd criminal and rioter. For too long, historians have focused exclusively on the extraordinary lives of exceptional women such as Joan of Arc or Duchess Mary of Burgundy. The heroines in this book played no role on the battlefields or at court. They worked in the shadows, trying to make the best of their lives. Yet their stories can tell us more about medieval society than the exceptional lives of their illustrious contemporaries. Still, we will not wholly neglect the lives of "famous" women. We shall thus consider the extent to which the ideas advanced by the famous Antwerp writer Anna Bijns or by Christine de Pizan about how men and women should behave corresponded to reality. In this book we will seek to answer these questions by looking at the lives of women such as Liesbet of Leuven, that is, ordinary women with no blue blood running through their veins.

Of course, we are not the first to write a book about women of the past. In the wake of women obtaining the right to vote across Western Europe after the world wars, and as a corollary of their growing presence in universities, there has been burgeoning interest in women's history. Historians did not simply study the women of the past, but also observed how ideas about masculinity and femininity fashioned relationships and power relations between the sexes within a society. In 1988, for example, Georges Duby published his bestselling *Mâle Moyen Âge*, which analyzed the relationship between men and women in the twelfth century in particular. Concluding his study, Duby notes that the Middle Ages were primarily "a masculine era": "The Middle Ages were resolutely male. All the opinions that reach and inform me were held by men, convinced of the superiority of their sex." Yet Duby adds that historians must do everything in their power to discover the "hidden part, the feminine" and, like many others, went on to put this recommendation into practice.[7]

Since the 1970s – an age in which women's rights increased in the medieval West – historians have been catching up, however. Today, there is even an *Oxford handbook of women and gender in medieval Europe* available to anyone studying the field. Its editors, Judith Bennett and Ruth Karras, explain the lack of attention to women in the historical literature as follows. Some medieval people considered "man" the human standard and "women" peculiarly capable both of extraordinary good, as with the Virgin Mary, and of evil, as exemplified by Eve.[8] For many centuries after the close of the Middle Ages, historians echoed these assumptions, characterizing women as both revered (ladies on pedestals) and maligned (witches at the stake). But no longer, Bennett and Karras argue. Since the 1970s, historians of medieval women have written more often about diversity and opportunity than pedestals or stakes, and since the 1990s, women historians have unpacked the many gendered languages of medieval Europe. We can actually refer to this handbook for a good introduction to the historiography of women in medieval Europe, an introduction that shows that the library on medieval women is becoming well stocked.

Nevertheless, "ordinary women" have been largely invisible in many of these publications focusing mainly on the period until around 1350, drawing on texts produced by the social elite. Yet "ordinary women" are just as absent in works by other well-known medievalists who have examined subsequent centuries. In *Hommes et femmes du Moyen Âge*, edited by Jacques Le Goff, for example, the authors set out to discover the "great figures of the Middle Ages".[9] Even so, only 17 on the impressive list of 105 people discussed are women. Le Goff acknowledges this underrepresentation and explains that looking at famous people from this period of history automatically results in a male group. Turning to works in English, Eileen Power's bestseller *Medieval People* describes in colourful detail the lives of six men and women who were representative of their age, though only two are women. Nevertheless, Power's efforts to turn away from queens, female saints, and exceptional figures such as Joan of Arc and to focus instead on "ordinary" women echoed widely. For the Low Countries, for instance, Martha Howell's work has been extremely influential. A glimpse at the bibliography of our book shows the extent of our debt to her, for in addition to boosting the gender history of this region, her work focuses on medieval wives, single women who made their own living, and women from the street.

In this book, we too seek out the "ordinary" women comprising the majority of the population. We leave the palaces and churches behind to visit the common houses of the medieval town instead. We discover individuals who, despite their less prestigious destiny, nevertheless played an active part in daily life in late medieval society. Given that ordinary women also took up their pens in the fourteenth and fifteenth centuries, it is possible to write a "female Middle Ages" in which we hear them speak in their own name. In the following chapters, we present hitherto unknown historical elements. Accordingly, you will read the results of our fascinating research into these anonymous women perpetually excluded from history books, yet who nevertheless shaped history. We will examine their social involvement and look at how their lives differed from those of their male contemporaries. We will be hearing from women like Liesbet with strong opinions, from women selling their products on the market, squabbling spouses, businesswomen undertaking negotiations, mothers dictating their will, beguines writing love letters, fishwives hurling insults, prostitutes hawking their services, and so on.

Not all female voices managed to get an equal hearing. While Liesbet of Leuven clearly knew how to approach the aldermen's court to claim her rights, many did not follow this path. Medieval society was characterized by great social inequality, which also occurred in legal matters. Just as for men, rights were not distributed equally. This observation leads to an important nuance: many types of women lived in towns, and some of them had more opportunities than their fellow townswomen. In principle, all citizens in a given town were equal, but prosperity, reputation, and origin determined their social rank. Some possessed privileges and thus had rights different to those of their neighbours. Craftswomen did not have the same privileges as those accorded to well-born women, yet enjoyed greater social protection than women not belonging to a craft guild. The medieval streets were also home to many destitute people. It is hard, though, to write their history, one of rural migrants and poor families affected by catastrophe or by temporary or permanent unemployment, and the like. Given that they were illiterate, there are few documents telling us about their existence. Presumably women belonging to these groups – certainly in a society in which they had fewer rights than they do today – found it harder to maintain themselves than privileged women did. Towns were an unequal place, but during the period in question this situation was of course equally true of men and of women.

General map of the Low Countries at the end of the Middle Ages (c. Iason Jongepier, GIStorical Antwerp). This book focuses on the Duchy of Brabant, which was under the sovereignty of the Dukes of Brabant, together with the Duchy of Limburg. It also included Mechelen, an independent lordship embedded in the heart of Brabant. In 1430, Brabant passed into the hands of the Dukes of Burgundy, as had the counties of Flanders, Artois and Namur. Hainaut, Holland and Zeeland soon followed.

Focus of this book

This book mainly describes the situation of middling social groups, that is, those between the elite and the lower strata of society. They belonged neither to the upper echelons of society (the nobility, the court elite, and the clergy), nor to the needier circles (such as the poor and beggars). These middling groups lived, quite literally, amidst the others, for towns were a melting pot. On the edge of society lived people who did not belong to the trade guilds, along with others who had fallen on hard times or into crime. The women mentioned in this book do not come from these groups, except perhaps a few criminals who ran into trouble with the courts and a few women in unfavourable circumstances (due to sickness or being unable to work, etc.). Generally, "our" middling women enjoyed relative wealth and prestige. They were also educated and therefore literate. For historians these attributes are invaluable, for it means they produced texts, hence sources enabling us to piece together their life stories.

A significant number of the sources used in this book have rarely been consulted over recent decades. That is another reason why this history of medieval women differs from those written previously. Traditionally, scholarship on medieval heroines has been primarily based on literary stories emphasizing and even reinforcing their particular characteristics. Some of these texts – often produced by men with ideas similar to Jan van Boendale's – deliberately portray women in a bad light and, as a result, are of little use for reconstructing how women lived. Additionally, various authors, such as monks, paid very little attention to working townswomen. And the same is true of court chroniclers. That is why we have based our book on unexplored sources, mainly texts written by women themselves or else documents that they had drawn up: deeds of sale, wills, court statements, witness reports, and a host of other papers relating to daily life. These sources shed light on various facets of their life that are largely absent in traditional sources. Indeed, in cases when a woman was holding the pen or getting a clerk to draw up a legal document, it was necessarily a matter of "ordinary affairs" of very little interest to previous generations of historians. In this book, these sources provide the underpinnings for a new and original approach.

The documents making up our study date mainly from the period between 1350 and 1550, with an emphasis on the fifteenth century. This period is usually referred to as the "Late Middle Ages", renowned as one of the darkest times when plague, famine, and war decimated the population. In the mid-fourteenth century, medieval Europe was in the grips of the Black Death, and hygiene in towns also left much to be desired. Still, the image of large sections of the population regularly dying from recurrent waves of plague, famine, and privation is a cliché wholly at odds with reality. While war and economic crises sometimes consumed Europe, the fifteenth century in particular was a period of relative stability. Earlier centuries are harder to study for few personal documents produced by women have been preserved. The growing complexity of society and increasing use of writing prompted contemporaries to set down ever more of their agreements on paper. Additionally, to better control their citizens, administrations set about improving how they monitored sanctions against them. Moreover, citizens themselves demanded that writing be used more and more systematically to record their rights, given that administrations tended to flout them.

It was in towns, especially, that women took up their pens. Leaving aside local differences, urban law provided women with greater scope for legal action and documentation than did rural law. Given the more complex economic situation in towns, men and women were quicker to turn to writing, for there were many transactions for which it was safer to have written proof close at hand. Additionally, urban life, in which people worked mainly in trade, industry, and services, created the conditions for different lives. Thanks to the many employment possibilities, many countrywomen migrated to towns to work there in the crafts – or sometimes as prostitutes – thus able to make their own living. Furthermore, due precisely to this economic organization and to migration, people's lives in towns were less family-centric, hence women more frequently "escaped" their families' control. From this point of view, the saying that "town air sets you free" also applied to women, even if it is hard to ascertain the extent to which women's social standing in urban circles differed from the situation of women in the countryside or from that of peasants. Concerning the latter, there are virtually no sources that have come down to us, meaning we cannot throw any light on the history of their lives. In matters of archiving and especially of conservation, town councils were far more meticulous than village communities. It is thus by necessity that this book emphasizes women in towns, though village women are not wholly absent.

Nowadays, the Low Countries are still a very urbanized region. This dense urban network emerged in the late Middle Ages: the growth of

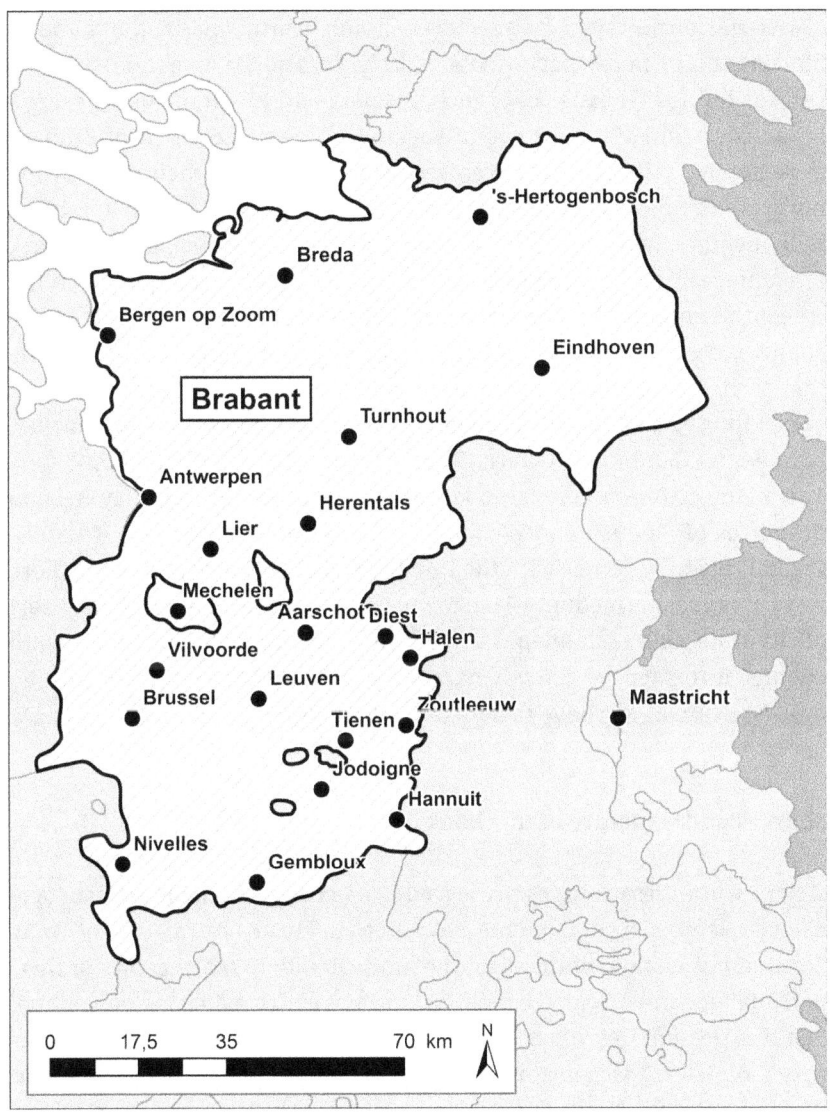

The Duchy of Brabant and the Lordship of Mechelen in the 15th century (c. Iason Jongepier, GIStorical Antwerp). Maastricht had two lords: the town depended on both the Duke of Brabant and the Prince-Bishop of Liège.

towns was encouraged by intense economic traffic and by the favourable location of many port towns and rivers. The archives thus include records for a wide range of French, Belgian, and Dutch towns, offering a broad spectrum of stories about working women. The duchy of Brabant in particular still holds vast archives throwing light on their lives. By the norms of the period, Brabant was a densely populated region and a key hub, together with the major towns of Leuven, Antwerp, and Brussels. The university town of Leuven was home to about 20,000 people in the fifteenth century. The population of Brussels, the political heart of the country, rose from 20,000 inhabitants in 1400 to 30,000 in 1500, while that of the port town of Antwerp rose from 10,000 inhabitants in 1400 to 55,000 in 1525. Smaller towns included 's-Hertogenbosch, Tienen, Nivelles, Zoutleeuw, Gembloux, Wavre, Vilvoorde, Breda, and Bergen-op-Zoom. The duchy of Brabant covered large districts in the present-day Belgian provinces of Flemish and Walloon Brabant, Antwerp, and the Brussels-Capital region, together with the Dutch province of North Brabant. There were also various medium-sized towns that were autonomous fiefs, a sort of city-state. One such town was Mechelen, but given that in the fifteenth century it formed, with Brabant, a union under the overlordship of the duke of Brabant, we have included it in this book.

Sources and structure of this book

Where were these sources preserved? The chests in which townspeople used to keep such documents have not survived the ravages of time. Fortunately, enough of them got the municipality to make copies of their personal documents, just in case. Aldermen's courts had legal power and, just like present-day notaries, registered documents for a fee in "aldermen's registers" (*schepenregisters*). People thus unwittingly generated many sources for historians, which are today held in municipal archives. The aldermen also issued judgments, as illustrated by the example of Liesbet in 1490. Other administrations likewise monitored citizens' behaviour and therefore produced evidence and judgments that may tell us about townspeople's lives. The bishop, for example, punished miscreant believers, and princely representatives sentenced criminals to fines. The princely administration employed local officials who maintained public order and who, among other things, were responsible for arresting criminals and ensuring that convicted criminals served their sentence or paid their out-of-court settlement. The name of these officials varied from one town to the next (*bailli* in Nivelles, *meier* in Leuven, *schout* in Antwerp, and *amman* in Brussels), but in this book we shall be referring to them as "bailiffs". These people left accounts books detailing revenue from fines. Taken together, all these administrative sources are a goldmine for unearthing the lives of "ordinary" people.

Our book starts by sketching the course of a medieval woman's life. What rights did women have as a child, as an adolescent, and as a wife, and what use did they make of them? We then look at the freedom available to women in an important stage in their life, namely, when choosing a partner. Medieval literature is full of legends depicting knight's ravishing obedient damsels. That is not wholly unfounded: abductions of women and forced marriages undoubtedly go back to the dawn of time, but going along with an abduction could nevertheless offer the advantage of escaping from one's parents' authority. Of course, marriage did not always mean freedom; conflict, divorce, and adultery were omnipresent in the world of married men and women. We then look at women in various social contexts: religious women (particularly beguines), married and single businesswomen, and women working at markets or in a craft guild. To what extent were they in competition with their male counterparts? Beguines, for instance, sometimes came into conflict with textile guilds, for they supplied similar work. Other conflicts could also erupt within a guild: men against women, the old against the young, the rich against the poor, and migrants against town citizens. Be that as it may, a sizeable number of women successfully ran their own business. Although there could be major social and economic distinctions between different groups of women, many managed to become relatively wealthy. This status can be particularly illustrated by beguines' wills, and the business transactions of wealthy women are no less surprising: there were many businesswomen working in towns, such as Liesbet in Leuven.

We also look at women living outside the law and those looking for love. Purportedly "bad women" – those who by nature sought to do wrong – figure in a series of tales in which seductresses exhort men to crime. There were fewer witches during the Middle Ages than the prevalent cliché suggests, but there was no shortage of women throwing punches, stealing, and squabbling. By listening to what they say, to their cries and their stories, we may learn what they thought about men holding the reins of municipal power, for on occasion these women rose up (together with men) against the (alleged or otherwise) misdeeds of their administrators. Sex workers also regularly had dealings with the court. Nowadays they are often associated with secret criminal organizations, but in the late medieval Low Countries prostitution was not so much on the margins of society as at its heart. There were various limitations on townspeople's sexuality: there were binding norms not only for married men and women, but also for single people, although men could turn to prostitutes. How did the two sexes perceive sexuality? How did towns manage prostitution? What was the inside of a brothel like? In answering these questions, we reveal a fascinating world of lust and passion at the heart of the late medieval town. In sum, we shall see whether men's and women's conduct and virtue were as perfect as Christine de Pizan had hoped.

Notes

[1] Quotation from *The City of Ladies* (cf. *infra*), translated by Hicks & Moreau, *Le livre*, 55. The original version reads: *la hauteur ou abaissement des gens ne gist mie es corps selon le sexe, mais en la parfeccion des meurs et des vertus* (De Pizan, *Le livre*, 250).
[2] In this book, quotations from works unavailable in English are given in translation in the main body of the text, with the original appearing in the footnotes. Hence Liesbet declared that she and her husband lived *in overspele* (adulterously) and that he was living an *ombequamen levene* (indecent life); see CAL, 7384, 270r-v. For references to the archives, see the explanation found in the bibliography.
[3] *Dwijf es van naturen loes, vrecke ende ghierech altoes*, taken from *Jans Teesteye* (Snellaert, *Nederlandsche gedichten*, 226). See too: Van Oostrom, *Wereld in woorden*, 167.
[4] On "La vision de Christine", a work she completed in 1405, see Paupert, "La vision", 510.
[5] "plus que les hommes meismement / es ars humains inventives", Bousmanne & Savini, *The library*, 164.
[6] "abille en science et vertu, gracieuse et humile, saige entre ung mile", Van Hemelryck, "La femme", 266.
[7] Duby, *Love and marriage*, vii. See the bibliography for the main history works about women in the Middle Ages.
[8] Bennett & Karras, "Women", 1.
[9] Le Goff, *Hommes et femmes*, 12.

CHAPTER 1

From girlhood to widowhood: On the rights of women and children

Andrea Bardyn & Jelle Haemers

On 28 May 1459, Jan De Custere and Katelijne Buelens went to Leuven Town Hall to inform the aldermen of decisions they had reached by common accord. Two children, a boy and a girl, had been born of their relationship. Jan and Katelijne were not united by the bonds of matrimony, however, and no longer lived under the same roof. This situation caused a problem: who was henceforth to look after the children? Jan lived in the countryside, in Kortelke (present-day Kortrijk-Dutsel, northeast of Leuven), while Katelijne lived in Leuven with the two children called Hanneken and Grietkin. In this case, the children had probably been baptized Johannes and Margriete, which their parents had turned into children's common pet names, resulting respectively in Hanneken and Grietkin, as in the fairytale Hansel and Gretel. Yet these two children did not seem predisposed to a happy ending. As their parents were not married, Hanneken and Grietkin belonged to the unenviable class of illegitimate children. Thus their respective futures did not augur well, for children born out of wedlock had fewer rights than those of married parents. Still, Jan and Katelijne found a solution by reaching a sort of amicable settlement. In the presence of the aldermen, Jan promised to look after Grietkin, while Katelijne was to take care of their son. Additionally, the parents were to set money aside for Hanneken. Jan paid Katelijne a reasonable sum, equivalent to four months' wages for a skilled labourer, which she was to invest in an annuity. This plan meant that Hanneken would receive a (modest) yearly income to meet his needs throughout his life. The fact that he would grow up alongside an unmarried mother meant his future was uncertain and risky. It is possible that Katelijne earned a decent living, though equally possible that she lived on the edge of society. Unmarried women living in town had to count on their own revenue without being able to fall back on the security offered by a marriage.

In the case of Jan and Katelijne, in addition to the arrangement about the children, there was a second reason for resorting to a contract. The sizeable sum agreed to by Jan was a sort of compensation for "depriving her of her virginity".[1] Was Jan really Katelijne's first partner? We will never know. After all, the passage about "virginity" may equally refer to the fact that Jan would henceforth be making a sort of maintenance payment for his unmarried girlfriend. Nevertheless, it was customary in the Middle Ages to indemnify young women for "damages" if a sexual relationship did not lead to marriage. Such damages were perceived not as a physical harm but as a social injury. Medieval society applied dual standards for men and women in many matters, including sexual relationships prior to marriage: it would be harder for Katelijne than for Jan to find a good match, for her dishonour was greater. The maintenance payment was a form of compensation and could even be an advantage should Katelijne wish to find a husband. Life was not easy as an unmarried mother. It is quite possible that Katelijne was the one who wished to leave Jan. Maybe mounting disagreements within the couple led Katelijne to choose to live on her own, and Jan may well have opted to return to Kortelke. In any case, the two remained on good terms and appeared together before the aldermen's court of their own free will. Furthermore, members of Jan's family came forward as guarantors. Should fate strike one of the two, these guarantors would be entrusted with fulfilling the parents' obligations. Thus while the children's future was uncertain, guarantees were nevertheless in place should problems arise. These measures were part of a broader mechanism: throughout a child's life, as well as during adolescence and adulthood, the family acted as a safety net.

What rights did children have, and to whom could girls like Grietkin and adult women like Katlijne turn? Historians were long obliged to rely on sixteenth-century legal texts to answer this question. In the medieval Low Countries, though, there were no general legal codes, partly because the law differed from one town to the next. Additionally, neither the town administrators nor the duke ensured that the laws and ordinances they promulgated were systematically followed. This situation only started changing in the sixteenth century, when the law had already evolved significantly. It is thus mistaken to project the sixteenth-century situation back onto the earlier period, as often used to be the case. That is why we will examine the legal situation of women here, using documents recording daily life. These will enable us to reconstruct certain contemporaneous practices, which had significant legal force. Indeed, daily life was regulated by common law. It was often a matter of orally agreed rules and customs. Everybody knew them, but they were not codified in legal texts. If we want to know how women lived in the period prior to the sixteenth century, the only source we have are the concrete examples of daily practice. Let us start at the beginning.

Birth

Presumably, the births of Hanneken and Grietkin were female events, for men were mostly absent at childbirth, as illustrated by an anecdote from Mechelen. There, in 1456, the bailiff sentenced a certain Hennin van den Damme to pay a fine after what counted as punishable behaviour at the time: spying on his servant when she was in labour. As the officer noted, Hennin had been caught *in flagrante* watching the girl "labouring hard" *(en grant travail)*. He added, moreover, that Hennin's behaviour was "indecent for a man".[2] Thus childbirth was certainly not a man's affair. According to custom, women were assisted during childbirth by a qualified midwife. Practitioners of childbirth were sworn in by the town and learnt their trade from one another. The earliest known recognized midwife in Leuven was Christine Liedekens. On 16 May 1481, she took an oath before the town council that she would carry out her profession in accordance with the established rules.[3] As we shall see in chapter 5, in Brussels there was even an association of midwives (composed exclusively of women). For the most part they helped expectant mothers in their homes, yet also provided their services in hospitals. There were also centres where care was provided for less wealthy women, as not everyone was able to pay for a midwife. Since 1396, women in Leuven had been able to turn to a private charity. Unfortunately this organization had to close its doors in 1489, due to lack of revenue, the military unrest of the period, and mismanagement by its town-appointed administrator.

A birth was a festive event to be celebrated. Celebrations could last for days on end depending on the parents' social status, but a newborn was always welcome. The stereotype that infanticide was current in the Middle Ages due to the high number of unwanted pregnancies was disproved long ago. The population of this period knew of various techniques to avoid pregnancies (the best-known being *coitus interruptus*). Infant and child mortality rates – probably between a third and a half of all children – did not prevent parents from grieving a son's or a daughter's premature death. In urban families an average of two to four children reached adulthood. They tended to be named after a popular local saint. Thus the three most common first names for girls baptized in Leuven were Catharine (or Katelijne), Elisabeth (or Liesbet), and Margaret (or Margriet). For boys, there was a preference for John (Jan), Henry (Hendrik), and Peter (Pieter). Over half of Leuven's inhabitants had one of these names because the eponymous saints were devoutly worshipped in the town. Their parents hoped their children would benefit from the protection of the saints solicited by these religious anthroponyms, especially during the difficult early years of their lives.

Were many children born into poverty? Out of the 3,500 or so heads of household (men and women) in Leuven in 1477, 1,464 (42%) had to earn their living as skilled labourers, while 264 (8%) received income from an annuity, trade, or official position. In other words, about half the heads of household earned a living by working as a semi-skilled or unskilled labourer, a servant, or handyman. Were they poor? A census conducted for tax reasons in 1488 by the Leven town authorities notes that about 700 people were living in poverty that year. These people received public assistance and thus did not pay taxes. If we suppose that all these people were heads of household – bearing in mind that some of them were certainly single – that would mean that one fifth of the population was unable to meet their daily needs. It should be noted, however, that there was an economic crisis around 1480. In contrast, circumstances were more favourable in 1437, when only one thirteenth of the Leuven population was living in poverty. Interpreting these figures from a positive perspective, it is striking that a large majority of families in Leuven were deemed to have sufficient income to pay local taxes. Overall, these figures thus seem to indicate that, on the one hand, the future offered opportunities for many, yet, on the other, there were also great social and economic inequalities.

It was better not to be abandoned as a child, for in that case there was no family safety net to rely on in the event of need. Even if it was punishable by law, a number of newborns were nevertheless abandoned, possibly due to the absence of effective contraception, poverty, and the dishonour associated with being a single mother. In May 1420, the Antwerp court sentenced Kateline Meeuws for having abandoned a child and even having paid another woman to carry out this base deed.[4] Even darker was the case of a newborn discovered rolled up in straw in an Antwerp dump in November 1490. The town's governors observed that the child must have been delivered using forceps for its legs were broken. To clarify the matter, a large sum was promised to anybody with further information, for the perpetrator of this malfeasance could not go unpunished.[5]

Nothing is known about the outcome of this affair, but steps taken in another case clearly show that the authorities did not abandon foundlings. In 1462 in Brecht (near Antwerp), the administrator for the charity known as the "Table of the Holy Spirit" took legal action against Willem van Backenbrugge before the Leuven court of aldermen. One of the purposes of the "Table of the Poor" was to assist inhabitants in need, in this case a girl called Aechte who had been abandoned in Brecht. Her mother, Lijsbette Claes, had died during childbirth. Yet the Table administrator had found the father, Willem, and was taking action against him to recover the childcare costs. Willem denied he was the father, though was contradicted by the midwife who had attended to Lijsbette. During the birth and subsequent agony, Lijsbette had sworn on her soul's salvation that Willem was the child's father.[6] In this delicate matter, the Leuven aldermen found in favour of the Table. Willem was to pay for the care Aechte had received from the Table, to wit: a half-shilling per day, a barrel of beer, and three shillings for bread. He was further tasked with educating the child. This ruling shows the importance the aldermen attached to having a family: Aechte was at least going to have one, despite not having been born under a lucky star.

Other towns also took measures concerning abandoned children. In 1463, for example, the town of Brussels hired a woman to look after abandoned infants, for their growing number was becoming problematic. In the oath she took on being hired, this carer for foundlings promised to look after these children as though they were the apple of her eye. The position tended to be held by a (rich) widow. She was entrusted with providing basic care to the infants and looking for a home for them. The town treasury paid for the foundling's first set of clothes, after which they relied on charity. Many of the children were taken in by hospitals; the earliest mention of a foundling appears in the regulations of the Hospital of Saint John in Brussels and dates from 1211. In this document the hospital expresses concern over the financial implications of taking in foundlings. Thanks to a number of donations, including bequests, it could indeed meet various needs, but according to the hospital these funds were insufficient. Eventually the town covered some of the costs, as was also the case in Leuven, where "women who assisted foundlings" received a sum of money from the town treasury; as a rule they took in three or four children per year, probably at home.[7] In Mechelen, there was a house for foundlings. It was paid for by the town and through charity. As of 1377, the town also hired a woman to tend to abandoned children, who was to look after them on behalf of the town. As a rule, children lived in a charitable home or institution until the age of seven, when they were transferred to a foster family. An abandoned child could be taken in by a skilled worker, for instance, who found the additional labour useful and taught his trade to the child.

Things were different for illegitimate children like Grietkin, mentioned at the beginning of this chapter. They still had a father or mother to look after them. For this care, it was essential to be recognized, as shown by the story of the foundling Aechte. Willem was not the only man to deny paternity of a child. When fathers and mothers confessed about their carnal relations, whether secret or not, the effect could be at times surprising. In the event of doubt, the Mechelen aldermen requested that the mother declare under oath who the child's father was. If she took the oath with conviction, stating that a child had been "engendered by his body in my body", then she was in a strong position.[8]

If, however, the man swore that he had never had "carnal relations with her [the mother]", then the two parties could call witnesses. If it turned out that the man had well and truly shared his bed with her, the Mechelen court obliged him to pay "childbed" maintenance. A similar arrangement was applicable in Leuven, though not all women resorted to it. In June 1490, Margriete Stockelpot confessed before the aldermen's court that her youngest child, Metteken, was not her husband's but had been fathered by a tailor from the neighbouring village of Veltem.[9] The fact that Margriete demanded no maintenance payment from the father of the extramarital child suggests that the illegitimate child was taken in by her family. Metteken, though, would never enjoy the same rights as her half-brothers and half-sisters. Illegitimate children were not allowed to inherit from their father and, in certain towns, not even from their mother. Nor were they allowed to go on to hold public office, and in towns such as Vilvoorde, for example, they were not even authorized to act as witness in a trial. The life of an unfortunate illegitimate child was thus severely handicapped by the public dishonour stemming from extramarital relations. Yet things were not uniformly bleak: parents were obliged to meet their needs. Under Antwerp custom, it was mainly fathers who were obliged to house and feed their illegitimate children, while in Mechelen and Lier it was usual for each parent to pay for half their education.[10] If one of the parents married, the child was to be taken in by the new family. Otherwise they could be raised by a single parent, as was the case for Grietkin in Leuven. In such situations, the couple generally came to an agreement to share costs.

Additionally, illegitimate children could be legitimized. At their request and in exchange for recompense, the duke of Brabant could grant illegitimate children the benefit of inheritance. Such fortunate individuals had to pay a substantial sum for this ruling, which explains why the procedure tended to be the privilege of wealthy illegitimate children, who otherwise ran the risk of seeing their inheritance elude them. The size of the indemnity depended on the fortune of the person initiating the proceeding; in exchange, the illegitimate child acquired full legal capacity. In Brabant in the second half of the fifteenth century, an average of 12 people per year paid money to be legitimized; four out of ten cases concerned a woman. Liesbet Breukentop, a beguine from 's-Hertogenbosch, was thus "legitimized" in January 1500.[11] She was the (illegitimate) daughter of a priest, Peter Breukentop, who had apparently not taken his celibacy too literally.[12] Among the list of legitimized illegitimate children, a striking number issued from a relation with a cleric. The mothers for their part could also obtain legitimacy for children born out of wedlock. In 1462, Janne Schuts paid the requested sum to legitimize both herself and her daughter Johanna. Janne was an Antwerp businesswoman whom we shall discuss in greater detail in a later chapter, in which we will examine her remarkable business activity. The fact that she died a few years after the legitimization proceeding suggests that she sorted this matter out to ensure the distribution of her estate. As observed earlier, however, this procedure was not within everyone's reach.

From infancy to girlhood

The family safety net was crucial for a child's future. Children grew up surrounded by their relatives, except in the wealthiest circles where a wet nurse would also sometimes feed the child. The two parents were involved in educating the child. At times this education could be heavy-handed. In Antwerp, the law accepted that parents "castigate [their children] appropriately".[13] Parents were only liable to prosecution if the child died or was mutilated. Although children's rights were very limited in this domain, other aspects of medieval law were more complete. If one of the parents died, the child's fate became precarious, whether or not they were legitimate. When the father or mother died, the relatives and close friends of the deceased parent gathered to designate a guardian (*mambour*). In agreement with the surviving parent – or with the other guardian if the other parent was also dead – the *mambour* managed the orphan's possessions until they came of age. The guardian was always a man, even when replacing a deceased mother. He had to swear that he would look after the children "as if they were his own children", as the formula used in Brussels stipulated.[14] Given the very large number of (semi-)orphans, the town exerted a degree of oversight. At the end of the guardianship, when the (semi-)orphan came of age, the guardians had to present the bills and other supporting documentation to the aldermen's court to confirm they had properly managed the estate of the deceased parent or parents. The aldermen thus monitored proceedings, and in various towns distinct institutions were even set up to oversee guardians, such as the chamber of orphans in Antwerp in 1496. If a guardian had failed to carry out his task correctly, he had to pay compensation to the orphan. Thus all children were guaranteed that on coming of age they would have their parents' estate at their disposal.

If one of the parents died, the children tended to stay with the surviving spouse, who sometimes arranged for the children to be placed with their grandparents or other relatives until they were able to meet their own food and housing needs. The challenge was greater if one of the children was mentally disabled. In Brussels, such children were customarily taken in by their guardian or surviving parent until their twenty-eighth birthday.[15] A document from Leuven dated August 1455 refers to the case of an "infantile child".[16] He was "of weak understanding" and lived with a couple, Jan van Raveschote and his wife Kateline. A widow (named Liesbet) helped look after his brother or sister. Every three months the two children changed home, but the two parties altered this interval in the above-mentioned document. They agreed that the exchange would henceforth take place once a year, and that annuities were to be bought to ensure the two children would have an income once they left the nest. The fact that they alternated between the two foster families was probably to avoid a single person or family having to pay all the costs and expenses for their education. It is highly likely that this arrangement was rooted in the solidarity binding together a circle of friends and family. Of course, it cannot be ruled out that the children's possessions may also have appealed to those involved (though we have no specific idea in this case).

Be that as it may, needy children could rely on the assistance of relatives and acquaintances. It was not an established right, but rather a broadly respected custom arising from need.

In most cases parents took precautions to ensure their children would have a small sum of money, should they have to fend for themselves. In the example used at the beginning of this chapter, it was a yearly annuity for Hanneken, the son born of Jan and Katelijne's relationship. The parents of Weynkin and Grietken Van Geldenaken from Leuven also thought of their children's well-being. In 1458, their father drew up a will in which he divided his goods. Weynkin was to receive a sum of money (a debt owed by a friend of his father), together with his armour, a double bed with sheets, and two of the best pillows.[17] These were precious goods which would certainly be useful in his subsequent life. The daughter, Grietkin, also received a small sum, a double bed, six seat cushions, new sheets and pillows, and a chest for valuable objects which her deceased mother had given to Weyne, the father. In this way the daughter would have a trousseau enabling her to get ahead in life.

> **Women's fashion**
> There is no doubt that clothing was a symbol of social status, while also reflecting age. Infants were swaddled in white or red cloth. Young children generally wore a long tunic with a belt, along with hose often rolled to just beneath the knees. The quality of the cloth was an indicator of social class. As children grew, their clothing became shorter. Girls as young as seven sometimes wore dresses with a low neckline. They wore their hair loose or else held in place by a hairband. Church authors through the centuries invariably lamented the amount of bare flesh exposed. Yet women could also dress more strictly, or else accentuate or restrict certain of their shapes. The good abbot Gilles li Muisis of Tournai even insinuated that the new fashion of the 1340s, with rows of buttons on the sleeves and plunging necklines, had been made fashionable by prostitutes. This aspect never changed. It was also ordinary to wear a hat or veil, and it was appropriate for married women to cover their hair. Rules were more flexible for men, but they generally did not leave the house without a hat or beret. The main item of work clothes was an apron; an undershirt was common and could also be used as a night shirt. "Clothes maketh the woman."

The transition to adulthood

When did a girl's childhood end? There was no single definitive criterion. Biological and psychological development mattered of course, but particularly in this domain signed and sealed agreements were decisive. In the Middle Ages, children came of age in stages, more so than today. A girl could thus escape her parents' authority by marrying, which was possible at the age of 12. Boys had to wait a further two years. In one of her books, Christine de Pizan warns young women that during festivities they must take care to behave with restraint and to dilute their wine with water at dances: "for a young woman, excessive consumption of food and wine is the ugliest fault possible".[18] And when it came to finding a match, a young woman's reputation was important, especially in the aristocratic circles in which Christine moved. According to her, it was also forbidden to marry without parental consent (whether or not young women in towns followed Christine de Pizan's advice is the topic of the following chapter). For the time being, we will simply note that the average age upon marriage was relatively high: ordinary men and women generally married in their late twenties. In the event of a political alliance, a marriage between children could sometimes be concluded in noble or courtly circles. The children took their vows at a young age, but the marriage itself (together with the associated "conjugal duties") naturally only occurred once they were older. A 1445 legal text from Brussels fixed the age of marriage at 28. In other towns this age was often around 24 or 25.[19] This Brussels ordinance also stipulated that an orphan's guardianship ended for girls on reaching the age of 15, and for boys at the age of 18. Girls were thus held to mature at an earlier age than boys, including in view of their future marriage (a topic addressed in the following chapter). Adolescents continued to live with their parents or guardians for as long as they were minors, though some left the family home earlier to go and live with their employer – a master craftsman, for example – or else as a maid or children's nurse in a family. In any case, parents and guardians were obliged to meet children's needs until they had their own income or a job.

Adolescents enjoyed a high level of protection from their parents. Their material wealth could be provided for by an inheritance or dowry, but their spiritual education was equally important. Given the economic role girls were called upon to play in their respective households, they received solid basic schooling, just like their brothers. Until the age of 14, girls and boys followed the same elementary education. They learnt to read, write, and count. In the southern Low Countries, the level of education was very high. A late-sixteenth-century Spanish commercial traveller remarked upon the high level of literacy among women in this region. He thus wrote, with a wont for exaggeration, that women could "write, read, and count in such a way that few men may copy them". Living during a period of religious unrest, this merchant was mainly interested in the girls' biblical knowledge, but on the basis of his observation that women had "lots of printed books at home" and "that they learnt and memorized them from their earliest years", we may deduce that a high level of literacy was the domain of women.[20] It is hard to reconstitute the book collections of urban women, for few private holdings were preserved. Still, research into wills shows that women owned and read books, especially vernacular prayerbooks. A striking fact is that women often left their books to other women, bequeathing them to a niece or granddaughter, for example. A manuscript left by Katrien Thomas from Antwerp, dating to about 1500, provides us with information about the level of women's learning. Katrien clearly belonged to a relatively wealthy circle, for illuminated manuscripts and the earliest printed books were very expensive objects. Katrien's prayerbook is for that matter a personal one, suggesting a specific commission from the miniaturist, and perhaps that she used this religious work intensely: on the page facing the first lines of a prayer to Saint Catherine, there is a figure representing the owner herself in a long pink gown with a rosary around her waist. Behind her is a churchman, perhaps her son Jacob, who was a member of a Dominican monastery.[21] Yet while these manuscripts illustrate the level of women's erudition, we must nevertheless note that young women rarely received any specialized schooling as they grew older. It was mainly boys who attended the Latin schools that prepared them for university study. University was for that matter a male bastion, with only clergy allowed to study there. Nevertheless, from time to time groups of girls received Latin lessons: wealthy girls might learn Latin at home or in convents, and in 1320 there was a Latin school in Brussels for girls from wealthy families. Many children, including girls, became apprentices to a craftsman, while others continued their schooling in a religious order, such as the beguines. All of them, though, had already received good basic schooling.

Lastly, to what extent were adolescents deemed competent to take fate into their own hands? In this domain there were various, more restrictive

Image from the prayer book that belonged to Katrien Thomas. The owner is holding out her hands towards her patron saint. Behind her is a clergyman, circa 1500. (Brussels, Royal Library of Belgium, IV, 190, 96v).

legal rules. In Nivelles, a 1429 ordinance forbade minors from conducting any transactions of a value greater than that of a pitcher of wine. In Lier, unmarried people aged 16 to 24 were allowed to buy and sell only bread, beer, and other basic foodstuffs.[22] Until that age, children continued to live under their parents' authority. This condition of course meant that the parents remained responsible for any criminal acts their offspring committed, as well as for any debts or accidents they caused. And it was no different for mentally disabled children, as Jan Bollaert's family discovered. On 1 February 1510, Jan's mother went with two friends to the aldermen's court in Leuven to try to find a solution for her son. He had gone on a tour around town after "losing his mind". What exactly had he done? "A lot of harm", as his mother succinctly put it, and we have no further details.[23] The despairing parents had placed their child at Rumst and at Geel for a while, where there were well-known homes for the mentally disabled. They had also incurred many debts to compensate for the damages inflicted. That is why they now turned to the town council for assistance, no longer wishing to assume responsibility for their son. The town decided they were still responsible for their son's acts, yet advised them to have him put away to prevent his hurting anybody. Certain aggressive, mentally ill people were interned in the former Sint-Michielspoort. The town paid its neighbours a fixed sum to take food and drink to the prisoners. Specialized institutions were very expensive, and any medical care dispensed at the time was not very effective. From a legal point of view, intellectually disabled people thus remained "children" throughout their life.

Adult women and their bodies

For girls, menstruation and their first sexual contacts were important stages on the path towards adulthood. How was menstruation perceived by the medieval population? Answers may be found in learned writings, generally by men, whose opinions varied considerably depending on the context in which they were writing. Medical treatises often described menstruation as a normal and natural phenomenon: it served to purify the female body and was thus a necessary mechanism for fertility. Several writings explained the function of menstruation by referring to the image of a plant which grows and renews itself: it is necessary to ensure the growth of new life. Other texts adopted a far more negative view, as if menstruation were the prototypical symbol of the sinful state of the daughter of Eve. An extreme example is an inscription figuring amid a translation of the Book of Genesis into Dutch at that time. The (anonymous) clerical author explains that "femininity" and the "monthly purification of women" is a time when they must be avoided due to their bad secretions. Sexual relations with a menstruating woman were to be avoided at all costs, as otherwise the man would come into contact with the "most evil poison", that is, impure blood.[24] There is in any case a whiff of misogyny to what this author has to say.

> **The ideal of feminine beauty**
> A painted panel by Hans Memling shows King David spying on Bathsheba, whose figure corresponds to the traditional medieval ideal of beauty. The veiled woman has a high forehead, fine eyebrows, small mouth, slender nose, and sensual lips. A fourteenth-century Brabant poet was even more explicit when praising the beauty of the "girl with beautiful braids": "she has a slender waist and breasts rounder than a ball". A beautiful woman had fair skin, a slim frame with little round breasts, long legs, a narrow waist, and a rounded belly. As few women naturally have such a body, there were numerous means available to attain this ideal: white powders, padding for skirts to enlarge their belly and hips, and so forth. It was of course mainly wealthy women who had the means to enhance their beauty in this way. The women painted by Memling thus correspond to the ideal of the elite, who did not refrain from asking painters to raise a cheekbone here or modify a bosom there. Thus Michaël Pacher touched up his portrait of Duchess Mary of Burgundy (1456-1482), shrinking her nose on the painting intended for her future husband, Archduke Maximilian of Austria.

Medieval society was forever ambivalent in its way of viewing the female body. Menstrual pain was thus linked to original sin. The biblical figure of Eve, the archetypal woman at the root of misfortune, had plunged humanity into sin, thus making women the easy prey of the venomous pens of many a cleric. While they viewed menstruation as symptomatic of women's "impurity", virginity was conversely the very summit of purity. The Virgin Mary and the "Virgin of Orleans" (as Joan of Arc was often called) were symbols of salvation and resurrection. All Christians were deeply marked by these powerful images. It is thus not surprising that virginity or "purity" was widely valued, including by young women and their families. In concrete terms that meant that, in principle, only a husband was entitled to the privilege of breaking this period of virginity. Still, the example with which we broached this chapter shows that the norm was not always followed. As for self-pleasure, though not punishable, it was taboo. Yet there are no traces of the anxiety-driven moral condemnation of masturbation which would crop up at later periods. Medical treatises disapproved of masculine masturbation on the grounds that it was wasteful. As for women, it was not explicitly discouraged and was sometimes even recognized as beneficial in that it could rid the body of toxic substances.

It is probable that girls (and boys) scoffed at these ways of thinking, and that it was a popular topic of conversation. Sexual morality was relatively free: premarital sexual relations were viewed tolerantly, provided that the parents provided for the needs of any children issuing from such relations – as in the case of Katelijne and Jan from Leuven. Despite the church condemning sexual relations out of wedlock, young people were active in this regard. Once married, a couple was in theory meant to respect marital morality. In practice, however, society particularly disapproved especially of men's extramarital relations should these threaten the social order, by disrupting another person's marriage, for example. Sexual relations with minors were subject to punishment. In 1483, the bailiff punished Jan van Hoeke for having lured a 12- or 13-year-old girl out of town to "satisfy his will". But, the bailiff declared, this attempt had failed "because of the young age" of his victim. Although the girl declared she had followed Jan voluntarily, the bailiff had him thrown into prison.[25] Such cases could sometimes lead to an amicable settlement without the courts being involved. In this specific case, though, the fact that the girl was a minor was clearly an aggravating factor explaining why Jan was imprisoned.

Sexual contact between people of the same sex was also strongly condemned. The concept of sodomy – the crime of "unnatural" sexual relations – included homophilia, bestiality, sexual relations with heretics, public masturbation, and cross-dressing. Men were more likely than women to be sentenced for sexual contact with a person of the same sex. Of the 300 people put on trial for sodomy between 1400 and 1550 in the southern Low Countries, one in ten were women, a higher proportion than in other regions.[26] Additionally, men and women ended up being burnt at the stake for this "sin" more frequently in the southern Low Countries than elsewhere in Europe. Nevertheless, a lesser sentence was sometimes handed down, such as a heavy fine or exile. Be that as it may, it would be wrong to conclude that the inhabitants of the southern Low Countries had illicit sexual relations more frequently than elsewhere. It shows rather that women there were more present in public life, thanks to their strong economic position, making their "crime" more visible. Overall, however, the total number of condemnations was relatively low (two per year on average), suggesting any such contacts were carefully concealed, only resulting in condemnation if public order was compromised. The authorities did not systematically hunt down "sodomites", nor instigate any witch hunt.

If sexual relations between a man and a woman did not lead to marriage, then this was a case of deflowering. This charge meant that the girl (or her family) was entitled to compensation in the form of a payment or maintenance support if children were born of these relations. The example of Katelijne and Jan from Leuven is thus part of a broader scheme. In October 1464, for example, Jan van Liere of Antwerp informed the aldermen's court that he would (voluntarily) be paying such compensation. He had had carnal relations out of wedlock with Liesbet Vlugs and, as the legal record puts it "had stolen her virginal purity". In compensation for this he would henceforth pay Liesbet a quantity of rye each year.[27] Had there been a birth? The certificate does not say. Sometimes the courts had to compel a man to recognize "theft of purity", with some clearly wishing to shirk their financial obligations. In 1434, Machtilde van Hulslaer de Rotselaar launched legal proceedings against Willem Vandenvelde before the episcopal court of Liège *in causa defloracionis* (for a case of deflowering). After having observed that Machtilde was pregnant, the court ruled that Willem was to pay for maternity care.[28] This trial was not an isolated case, although such proceedings were fairly rare. Between 1448 and 1458, a total of 69 heard by the episcopal court of Brussels resulted in compensation for deflowering. In this large town, an average of only six trials per year were heard for such cases. This figure suggests that many situations were – literally – settled amicably.

Once married

Marriage had a considerable impact on a woman's life, at least legally, for her field of action was thereby restricted. For example, many contracts could no longer be concluded without her husband, such as contracting a loan or selling property, for which her husband had to be present. This stipulation had both positive and negative consequences for women. On the one hand, the husband provided complete protection to his spouse, even in the event of debts. On the other hand, this rule meant that the wife's sphere of action was severely curtailed. One rule was universal, as set out in sixteenth-century common law: "The man is lord and master in his household throughout the marriage."[29] This rule was categorical: once married, a woman was placed under her husband's guardianship for most legal acts. A married man, conversely, was free to act and manage all the couple's assets independently. He was not allowed, however, to dispose of his wife's assets without her approbation. The rules followed the principle that the household was perceived as a single unit: according to the fourteenth-century Antwerp clerk Jan van Boendale, the man and woman "form a single will, as they in fact form a single body".[30] Marriage conjoined two people sharing the same interests, which were managed by the husband in public life. According to the clerk, the woman's job was to look after household tasks.

Yet in practice many wives carried out transactions themselves. A different reality thus lay behind the façade of strict rules. As there is a separate chapter about women's business activities (chapter three), for the time being we shall only mention that men and women ran the household in concert. It is important to bear in mind that at the time, a household functioned as an economic structure far more than it does today: all the family members worked together in the family business. Admittedly, given that we cannot directly observe life as it occurred behind closed doors, we shall never know what (private) power relations looked like exactly. Regardless, a common saying in Brabant had it that it was better for a man be ordered about in the house if he wanted to live in peace: "Whoever wishes to live in peace will allow his wife to be the head."[31] Independently of this saying, it is striking to observe that men and women officially formed a single entity. With her husband's consent, a woman could replace him when he was unable to represent the household. Such occurrences concerned wives whose husband was ill, or developed problems, or else was absent for a long period. The Leuven cobbler Joes Wils had recorded in 1490 that he was authorizing certain people to manage his goods in his name. The people in question were his wife Katelijne and their adult daughter, also called Katelijne, along with two male friends. Each was free to act separately.[32] Nevertheless, over the course of the fifteenth century men and women increasingly turned to professional legal representatives – who were always men, given that they generally had a university diploma and that higher education was a male preserve.

While the family officially formed a united entity, there could be clashes. A woman was fully entitled to lodge a complaint against her husband, for example, should domestic violence become commonplace. In 1432, Jasper Kympe of Leuven had to explain himself before the aldermen after having treated his wife Barbele, who was pregnant with their child, "unreasonably" and brutally. The aldermen intervened and allowed Barbele to go and live at her mother's home. They forbade Jasper from contacting her until he corrected his behaviour and behaved with her "as a husband is obliged to treat his wife".[33] Wives facing such problems often appealed to their family, acquaintances, and friends. On occasion, this type of guarantee was provided for in a wedding contract. In Nivelles in the fifteenth century, one such contract stipulated that a woman's friends and close acquaintances had the power to intervene should her husband mismanage the matrimonial property. A certain Anne and her husband thus recorded in March 1421, that Anne was authorized to sell property should her husband behave poorly. In the event of such poor governance, Anne would be assisted by close family members.[34] This case thus presents a wife who was in no way under her husband's yoke. Another contract dating from 1414 even stipulates that the woman was allowed to divorce should her husband become involved in their child's education. Furthermore, the text adds that the woman is entitled to leave the marital home taking all property and acquired annuities should her husband "have sexual relations with another woman during the marriage, at least if that is known publicly."[35] Hidden adultery was thus tolerated, but openly living with another woman would lead to divorce. Was the husband in question suspected of loose morals?

As we saw in the case of the businesswoman Liesbet in the introduction to this book, divorce was one possible option. Yet divorce as we know it today was impossible. It is true that since the thirteenth century a married couple had been able to separate physically and thus live apart, but the religious bond of marriage remained. In such cases, possessions were generally divided equitably, and the matter of who was responsible for the children was examined on a case-by-case basis, with mothers being more likely than fathers to be entrusted with this responsibility. Should a couple get on no longer and envisage divorce, the aldermen tried to intervene and urged them to stay together. To this end, they called on the assistance of the couple's friends and family. Yet at the end of the day the aldermen recognized that the ultimate choice lay with the partners concerned. A good illustration of this situation is a trial heard by the aldermen in 1492, opposing Jan de Poorter, a Leuven brewer, and his wife Margriet Ingelrams. The couple had been living separately for a long period of time, but for some unknown reason Jan stated during the trial that he wished to return and live with his wife. He took a solemn oath before the aldermen to improve his life and leave his girlfriend. So apparently there was a mistress. Was this the reason why Margriet had left him? It is quite possible. Be that as it may, she clearly did not place much faith in Jan's promises. On hearing his request she cried out *Genoech geseyt!* ("Enough said!"), retorting that she did not believe a word he was saying.[36] For if what he said were true, why had he made no effort to find their child, she argued. Indeed, their child had fled and was wandering about the surrounding countryside. In the presence of the aldermen, Margriet suggested that she return to live with him if he found their child, and if he obliged his mistress to settle at least five miles outside the town. Jan deemed these conditions excessive, answering that he could not oblige his girlfriend to leave town. He was quite prepared, though, to promise he would never see her again. Margriet finally decided before the aldermen's court that they would meet their friends in order to reach an agreement. Unfortunately we do not know the outcome of the case.

Where applicable, a marriage could be dissolved if one of the partners proved there had been no consummation. This condition was a hard thing to establish, and any cases were marginal. On 21 May 1450, however, the ecclesiastical court of Brussels annulled a marriage on these grounds. Elisabeth Kemerlinx had filed the petition given that seven months after the wedding, her husband, Jan van Plessendonc, had not yet been capable of having sexual relations with her. We do not know why Jan failed in his duties, but he probably suffered from some form of impotence. In any case, he admitted under oath that he had not had relations with any other woman, either. The judge ordered that the two were to be physically examined by a doctor – an image of such an examination has been preserved. As Elisabeth's virginity was confirmed (the record states that an examination was carried out *per aspectum corporum et membrorum* – i.e., inspecting bodies and limbs), together with Jan's incapacity to have sexual relations, the first option was medical treatment. Though we do not have any further details, we know that the ecclesiastical judge ended up advising the couple to live together for a while to make sure that *copula* was indeed impossible. This experimental phase did not produce the hoped-for results, for, as the record states, Jan was apparently *naturaliter impotentem*. After Elisabeth had once again expressed her fervent desire to have children, the ecclesiastical judge decided to dissolve the marriage: in such an exceptional case, a complete *divortium* was thus possible.[37] In such cases, the spouses could continue to live separately for their entire lives and look for another partner.

Unmarried women: Spinsters and widows

In most towns, single women enjoyed total independence. There was nevertheless a significant drawback: in certain cities, such as Antwerp, unmarried women had to be assisted by a guardian when concluding transactions. It is probable that a male adviser was designated on the spot. There could be a sizeable number of single women in a town. A calculation for the year 1503 shows that one fifth of the population of 's-Hertogenbosch consisted of single women or widows.[38] This finding was partly because people married relatively late. Additionally, living alone was regarded as perfectly socially acceptable. Certain women opted for a life in a convent or as a beguine, while others had not yet married. Many earned a little as young women, which would eventually enable them to present themselves as a financially attractive match. A small group of urban women never married. Was it the circumstances of, for instance, an unwanted pregnancy which led them to isolation? Or was it rather because they did not find a good match? Or perhaps it was a deliberate choice to live alone. No doubt the response varied from one person to the next. Still, we cannot rule out that, should their financial situation so permit, celibacy was preferred over marriage. The Antwerp teacher Anna Bijns, who remained single throughout her life, praises female celibacy in one of her poems, though without denying the drawbacks of such an existence. Once married, she notes, a wife lives in chains, whereas a woman who does not marry is her own boss. She thus advises her contemporaries: "it is better without ties, a happy woman without a husband". At the same time, though, she acknowledges that marriage may be the best option for widows. For example, if it enables them to be "fed and housed", then it is better for them to search a man's protection without delay.[39]

> **Women and poverty**
> Single women were at great risk of falling into poverty, especially if they had children. Those facing difficulties could call upon what were known as the "Tables of the Holy Spirit", secular institutions which assisted the poor in each parish. A daily meal was provided mainly for women who had been impoverished by a stroke of fate (because they were incapable of working or temporarily unemployed, or else had lost their spouse). Many people were helped by charitable friends and family. In 1305, for example, the rich widow Ida van Wijnegem founded a temporary shelter in Antwerp, the Sint-Juliaansgasthuis, for poor men and women reduced to vagrancy. Yet despite private charity, in 's-Hertogenbosch, for example, there were twice as many single women receiving municipal assistance as men. Equally, in various villages in Kempen, such as Rijkevorsel, it was mainly single women and widows who requested assistance, suggesting that this form of charity was devised specifically for this target group.

One category of single women clearly did not live alone, but cohabited with a man unable to marry before the law, such as a divorced husband or churchman. Even if the latter generally respected celibacy, it was not rare for them to have contact with a woman. In May 1464, Jan Cornet – a priest affiliated with the University of Leuven – and his girlfriend Margriete van Cockelberge signed a contract with the prior of Sint-Maartensdal monastery in Leuven,[40] donating the rents they jointly managed to the prior, in all probability because Jan felt his strength was deserting him. The two were acting like a married couple drawing up a will. On top of this, they had two children and thus formed a family. They included a clause in the will stipulating that after Jan's death, Margriete was to receive a yearly income of 30 Rhenish guilders, a considerable sum equivalent to six months' salary for a skilled labourer. The couple also recorded that there was a condition linked to this rent: Margriete was to receive the sum if she lived "in purity", that is, for as long as she did not embark upon a new relationship. If, however, she decided to tie the knot with someone else, she would only receive half the rent, and it would be her new husband's responsibility to see to her upkeep. They also fixed the future of their two children in the contract: their son, a minor, was henceforth to receive religious education in the same monastery his father had attended, while their daughter Magdalena was to find refuge at the Sint-Nicolaasberg convent in Aarschot. Lastly, Jan and Margriete also settled their two children's inheritance: the prior was to invest the generous sums of 200 Rhenish guilders in annuities, the proceeds of which were to go to them. Thus, though not married, the parents of these children lived practically as a couple, albeit in "sin" and "impurity".

Jacob van Deventer and Barbara Smets showed less foresight. This couple lived in Mechelen in the 1540s, behaving like a married couple despite not being so. Jacob and Barbara were not ordinary folk, but together ran an engraving and colouring workshop that sold geographical maps. It was Jacob who drew the maps – often commissions for the Habsburg imperial court – while Barbara, the daughter of a painter, saw to their finishing and tended to her husband's commercial interests. Jacob van Deventer ended up one of the most celebrated cartographers of his day, and together with his wife produced a large collection of maps of towns in the southern Low Countries, which are among the oldest still in existence. When political unrest forced Jacob to move from Mechelen to Cologne in 1572, Barbara had, in her words, "begged" him to marry her. Jacob had replied that of course he considered her as his "married wife", but wished to prioritize the trips he had promised to undertake for the Spanish king, Philip II. When he died a few years later, it was extremely difficult for Barbara to inherit, given that the couple were not married.[41] She therefore travelled to Cologne with the paperwork to prove to the aldermen that she was entitled to Jacob's estate, since they had run a workshop together. While unfortunately we do not know the aldermen's verdict, the case shows in any event that it was important for an unmarried couple to legally settle their affairs before one of the two partners died.

Like unmarried couples, blended families are an ever-present phenomenon. The high mortality rate meant that there were many young widows. They often married, especially if they had any minor children. The children from a first marriage generally came with their mother into the new family. In 1445, it was decided in Brussels that a widow, should she remarry or fail in her duties, could lose custody of her children. In this case, a person previously designated by the father became their guardian. In practice, however, children often lived with their mother. The aforementioned marriage contracts drawn up in Nivelles show that the stepfather, even if not overflowing with love for a child who was not his own, nevertheless provided for its upkeep. The marriage contract of the widow Jeanne le Marchand and the blacksmith Jacquemart Durant, dating from 1472, stipulates that Hanno – Jeanne's son by a previous marriage – was to learn his stepfather's trade from him. To this end, the blacksmith donated a few essential tools to Hanno, such as bellows and an anvil. Obviously, Hanno was allowed to decide for himself in consultation with his immediate family whether he would rather pursue a different career.[42] It is thus clear that the new father of the family was to take care of the son of his new bride. Daughters-in-law were also well provided for in Nivelles to enable them to find a suitable match on the marriage market. Under the marriage contract drawn up between a woman named Jeanne – whose family name is unknown – and her new husband, Jeanne's daughter was to receive all the household furniture when she married: two beds, a bathtub, copper pans, tableware, and two coffers full of silver.

One of the challenges in a widow's life was to manage the inheritance from the preceding marriage. It is not surprising that this event could give rise to conflict with the children. This is what happened to Margriet Van Veltem from Leuven, the widow of Hendrik 't Syngels. In February 1455, the aldermen's court ruled that she could sell part of the inheritance she managed for her children, in order to live off the resultant income. She had argued that her son Hendrik, because of his "madness", had caused extensive damage about which no details are provided, other than that it resulted in his being incarcerated in the town. It is likely that Margriet had to pay damages to third parties, thus obliging her to draw on her children's inheritance. She still had two daughters and her meagre revenue as a "poor widow", as she describes herself, no longer sufficed to feed them.[43] As the surviving parent had to manage the children's assets to the best of his or her ability, Margriet asked and obtained permission to sell part of these goods. She promised to use the proceeds of this transaction to buy an annuity which would initially go to her, then to the children after her death. Given the circumstances, the aldermen's court enabled a breach of the law in favour of a needy woman. This affair illustrates the understanding the authorities displayed towards the disastrous situations facing ill-equipped widows, especially the poorest among them.

Conversely, wealthy widows were the single women best placed to partake autonomously in public life: they enjoyed full legal capacity and obtained a share of the matrimonial property. Setting to one side any personal suffering that may have resulted from her husband's death, a widow could, in the best-case scenario, have considerable assets at her disposal, sometimes even continuing to run the family business. After her husband's death, Kateline Petit, assisted by her son, continued to run *Den Aer* Tavern near the duke's palace in Brussels for at least 30 years.[44] In towns of various sizes in Brabant (such as Lier and Herentals), widows were entitled to carry out all legal actions relating to trade. Furthermore, a widow obtained custody of her children. In this respect, the common law in the southern Low Countries was very generous towards widows in comparison to what was prevalent elsewhere in Europe, where in many regions a deceased father's business was immediately taken over by the children or heirs. The relative independence of widows in the southern Low Countries further implies that they were often an attractive marriage party, especially for young men seeking to rise rapidly through one network or another. Marrying the widow of a renowned craftsman often literally resulted in a flourishing partnership for both parties.

Conclusions

Not all women enjoyed comparable rights, for three reasons. First, a woman's rights were regularly altered throughout her life. Grietkin, the daughter of Jan and Katelijne from Leuven, had no choice other than to accept the course of events when she was entrusted to her father. Her mother, on the other hand, was able to autonomously negotiate the terms of this decision. In this context, Katelijne profited from the relatively favourable position of Brabant women: as a single woman, she presented herself independently before the aldermen's bench. Second, a woman's civil status determined her degree of legal capacity. Katelijne was able to conclude contracts with relative independence. Yet a married woman, however important her word might be within the household, generally had to be assisted by a guardian if she wanted to sell or rent anything. In practice, however, such rules were often interpreted flexibly, or else circumvented, and they differed from one town to another. Third, a woman's wealth and social position had a strong impact, for it was a fact of life that there were strong social differences between citizens. Less wealthy women not only found it hard to make ends meet, but clearly also did not have the means to take their fate into their own hands. They no doubt enjoyed more freedom in their daily lives in comparison to well-born women. The latter were far more closely controlled by their families, who managed their sizeable fortunes. Yet most wealthier women received an education. Furthermore, they were able to obtain legal assistance and hence initiate legal proceedings to counter injustices. So while women generally enjoyed the same rights, their wealth and social milieu determined what they could do with these rights. There is no doubt that marriage was a key link in medieval justice. It conferred specific rights and obligations to a woman (and her husband), as well as constituted a form of social security in a difficult society. Nevertheless, conjugal life could also cause emotions to run high, as we will see in the next chapter.

Notes

[1] *Ontsetten van hueren maeghdomme* (CAL, 7752, 323v).
[2] Mentioned in Bousmar, "Een historisch-antropologische kijk", 46-7.
[3] CAL, 1524, 13v.
[4] CAA, VS, 234, 12r.
[5] CAA, PK, 913, 97r.
[6] CAL, 8132, 248v.
[7] For example, three children in 1471 (CAL, 5098, 45v).
[8] "I hereby certify and state on my faith and my honour, on my truth as a woman, and on the Christianity I received at the baptismal fonts, that the man present before my eyes engendered by his body in my body the child present here" (*Hier zekere ende affirmeer ic, bij mijnder trouwen ende eeren, ende bij mijnder vrouwen waerheyt, ende bij der Christdomme dat ic over de (doop) vonte ontfangen hebbe, dat hij die dair voir oogen es, dit kint dat hier es met zijnen lijve aen mijn lijf gewonnen heeft*); Maes, *Costumen*, 94.
[9] CAL, 7776, 1v.
[10] Godding, *Le droit privé*, 117.
[11] See chapter 4 for discussion of the beguine movement.
[12] Van Cauwelaert, "Wettigingen", 61.
[13] *Tamelijck castijen* (De Longé, *Coutumes*, II, 210).
[14] *Gelijc oft sij waeren mijns selfs kinderen* (Godding, "L'ordonnance", 168).
[15] *Ibidem*, 166.

16. *Kintsche kint* (CAL, 7749, 40v).
17. CAL, 7752, 94r.
18. Dulac, "Le livre", 679.
19. Godding, "L'ordonnance", 152.
20. Vasquez, *Los sucesos*, 462.
21. Wijsman, *Handschriften*, 166.
22. Godding, *Le droit privé*, 73.
23. CAL, 7403, 310v.
24. "Women's thing" or "the monthly purification of women" was "the worst venom" (*Wijflicheit* or *vrouwenmaentsuveringhe* was *dat quaetste venijn*); Van Oostrom, *Wereld in woorden*, 220.
25. "To satisfy his will" (Sijnen wille te volbringen); "due to the young age and small size" (*mids der joncheyt ende cleynheyt*); GSAB, CC, 12904, 53r-v.
26. Roelens, "Visible women", 9.
27. *Maeghdelike reynicheit berooft* (CAA, SR, 67, 125r).
28. SAL, AOL, 1, 14r.
29. "Den man es heere ende meester van sijnen huyse, 't huwelijk gedurende" (Gilissen, "Le statut", 289).
30. *Van énen wille, ghelijc dat si sijn één lijf* (De Vries, *Der Leken spieghel*, III, 113).
31. *Die met paeyse wilt leven, late zijn wijf sijn overhooft wesen* (Goedthals, *Les proverbes anciens*, 39).
32. CAL, 7776, 19v.
33. *Als een man sijnen wive schuldich is te doen* (CAL, 1523, 104r).
34. Godding, "Le droit", 87.
35. s'il advenoit cose que li dis Gilliart tenist en son mariaige aucune femme carnelment et ce fuist seut publicquement (*Ibidem*, 103).
36. CAL, 7386, 163r-164r.
37. Vleeschouwers-Van Melkebeek, "Aspects du lien", 81; Vleeschouwers & Van Melkebeek, *Liber sentenciarum*, 180-1.
38. Blondé, *De sociale strukturen*, 55.
39. Without ties it is better, happy woman without a husband, you can have food and clothes (*Ongebonden best, weeldig wijf zonder man; ghecrijgen can cost ende cleere*); Pleij, *'t Is al vrouwenwerk*, 7.
40. CAL, 7357, 215v-219r.
41. Rutte & Vannieuwenhuyze, *Stedenatlas*, 21.
42. Godding, "Le droit", 101.
43. CAL, 7748, 208r-v.
44. SAA, AEB, 6926, 12r.

CHAPTER 2

Women and marriage: Choice of partner, matrimonial conflicts, and relations

Chanelle Delameillieure

On 4 May 1435, Adriane Vander Rijt and her parents went to the aldermen's court in Antwerp to register a surprising contract. Under this agreement, Adriane solemnly undertook not to marry without the express consent of her father, mother, and several other family members.[1] This contract thus guaranteed that Adriane's relatives would be involved in choosing her future partner. Such a procedure was not in fact unusual. Indeed, marriage was not just an important step in the life of a young adult; it also had major consequences for the family. It could harm the entire family's honour and prestige, or imperil its wealth, part of which the other family were legally entitled to. That is why parents started preparing their children for this event from infancy, reminding them of the importance of a good partner and alerting them to the consequences of an ill-considered marriage. Contracts drawn up in Leuven thus often contained a stipulation that to marry the children had to have the approval of at least four relatives, two from their father's side and two from their mother's. Parents generally restricted the range of options available to their daughters, but sons and even widows could at times be subject to similar measures.

There were good reasons for parents to seek to protect themselves in this way. Young people could neglect their families' wishes and wed an "inappropriate" partner in secret. Such a nightmare scenario was threatening Adriane's parents: one month before the above contract was registered, she had been carried off by an anonymous man and his accomplices.[2] It is true that the authorities sanctioned this abduction, that is, that a man had carried off a woman – with or without her consent – with the purpose of marrying her. Did Adriane consent, or was she a victim? We do not know. What we do know is that her abductors' attempt failed. If Adriane's marriage to one of them did not take place, it is doubtless because the authorities were swiftly informed of the offence. Given the Vander Rijt family's high social and economic status in Antwerp, the town moved heaven and earth to find Adriane and bring her back home. Nevertheless, the abduction was a stark warning for her relatives, who became aware of the "danger" their single daughter posed. And so one month after the incident, Adriane's father had a contract drawn up in the hope of avoiding any renewed secret attempt at marriage. Were Adriane to break her contract and wed in secret, she would immediately be disinherited. This condition was the severe, though unconventional measure for daughters who sought to sidestep parental involvement.

The example of Adriane shows that families used marriages primarily for strategic reasons: to forge networks and protect assets. Any attempt by the youngsters to oppose this mechanism was in principle severely punished. In Adriane's case, there was a threat she would lose her inheritance. Yet in the late Middle Ages marriage was not necessarily a cold and irrational alliance in which daughters were always the consenting victims of matrimonial policy. First of all, Adriane came from a high-ranking Antwerp family. Her father, Jan Vander Rijt, was even mayor of the town on several occasions. Within important families of this standing, the freedom to choose one's partner was obviously more limited. Historians still do not have any clear and unambiguous answer as to whether people in the Middle Ages were free to choose their partner. It is hard to hear the voice of the dead, and people tended not to leave any personal documents. What is certain is that men and women from lower social groups were freer to decide about their marriage for themselves, given that their families were less constrained by the wish to safeguard their wealth. Second, the contract between Adriane and her parents was in all probability a response to her abduction. Although this one had failed, many other abductors succeeded in marrying the woman they had carried off. Obviously, an important question here is the involvement of the woman: was she carried off against her will, or was she voluntarily accompanying her beloved? In other words, was it a couple who were fleeing to avoid parental control, or was the abduction perpetrated by force?

Marriage: Legislation, preparations, and ceremony

How did people marry in the Middle Ages? Civil marriage did not yet exist – it was a nineteenth-century invention – for under the principle then in force, a union between two people could only take place in the presence of God. In the twelfth century, marriage became an ecclesiastical competence, with the Church henceforth determining the steps for entering into a union with someone. The new ecclesiastical rules were both simple and complex. Simple, because marriage became a sacrament devised around the central idea of consent between two partners. Thus in principle, consent henceforth sufficed to marry, meaning that, for the first time, the ball was in the spouses' camp. A couple could thus wed *per verba de praesenti* (by "words of consent in the present"), that is, by simply exchanging the words "Yes, I do." Second, it was possible to conclude a marriage *per verba de futuro* (by "words of consent in the future"). A wedding concluded in this way was a promise to wed in the future, which promise equated to a betrothal. The betrothal became a truly indissoluble marriage after the fiancés first had sexual relations. The approbation of family members was not required.

The church rules were also complex in that they distinguished between legitimate marriages on the one hand and valid marriages on the other. A seemly marriage came with many requirements and ceremonial rules. For example, it was obligatory to publicly announce the marriage well in advance. It was the duty of each member of the community to voice any objections, such as there being too close a degree of consanguinity, which was forbidden. The diocesan court then examined each allegation to determine whether the marriage was to be authorized or not. Additionally, marriages had to be celebrated in public in the presence of a priest and several witnesses. Only marriages concluded by mutual consent and respecting all these supplementary rules constituted legitimate alliances.

Yet many couples paid scant attention to these supplementary provisions. They might marry in secret, for example, without previously voicing their intent, or even without a priest and witnesses. Such marriages were contrary to canon law. Known as clandestine marriages, they were illegal and a punishable offence. Yet such marriages were valid, for the simple fact of exchanging *verba de praesenti* or *de futuro* sufficed to accomplish the sacrament of marriage. Nobody could break these undertakings "before God". Nevertheless, the Church was empowered to punish those concerned. In 1454, a couple who had clandestinely married, Christiaan Vanden Scilde and Maria Pellemans, were summoned to appear before the episcopal court of Brussels (part of the diocese of Cambrai) because of their clandestine wedding contracts, their *conventiones matrimoniales clandestinas* as the solemn verdict in Latin puts it.[3] Not only did the couple have to pay a fine, they were also obliged to solemnize this illegal marriage by conducting an appropriate celebration within 40 days.

Such financial sanctions were meagre consolation for the parents, of course. Whether clandestine or not, a marriage was indissoluble once it had been contracted. Many took a dim view of the importance placed on consent, which was likely to disrupt the normal course of things. The couple and their families were normally meant to go through a long process before the marriage was truly sealed. The first stage was discussion and negotiations, which took place both within and between the respective families. After selecting an appropriate partner, families had to determine what assets the new couple were to be assigned on marrying. While the two partners were most probably involved in these conversations, it was the parents who had the final say. On 28 December 1416, Mathieu le Corbesir and Baudion of Fexhe, a fur merchant, appeared before the aldermen of Liège to establish the terms of the planned wedding between their respective children. The future husband, Mathieu's son, was present at this important event, unlike his future wife, Baudion's daughter.[4] The choice of assets for the spouses and the attendant conditions were discussed and registered well ahead of the wedding. All sorts of other agreements could likewise be registered, concerning any stepchildren, for instance, or the death of one of the partners. A contract drawn up in 1452 in Nivelles stipulates that the wedding expenses were to be paid by the groom's father and a cousin of the bride.[5] The more assets a marriage party had, the more attractive they were on the marriage market. Under these circumstances, a family of more modest origins had to be careful that a child was endowed with sufficient assets to join the circle of potential matches for families seeking an acceptable union.

> **Gift on marriage**
> Unlike elsewhere in Europe, dowries were not common practice in the southern Low Countries due to the law on equality of inheritance which applied in this region. Daughters and sons both received a gift from their parents, also known as a "marriage condition". Unlike a dowry, this gift did not hypothecate the subsequent division of the inheritance into equal shares. When the time came to share out the inheritance, each child had to "give back" their marriage gift so that everything could be shared out equitably. In wealthy families this

> gift could be a place of residence. In the mid-fifteenth century, Louis Pynnock of Leuven gave the "Moriarsart" estate at Moustier-sur-Sambre to his daughter Katelijne when she married Lord Librecht of Meldert. This estate, where 200 sheep were reared, comprised a fortified farm, meadows, and a forest. On his death in 1457, Louis in fact bequeathed this estate to his daughter, who also inherited a gold necklace, some annuities, and three golden cups that had belonged to her mother. From this point of view, a marriage gift was a downpayment on the inheritance, providing the new couple with an income or dwelling.

Once the negotiations had been successfully concluded, it was possible to move on to betrothal. This proceeding took place at the entrance to the church and in the presence of a priest. It provided a way of informing the entire community that a couple was soon to wed and of inviting people to come forward with any objections. Marie de Fauchamps of Liège and Wincelien of Oupeye were betrothed in 1434, exchanging the following words: "Wincelien, je vous ay encouent par ma foid que je vouz prenderay a marit et que jamays n'aray autre marit de vouz," to which Wincelien replied: "Et pareilhement, je vous ay encouent par ma foid que je vouz prenderay a femme et que je n'aray autre femme de vouz."[6] Subsequent to further investigation the episcopal court decided whether or not the marriage could take place. The verdict was not always favourable. In 1438, the diocesan court of Cambrai annulled the betrothal between Jan Vanden Putte and Katherina Cousaerts because the latter was reputed to have had relations with her fiancé's father.[7] In 1442, another Katharina objected to the marriage between Nicolas Papeleu and another woman on the grounds that Nicolas, the father to Katharina's three children, had previously promised to marry her. However, in the absence of proof, the court overruled this objection, thus enabling Nicolas to go through with his projected union, leaving Katharina on her own with her illegitimate children.[8] As she had not previously entered into a betrothal – or in any case could not prove it – Katharina was unable to prevent Nicolas's acquittal.

In the absence of objections, or if the couple got the nod from the Church (as was the case for Nicolas and his new spouse), the wedding proper was then celebrated. To make the event more resplendent, couples tended to get married in their finest clothes, in front of the parish church, and with a group of friends and relatives. Like betrothals, weddings were often celebrated not inside the church but outside on the forecourt. A priest awaiting the future spouses would direct the ceremony in their honour. He would ask the fiancés if they accepted to be the husband/wife of the other and join their right hands, thus symbolizing their agreement and choice of each other. The couple would then pronounce the wedding vows. In 1434, Arnold van Loet thus said to Maria Smeedts of Tilburg: "Mary, I, Arnt van Loet, give you my Christian fidelity and take you as my lawful wife," to which Maria replied in similar terms: "Arnt, I give you my Christian fidelity and take you as my lawful husband and will never leave you and promise to continue my journey with you."[9] After the priest's blessing, the man would slip a wedding ring around his wife's ring finger. Once the ceremony was over a mass might be celebrated inside the church.

> **"Drink money" and colour codes for weddings**
> Brides did not wear white in the Middle Ages. Weddings were very colourful events, for the different shades of colour in wedding outfits revealed a couple's social class and even how large the gifts dispensed were. A 1484 provision in Leuven establishes a link between the colour of the bride's dress and the amount that could be spent on "drink money" to please those attending the celebrations. As it was not rare for people to drink too much – and with third parties (such as people working for the Church) sometimes expecting larger sums – the town fixed the amount for alcohol consumption. If the bride wore a dress of baldachin (a precious fabric made from gold thread and silk), the "drink money" could be up to two florins. For brides wearing a dress made of scarlet (a fine fabric that was generally red in colour), the sum was reduced to one florin. Lastly, "drink money" was capped at half a florin if the bride wore a simple black dress. Most women got married in black, for rich golden fabrics were of course a lot more expensive than a simple black dress. Distinguished couples stood out from the grey crowd thanks to their delicately dyed, deep-hued clothes.

The ceremony generally ended in a sumptuous dinner and evening ball, for which wealthy families did all they could to display their wealth and status. The celebrations could even last several days, sometimes resulting

WOMEN AND MARRIAGE: CHOICE OF PARTNER, MATRIMONIAL CONFLICTS, AND RELATIONS 55

A symbolic depiction of a medieval family tree of a married couple (Bibliothèque nationale de France, ms. fr. 202, 15v). https://gallica.bnf.fr/ark:/12148/btv1b8470041x/f38.item#

in excesses against which towns issued ordinances seeking to curb the decadence. Accordingly, in 1443, Antwerp Town Hall announced that guests would henceforth be forbidden from giving excessive sums at a wedding. Only the "father and mother, sister and brother, uncle and aunt, and nephews and nieces may give what they wish," it states.[10] Once the celebrations were drawing to a close, the young couple headed off to the bedchamber to "know each other carnally" (*carnaliter cognoscere*) in the Church's terminology. After the wedding night, the couple were truly married and allowed to live together and establish a family. Many couples, particularly from lower social classes, did not follow this scenario and cohabited before marriage.

Abductions and (forced) marriages

Marrying after 20 tended to be the norm. Parents thus found it difficult to impose their choice. As their sons and daughters were young adults, they were protected by the law on free marriage and could choose to take things into their own hands and organize a (clandestine) marriage themselves. Even in the event of legitimate unions following the normal procedure, the parents' consent was not an explicit condition. Of course, when the community was informed of any marriage plans, it was harder for the young adults to escape parental control. Yet there are still examples of legitimate weddings opposed by family members.[11] The diocesan court of Cambrai thus found Jean Cornut guilty of having proclaimed to give his soul to the devil were his daughter, Jeanne, to marry a certain Pierre. Hoping to get the marriage dissolved, he further attempted to question the bride's freedom of choice by wrongly claiming that Jeanne's aunt had forced her to marry Pierre. Jean was punished for his "bad words" and for having raised a false objection. In 1444, the same court sentenced Jean Brisemoustier to pay a fine for having sought to sabotage his brother's marriage to a certain Hanette: he had disrupted the church ceremony, stating that he would prefer to be flayed alive than see his brother marry her. As for Pieter Vanden Bossche, he disrupted his sister's betrothal in the church at Opwijk in 1446. He had threateningly brandished a cudgel in the cemetery before entering the church to strike his sister. Pieter was taken into custody by passersby and punished for "his lack of respect for the Opwijk cemetery and for the sacrament of marriage", as the verdict states.

The fact that the Church's matrimonial law did not recognize the importance of parental consent was a source of frustration. That is why town authorities were quick to draw up their own legislation. Municipal councils tended to count a good number of members from the wealthiest families, precisely those with the most to lose from the free choice of partner. Starting in the thirteenth century, Brabant towns promulgated new laws focusing not so much on marriage itself as on abduction – the "kidnapping" of a willing or unwilling woman. An abduction was often preparatory to a clandestine marriage. In 1451, Margareta Brisons was abducted of her own free will by Herman Ruedinx after Margareta's friends and family refused to let them marry. After this abduction, the couple became clandestinely betrothed in front of St Martin's Church in Lennik.[12] Abduction could thus be a way of escaping parental control. By making this springboard to clandestine marriage a punishable offence, towns were hoping to dissuade potential abductions and so reduce the number of unions without parental consent, such as Herman and Margareta's.

It is hard to estimate the scale of the phenomenon of abduction. The bailiff and aldermen in Leuven registered over 100 abductions in the fifteenth century, whereas only 37 were recorded for Antwerp. While it is perfectly possible that abductions were more frequent in one town than another, the size of the difference is probably attributable to the sources. The registers of the Antwerp bailiff are generally more concise than those of his counterpart in Leuven. Additionally, for certain years, the sources indicate up to six abductions, whereas for other years none are recorded. Given that families and the authorities often reached an amicable settlement in cases of abduction, we may suppose that many cases were probably never recorded. Nevertheless, the severity of the laws against abduction in force in several towns suggests there was considerable concern. While it would no doubt be exaggerated to claim that abduction was a frequent phenomenon in late medieval society, it was probably an offence that legislators and judges had to confront relatively regularly.

What does the legislation on abduction tell us about secret marriages? Most of the texts make a distinction between the abduction of adult women on the one hand and of minors on the other. Abducting underage girls living under their parents' or guardians' authority was always a crime, irrespective of whether the girl consented. Yet the abduction of adult women was only an offence if coercion had been used. Adult women were indeed authorized (at least in theory) to marry whomsoever they wished. The legislators used the criterion of whether the woman had called for help to determine whether the abduction had been with or without consent, for a call for help was a possible indication of coercion, violence, and rape. Town laws were extremely severe towars abductors and abducted women. Abductors were to be beheaded or, under a Leuven charter, to undertake a punitive pilgrimage to Cyprus. Abducted women were disinherited. This latter measure sought primarily to dissuade fortune-seekers planning to marry a wealthy woman by abduction in the hope of gaining joint ownership of her future inheritance. In practice, though, abductors and "victims" only rarely received harsh sentences, with the provisions in this domain acting mainly as a warning. The overwhelming majority of abductors (80% in Leuven in the fifteenth century) got off with a fine, while others were mainly sentenced to a pilgrimage. It is true that Cyprus was a pilgrimage destination for many abductors, but other destinations were also possible, such as Aachen, Cologne, Paris, and Rome. It was also rare for a woman to actually be disinherited. In many cases the aggressor and the "victim" got married and a reconciliation with the family then took place.

In granting a central place to cries for help, judges nevertheless managed to punish false abductions on occasion. After being abducted by Gielken Vanden Gersse and his accomplices at Wezemaal around 1406, Machtelde Ellemoens, an adult daughter, declared several times before the aldermen that she had left with them of her own free will. The couple married and could no longer be prosecuted under the law, but the bailiff of Leuven did not see things that way. He presented two witnesses who declared that Machtelde had called for help at the time of the offence. The officer thus deemed that the abduction was a kidnapping "without consent", after which the Leuven aldermen sentenced Gielken to three pilgrimages, to Cyprus, to Santiago de Compostela, and to Rocamadour.[13] The importance attached to cries for help thus gave the courts a way of sanctioning affairs that, while not really crimes, ran counter to the social order. This ambiguous approach to female consent shows that the authorities' main concern was protecting the wealthy families' economic interests rather than repressing violence against women.

The key question in court cases was to know whether the woman had consented to her abduction and, therefore, whether she was an accomplice or a victim. Many abductions were not romantic affairs, but well-organized joint undertakings in which the members of a given family abducted a wealthy woman in the hope of getting her to consent to marriage. In 1407, the bailiff of Brussels found four men guilty of a single abduction, while in 1434 his counterpart in Leuven sentenced seven men for a single abduction. At Lubbeek, near Leuven, Willem De Smet was able to count on his brother, uncle, and two cousins to kidnap Liesbeth Winters.[14] And in 1476, when the widow Katharina Meulenpas went to morning mass at St Gertrude's church in Leuven, Dirk van Langenrode called on the assistance of no fewer than nine accomplices to abduct her.[15] In the event of group kidnappings, the victim was generally not consenting, and the abductors had to go to great lengths to get the woman to accept marriage. In such cases, abduction was thus often accompanied by violence, aggression, and even rape to put pressure on the victim and so extort a "yes". In 1419, a girl was abducted at Zoutleeuw, where she was dragged "forcibly through the hedges and verges". The victim managed to escape and filed a complaint, showing her injured legs to back up her account.[16] About 50 years later, Ruelen Van IJsere and a few accomplices abducted Machteld Trudens of Leuven with great violence. The men took the poor woman to Meerdaalbos in Heverlee where she was raped and brutalized. Ruelen asked her several times to marry him, but Machteld refused and finally managed to escape.[17] Ruelen and his accomplices had to pay a large fine as punishment for their crime.

Nevertheless, it was not unusual for an aggressor to succeed in his undertaking and to marry his victim. The sources provide examples of women who, having been abducted against their will, declared after a while that they were nevertheless "satisfied" – or ended up marrying. Even if there was initially abduction in such cases, the victim subsequently went along with her abductor's wishes in order to save her honour. Women's sexual behaviour largely determined their honour and their reputation, two factors of vital importance in late medieval society. It was essential for girls to preserve their virginity if they wished to attract a good match. An abduction, though, often led to something irremediable. Victims were then compelled to accept to marry their abductor, a step they would doubtless not have taken in other circumstances. Of course, the woman's consent was essential in these cases, too, so as not to compromise the validity of the marriage. In rulings by the episcopal court, a judge might annul a marriage or betrothal on the grounds that the woman had consented under coercion. In Mechelen in 1452, Hendrik Tieselinc violently abducted Margareta of Outerstrate before forcing her to become betrothed to him. The judge nevertheless ruled that Margareta had not pronounced the vows of her own free will. He annulled the betrothal, and Hendrik had to pay a fine and legal costs.[18]

Other women, such as the minor Ydeke Roenvox, used abduction to marry a partner of their choice. Ydeke was still living with her father Willem Roenvox in Leuven in 1418, when she secretly ran away to Hendrik van Calsteren's house in nearby Kessel-Lo. After a complaint no doubt filed by Willem, Ydeke declared before the court that she had gone to Hendrik's of her own free will and would not hesitate to do the same thing again. The couple married, and the aldermen decided that Ydeke had left voluntarily "under the appearance" of an abduction. Her father thus failed. Woyeken Hagen of Antwerp was also carried off of her own free will to marry without her parents' consent. On being asked by the court why she had gone off with her abductor, Woyeken immediately declared that she had done so because she feared that her family might marry her to "another man, who was bearded and ugly".[19] The episcopal court of Brussels regularly heard cases in which girls, after becoming betrothed, willingly allowed another man to carry them off and marry them. Margareta van Londerzeel, for example, was betrothed to Jan Swaden in Brussels. She then allowed herself to be abducted by Pieter Vander Heyden, with whom she became betrothed once again, in front of the parish church in Heffen (in present-day Mechelen). After the betrothal, she had sexual relations with Pieter on several occasions, meaning that the couple concluded a clandestine marriage *per verba de futuro*. In 1453, the judge ruled that the second union was stronger than the first, after which he annulled Margareta's betrothal to Jan and compelled Pieter to convert their clandestine marriage into a legally valid one.[20] Although these concise rulings do not give the context, it is likely that Margaret was dissatisfied with her first engagement (which had perhaps been arranged by relatives?) and of her own accord entered – successfully – into a second.

Young people thus managed to go against their parents' matrimonial policy. Still, it was not a matter of unruly youngsters indulging massively in abductions for romantic reasons. Mention of consent does not necessarily mean that an abducted woman was running to her beloved, or that there was a conflict with her parents. The only court reports we have tend to be for cases that resulted in punishment. These documents are often biased, only telling one side of the story as they need to justify the authorities' decision to issue a severe punishment or, on the contrary, to intervene more moderately. Thus if the aggressor only had to pay a fine, the reports are swift to justify it: the victim was involved, the aggressor was very poor, or he was drunk during the punishable deed, and thus deserved clemency. We must therefore not generalize from exceptional cases in which children decided on or were forced into marriage. The exact scale of these phenomena is wholly unknown. What is clear, however, is that young people did not fundamentally question the system in which the choice of partner was a family matter. In any case, it was perfectly possible that children themselves opt for a strategic as well as financially and socially beneficial marriage, just as there must have been parents capable of taking their offspring's wishes into account. Accordingly, we must shun any dualistic vision, especially as it is impossible to discover the feelings the two partners may or may not have had for each other.

Love, lust, and jealousy

Even arranged marriages were not necessarily devoid of friendship and love. As Jan van Boendale states: "husband and wife will love each other with all their senses". The ideal of a love match certainly had its supporters, even if Boendale also underlines the socio-economic importance of the union between a man and a woman, for "too dissimilar oxen [i.e., dissimilar partners] rarely pull the same cart".[21] At the episcopal court, the judge sometimes ruled that married couples had to live together in dignity and, in this context, often used the phrase *affectio conjugales* (conjugal affection). Margriete Pasteels and Heilwijch Vanderlinden also attached much importance to love in their marriage. In 1453 and 1456, respectively, they forthrightly asserted to the aldermen of Leuven that they had voluntarily accompanied their abductors and had married them out of love.[22] According to their declarations, both Margriete and Heilwijch chose to marry a man for love. A 1456 ruling by the episcopal court of Brussels shows that the Church likewise considered that some degree of affection was a requisite for a marriage. It thus sentenced a couple from Herenthout, near Antwerp, to a fine because they had clandestinely married after an abduction without their families' approval; yet the couple was further obliged to solemnize the wedding for, the judge explained, they had acted out of reciprocal love, *ex mutuo amore*.[23]

> **Attentive to ordinary people?**
> Court documents about marital conflicts sometimes contain descriptions of events as told by the parties involved. In 1434, Goeswijn Wevers of Bocholt sued his alleged fiancée Heilwige Comans before the episcopal court of Liège. He asked the judge to grant him Heilwige as his wife. Shortly before, he had abducted her with her consent. Subsequently, the couple had been betrothed, and on several occasions they had shared the same bed, "naked man with naked woman and single man with single woman", as the text puts it.[24] Heilwige, however, told a different story. She had been misled by Goeswijn and had become betrothed to him against her will. Additionally, this engagement had not been consummated, despite Goeswijn's repeated attempts. She thus considered that there had been no marriage. In the intervening period, Heilwige had married a knifemaker from Liège. She asked the judge to recognize the union and oblige Goeswijn to pay the legal costs. These two contradictory statements clearly show how subjective court documents are. They do not always contain true accounts, but cleverly constructed strategic stories. Both Goeswijn and Heilwige were assisted by lawyers who knew exactly what points to make to increase the likelihood of a favourable verdict. Additionally, reports drawn up by highly qualified clerks are not necessarily exact transcripts of what was said in court. While town court records were composed in the vernacular, those of episcopal courts were in Latin, a language that the plaintiff and defendant did not master. Even if it is hard to catch the voices of ordinary people, it is important to bear in mind that the accounts contained in these sources are fashioned by legal strategy, cultural expectations, and the language of the court and the law.

Feelings between the spouses may appear even in solemn court sources. In Balen, Griet Steynen had relations with Meeus Ghijlincx, but the couple had not (yet) wed. Meeus was soon letting his eye wander and cheated on Griet with another woman. Griet went to that woman's house to threaten her and instruct her to stop seeing Meeus, or else her house would be set on fire. Meeus went back to her shortly afterwards, though. Griet then took action and set fire to the roof of her rival's house. Meeus and his girlfriend escaped unscathed. We do not know exactly when the fire was, but in 1429 Griet was prosecuted for her criminal act and fled from Brabant.[25] In another case dating from 1453, Hennen Van Opstal of Herentals threatened his girlfriend who had just married another man. Hennen had had a long-term relationship with her, but she had ended up leaving him, to Hennen's fury. He threatened his rival and mutilated his girlfriend's face: "he wanted to cut off the girl's nose".[26] Griet and Hennen were both sentenced for their violent behaviour, for the authorities did not tolerate acts of revenge. Cheated partners thus frequently called on courts to deliver justice. Many of them (nearly always women) had been about to marry and sued their partner for having suddenly walked out on them. The anger, jealousy, and indignation these men and women felt are very recognizable today, showing how high emotions could run.

Was it possible to cohabit without marrying? We have already addressed the problem of women deprived of their virginity before marriage. As we shall see in the final chapter, the Church only tolerated sexual relations within marriage. Yet practice shows that many people's norms differed from those prescribed by the Church, and they lived with their partners without being married. As we have just seen, Griet Steynen and Hennen Van Opstal had three children together without legally marrying. Another telling example is that of the relationship between Heylken Lappaerts of Helmont and Jan Haddaerts. This couple had been cohabiting for five to six years when one day they had a fight and Jan slapped Heylken. Heylken immediately left Jan and fled, taking her companion's jewels with her. The source states that Jan felt the loss of Heylken more keenly than that of his jewels ("he was more worried about the woman than his other loss"). He immediately set off looking for Heylken, and "went so far that he recovered her". The couple patched things up and started living together again.[27] We only learn of such relations indirectly, in this instance because Jan appealed to the court after his jewels were stolen. That is why it is hard to determine how widespread this phenomenon may have been. There was a sizeable difference between, on the one hand, the norm of marriage as validated by the Church and, on the other, the practice of cohabiting informally whilst promising mutual loyalty, or clandestinely marrying.

Such unions could be prejudicial to any offspring, who were thus illegitimate and thereby not entitled to any inheritance. That is why many couples opted for the legal security of marriage. Given that there was no obligation to register marriages with the Church – a measure only introduced in the sixteenth century – legal proceedings could arise concerning the validity of unions. In 1445, a certain Jeanne Cabotte successfully sued several members of her family before the diocesan court of Cambrai for having threatened to exclude her from her parents' inheritance, as she was an illegitimate daughter. The court examined whether her parents, who had cohabited for a long while, had ever officially been married. After enquiries, the judge discovered that the couple had exchanged marriage vows prior even to Jeanne's birth. He concluded that there had been a marriage: the birth proved that sexual relations had occurred and that the marriage had been consummated. Furthermore, the ruling stipulates that the relatives who had sought to exclude Jeanne from the inheritance were ordered to forever keep their silence on the matter, and they had to pay Jeanne's legal expenses. In all likelihood, Jeanne managed to present witnesses to her parents' exchange of vows. In any case, this example shows that even for contemporaries, there could be doubts as to whether a formal marriage existed or not, and that two parties could claim the contrary in a bid to obtain the most favourable court outcome.[28] Even though an exchange of vows sufficed to make the difference between being married or cohabiting, this finding made all the difference for children such as Jeanne.

Matrimonial disputes: False promises and adultery

If men and women enjoyed a certain degree of freedom to act as they wished, the norms of consensus wielded by the Church also led to misunderstandings and infidelity. As it was relatively easy to wed, it was also easy to then deny any matrimonial bond. A relationship could thus seem like a marriage for one party, while the other viewed it as of no real importance. Women could even be victims of cunning playboys who used the promise of marriage to have their way. Afterwards, the man would hear no further talk of union and would abandon the duped woman, either single or with child. Historians call this phenomenon "self-divorce". Such men, by denying any matrimonial bond, unilaterally separated from their wives. In 1434, for example, Peter Moeren left Aleyde Andrée, who subsequently complained to the episcopal court of Liège that Peter had made the following promise: "I promise I will marry you in six months or a year at most." Although the combination of a marriage vow and sexual relations meant the couple were married by *verba de futuro*, Peter had left Aleyde and married another woman. And poor Aleyde was unable to prove that Peter had promised to marry her.[29]

Nevertheless, young women were not the only victims of cunning individuals. In Lubbeek, a widow had a relationship with Hendrik de Beer which lasted several months. Throughout that time she was under the illusion that he would marry her, for that is what he had promised. Hendrik had only led her to believe it, however, to obtain sexual relations: "he had promised it in order to obtain what he wanted from her." When Hendrik ended up marrying another woman without asking for the widow's approval and without even informing her, she was sore about it and in 1492 appealed to the authorities to sanction Hendrik for his misbehaviour.[30] Even though such men abusively exploited the law on free marriage, the authorities recognized what the suffering caused to their victims. The latter were entitled to compensation and maintenance upkeep. While it is true that women tended to be the injured party in "deflowering" cases, some resorted to ruse or lies. Thus certain women, such as those described above, were voluntarily abducted to get out of an engagement. In Bruges, there was even a case of two women who, wishing to be rid of their respective husbands, took the radical step of accusing them of sodomy in the hope they would end up at the stake, the standard punishment for this type of "crime".

Apart from false marriage vows, adultery was a common practice affecting married couples. While the ideal of domestic love inspired poets, marital life was not without its defects. Historians used to hold that adultery was condemned especially when committed by wives, whereas male infidelity was more or less tolerated. Recent research shows, however, that many men were also sentenced for adultery, particularly when they had extramarital relations with married women. There is one exceptionally striking dossier kept in Antwerp, about a court case from 1448. In its pages, a cheated husband accuses not his wife but her lover of adultery.[31] The wealthy steward Claus de Herde sued his good friend Wouter Breem before the ducal council (because Wouter was in the duke's service, as clerk and bailiff of Antwerp). Claus meticulously explains how he returned home one Sunday evening at about 8 o'clock, intending to go to bed. He knocked on the bedroom door but his wife Polixie, the illegitimate daughter of an eminent Antwerp figure, answered that he was not allowed to come in. Sniffing a lie, Claus burst into the room. Polixie ran out and Claus found his friend Wouter Breem "hidden behind the bed". Claus lodged a complaint on the dual grounds of adultery and of the shame Wouter had inflicted on him by abusing his friendship with his wife. We read that Claus was "an honourable man" who had been "honourably married" to Polixie for 24 years, a marriage which, because of Wouter, was now defiled by "eternal and pernicious shame and scandal". Moreover, Wouter was also married, further aggravating his case. When able to defend himself, Wouter swore on the Bible and on the "damnation of his soul" that he had never had any sinful carnal relation with Polixie. Wouter and his wife were good friends with Claus and Polixie, and the two couples often went to visit each other. So, too, according to Wouter, his own wife and Claus got on very well. Additionally, according to Wouter's statement, the pair had even played a "table game" (a sort of board game with bets) while he had slept, but he did not have a suspicious mind and had never suspected any infidelity. Wouter thus argued that Claus should have trusted him and should understand that his relationship with Polixie was likewise clearly friendly, instead of believing gossip and accusing him with his "jealous words". The duke passed the case on to the aldermen. They did not rule on whether Wouter was guilty of adultery, but nevertheless sentenced him to three different punitive pilgrimages because he had entered Claus's bedroom without his authorization. There is no doubt that this result put an irremediable end to Claus and Wouter's friendship. Likewise, the presumed adultery caused Claus to feel bitterly towards his wife. Polixie left, taking clothing and jewelry, and the couple opted for a "physical separation", a phenomenon we shall shortly examine in more detail.

> ### *Domestic love... on paper*
> Just like today, the theme of love was a source of inspiration for songs, poems, and writings. The Bruges poet Anthonis de Roovere, among others, wrote a poem praising the love between man and wife in a household. He gave four pieces of advice to married couples on how to avoid gossip and backbiting. First, he recommends devotion, then advocates honourable behaviour: temerity and insults have no place in a home. He additionally recommends gaiety, a ray of sunshine always being appreciated at home. Lastly, he wrote rhymes on love-making: "you will be kind, secret, and not too valiant in bed. Skilful in the work of love, firm, strong, loving". And, last not least, not "outside the rules but just the two of you", that is, stay with your own partner and do not go looking for love elsewhere.

This case reveals a remarkable degree of sensitivity. It is striking that Wouter was found guilty but not Polixie. It was a regular occurrence for the authorities to condemn the lover and not the adulterous woman because of the shame adultery would inflict on her husband. When a woman cheated on her husband, the popular imagination would seize upon the image of a man wholly unable to control his wife, or not up to the task sexually, who thus became a public laughingstock. By attributing a passive role to the woman and full responsibility to the lover, this trial, which was doubtless on everyone's lips, spared the cheated husband.

A fourteenth-century fable illustrates this sentiment well. The story is about a male prostitute, one of whose clients is the bailiff's wife. One day the woman is unable to pay, so the prostitute refuses to leave her bed. When the bailiff finds his wife in gallant company, he is afraid of losing face. He therefore pays the man for the services rendered to his wife and even allows him to complete the romping in exchange for a promise, that he never breathe a word about this paid-for gallant encounter.[32] Popular culture had a wealth of such stories, plays, and jokes in which spineless simpletons are the victims of their pitiless, authoritarian wives. This type of jest was very popular, for it conveyed the image that wives were meant to be subordinate to their husbands. Such fictional caricatures thus depict a topsy-turvy world, heaping ridicule on the henpecked antihero. The classic division of roles within a couple was thus undermined, seizing upon and exaggerating the additional idea of "shame", a very sensitive topic at the time. Nevertheless, many texts depict a courageous male head of family, thereby seeking to criticize strong women. Yet adultery committed by women was also punished. For them, too, infidelity led to shame, and the public nature of an extramarital affair was fully capable of overthrowing the established order, something the town authorities could not tolerate. Whoever it was who received punishment, adultery caused much resentment and sorrow within couples. If the waters became too deep, the miserable spouses could take refuge in adultery to no longer spend their lives together, as in the case of Claus and Polixie.

Divorce and remarriage

Once concluded, a marriage could not be undone: it was a sacrament, an eternal divine union between two people. The only way to be released from a marriage was to have it annulled by arguing that there had never truly been any legally valid union because one of the partners, for example, had been forced to marry or was already married. Tales about kings like Henry VIII of England seem to suggest that it was not too difficult to get a marriage dissolved, but in fact such annulments were rare among ordinary people. If there was no proof of marriage, though, because it had been contracted in secret, and if one of the parties then denied that this union had taken place, "self-divorce" was possible.

The fact that divorce did not exist does not therefore mean that medieval couples had to stay together until death. Married couples could proceed to a "separation of bodies". This meant, in theory, that they remained married (they could thus not remarry, and any new relationship was still considered as adulterous), but in practice they lived singly and were freed from marital obligations. Husband and wife could thus live separately, with each disposing of their own goods. Though the ex-spouses could not remarry, they no longer had any obligations to one another. To live separately, it sufficed to obtain the permission of the episcopal court and to pay a modest sum. Yet not all reasons were accepted to obtain separation. The main legal reasons were adultery and violence, but separation due to a wasteful or impotent husband were also recognized grounds. Sources kept at the episcopal courts in the southern Low Countries record about 300 cases of separation in the mid-fifteenth century. Between 1448 and 1459 in Brussels, about 80 couples obtained separation of bodies. In three quarters of cases it was the woman who requested separation. The Church thus sympathized with many women in unhappy marriages by approving legal separation. In one highly exceptional case, a judge refused to accept a separation based on a husband's adultery: given that the woman was having a liaison with a priest, the judge ruled that she, too, was guilty, and that the couple thus had to remain together.

Another, surprising ground for separation was *incompatibilitas morum conjugum*—"incompatibility of character". In the late Middle Ages, couples wishing to separate by mutual consent often used this argument. This argument is remarkable, for in most parts of Europe the courts did not accept it as a reason. On occasion, couples even invoked incompatibility of character to annul a betrothal. The 1453 records of the episcopal court of Brussels record the eventful history of Pieter van Stenere and Elisabeth Bollens, who fled secretly then separated before any marriage took place. Pieter abducted Elisabeth with her agreement in order to marry her, though without her parents knowing. Shortly afterwards, their relationship seemed to be in trouble, for their freshly sealed betrothal was dissolved on the grounds of incompatibility of character. Since the marriage in question did not take place, Pieter and Elisabeth were subsequently able to go their separate ways and marry another partner. The ruling explicitly mentions that Pieter was authorized to do so, whereas the judge advised Elisabeth to examine her conscience with the assistance of a discreet priest. The judge justified the end of the betrothal is follows: "for fear that someone should have to marry a woman he hates, for unwanted marriages often end in bitterness."[33] This addendum to the ruling once again suggests that affection – or at least some degree of respect and amicability – was both expected and desired in the relationship between two partners.

Repeated adultery was one of the obstacles that could lead to "divorce". In 1456, Elisabeth Voesdonck successfully requested separation before the ecclesiastical court of Brussels. Her husband, Antoon van Brabant, had been unfaithful to her on several occasions with a certain Katrien Goerijs. Given that it was no longer feasible to live together, the court authorized the two partners to make their separation official.[34] While there were also cases of domestic violence, it is striking that spouses separated amicably and drew up concrete arrangements to live separately. Once physically separated, a woman obtained a new status in society. She was no longer subordinate to her husband and became "her own woman", meaning she was able to initiate legal proceedings and to enter into contracts in her own name.[35] Yet a separation could weigh heavily on the life of women finding it hard to make ends meet without their husband's support. Others, being unable to ensure their children's upkeep, were sometimes compelled to entrust them to a friend or relative. Still, a fair number of them became prosperous businesswomen and very active economically and legally.

Remarriage was only an option in the event of the spouse's death. Certain widows were very wealthy, for inheritance law in the southern Low Countries was favourable to them, giving them the same advantages as widowers. Additionally, taking over their deceased husband's business could act as a springboard to an active and prosperous life in business. Furthermore, they sometimes attracted interest on the marriage market, as illustrated by instances of their being abducted by men lured by their fortune. The reader will remember the widow Katharina Meulenpas, who was abducted by Dirk van Langenrode and his nine accomplices at St Gertrude's church in Leuven in 1476. Katharina came from a wealthy family of craftsmen who enjoyed a good position in town. While it was true that a widow, as an independent woman, could in principle freely decide to enter into a new union, it would seem that her children and other family members were often still involved in sensitive projects of the sort. After all, remarriage could endanger their own inheritance. The choice of partner for a widow thus often equated to family interference. In 1405, a widow even entered into a contract of the same type as that signed by Adriane Vander Rijt, with which we opened this chapter. In this contract, Kateline, the widow of Antwerp tanner Jan Smeets, promised she would never marry without obtaining the approval of her relatives.[36] Although in theory widows were independent, it would appear that their families sought to control their choice of subsequent partner out of fear for their inheritance.

Conclusions

In 1449, Herman Diericx of Antwerp, being worried about the future of his niece Janne, promised her a sum of money if she either married or opted for a monastic life.[37] We do not know what she chose, but both were equally honourable. Married women were much respected, and the choice to marry was considered as equally valid as opting for a spiritual life. In any case, for both boys and girls, a legal union was a turning point in their life, having a significant impact on both their private situation and their family's wealth. That is why marriage was accompanied by a set of rituals, as well as negotiations and carefully thought-through projects. Concluding on this basis that girls were puppets deprived of their will in matters of family matrimonial policy, that there was no place for love and happiness, would amount to reducing complex historical reality to a cliché. The world of marriage and liaisons in the late Middle Ages was far more diverse than is often imagined: it was mainly conflictual situations which left traces in the records, particular those concerning the choice of partner. Still, it would be entirely wrong to conclude on the basis of these exceptional cases that girls resisted marriages arranged by their parents en masse, by opting to rebel or by fleeing with their beloved. Of course one should not, on the contrary, minimize the scope available to young people in determining whom they were to wed. Backed up by ecclesiastical law on free marriage, girls and boys could choose their partners themselves.

And once the couple were married, the parents had no choice other than to resign themselves to the facts.

This chapter has further shown that alongside traditional Christian marriage, there existed a wide range of alternative relationships between men and women. These could take different forms: adultery, clandestine marriages, lengthy or brief liaisons between unmarried couples, and prenuptial adventures eventually leading to "self-divorce". Nor should we forget that a relatively large proportion of the population remained single. Love or at least respect and friendship was of prime importance for married couples, even when the union had been arranged. This position was more or less ingrained in custom and expectations, as demonstrated by the fact that the Church looked favourably upon women's requests for separation on the grounds of adultery, cruelty, or incompatibility of character. While marriage was often the best option for women, both from an economic and social point of view, their role went beyond that of good wife and mother tacitly accepting their parent's and husband's projects. Indeed, the law enabled them to make choices going against what was expected of them, to leave their husband if the marriage was an unhappy one, to denounce infidelity, and to remarry. In medieval urban society, to be sure, women regularly made use of these legal protections.

Notes

[1] CAA, SR, 21, 500v-501r.
[2] CAA, VS, 234, 57v.
[3] Vleeschouwers & Van Melkebeek, *Liber sentenciarum*, no. 704.
[4] Demonty, "Documents", 125.
[5] Godding, "Le droit", 81.
[6] "Wincelien, I pledge by my troth that I will take you as my husband and will never have any other husband than you." "And similarly, I pledge by my troth that I will take you as my wife and will never have any other wife than you." SAL, AOL, 1,38r.
[7] Vleeschouwers & Van Melkebeek, *Registres de sentences*, no. 75.
[8] *Ibidem*, no. 368.
[9] *Mary, ick Arnt van Loet gheve u mijn kerstelijck trouwe ende neme u te mijnen wettighen wive* (SAL, AOL, 1, 70r-v).
[10] CAA, PK, 913, 5v.
[11] Vleeschouwers & Van Melkebeek, *Registres de sentences*, no. 420, 596 et 866.
[12] Vleeschouwers & Van Melkebeek, *Liber sentenciarum*, no. 317.
[13] GSAB, CC, 12653, 87v-88v.
[14] GSAB, CC, 12655, 209r, 223v et 12653, 68v (see too Vanhemelryck, *De criminaliteit*, 175).

15 Prevenier, "Huwelijk en cliëntele", 85.
16 GSAB, CC, 12654, 190v.
17 GSAB, CC, 12658, 106r-108v.
18 Vleeschouwers & Van Melkebeek, *Liber sentenciarum*, no. 370.
19 GSAB, CC, 12659, 89rv; and 12654, 209r, 251v; CAL, 584, 125r.
20 Vleeschouwers & Van Melkebeek, *Liber sentenciarum*, no. 526.
21 Jan van Boendale, *Der leken spieghel*, III, 95
22 CAL, 7746, 241r and 7747, 8r.
23 Vleeschouwers & Van Melkebeek, *Liber sentenciarum*, no. 968.
24 SAL, AOL, 1, 83rv.
25 GSAB, CC, 12903, 403v-404r.
26 GSAB, CC, 12903, 54rv.
27 GSAB, CC, 12903, 42v-43r.
28 Vleeschouwers & Van Melkebeek, *Registres de sentences*, no. 835.
29 *Ick ghelove u dat ic u binnen enen halven jaer of bynnen eenen jaer ten lenghsten truwen sal teenen wijve* (SAL, AOL, 1, 65v.)
30 GSAB, CC, 12659, 277r.
31 CAA, PK, 913, 29v-30v.
32 *Klein kapitaal uit het Handschrift van Hulthem*, 100-112.
33 Vleeschouwers & Van Melkebeek, *Liber sentenciarum*, no. 507.
34 *Ibidem*, no. 683.
35 A status referred to in the Dutch from the time as *haers sellefs wijf*.
36 CAA, SR, 1, 350v.
37 CAA, SR, 41, 431v.

CHAPTER 3

Industrious women and their life in business

Andrea Bardyn

Katlijne van Brussel was a businesswoman in Leuven in 1430, driven by circumstances to make her own living. Having decided to leave her husband, Hendrik van Schore, she was forced to be financially independent. On leaving Leuven, she settled in Kortrijk and set up her own business, making a success of it: three years later, she had amassed a savings of 15 Flemish pounds, a substantial sum amounting to more than a labourer earned in one year.

Yet Katlijne's life then took an unexpected turn. Having heard how wealthy she was, her (ex-)husband wrote her a letter. "With nicely turned words", he begged her to return to her hometown and resume their life together.[1] What went through her mind? Did she miss Hendrik? Or was it rather the little boy she had had with him who had stayed with his father? Was her solitary life too hard, or was she unhappy in Kortrijk? Whatever the reason, Katlijne packed her bags and went back to Leuven, imagining she would receive a kind welcome from her husband and that "henceforth they would live peacefully together as husband and wife". In what looks like a very naïve impulse, she sold all her assets and immediately sent him the sum of 15 pounds, as he had requested. Though Katlijne was clearly a shrewd businesswoman, her decisions were not so wise in matters of the heart.

On arriving in Leuven, she found Hendrik at home in the company of a woman named Anne. Her husband observed that it would be inappropriate to send his "friend" away, for she had been living with him for a long while and had always been faithful.[2] He dismissed Katlijne with these harsh words, refusing to say anything further to her, even though she had handed him her savings. Luckily, Katlijne was able to fall back on her network in Leuven and, with the support of her friends, went before the town council to tell her story. She begged the councillors to intervene "for the love of God", and to either oblige Hendrik to keep his promise and join her once again or else compel him to invest the 15 pounds in an annuity for her and their son. Hendrik presented his defence, but apparently it left the town council unmoved: the aldermen did not even bother recording his arguments and simply declared that the "long story" he had come up with made little sense.[3]

The aldermen ruled that the couple were to live together once again, urging them to treat each other with mutual respect. Hendrik was ordered to invest in an annuity for Katlijne and himself. The town was careful to add a safety clause, however: should Hendrik revert to his bad ways and leave Katlijne, then the annuity would be hers alone. This finding looks like a most judicious step given that six months later Katlijne had to appeal to the court once again.[4] The aldermen noted that Hendrik was still behaving "incorrectly" towards his wife: he wasted money, refused to grant her access to her savings, and was still living with a "woman of no honour and no use", public opinion showing little leniency towards women in relationships with unavailable men. Additionally, it was not only Katlijne's well-being which was in jeopardy, but also that of their son Woutertje. The boy was suffering both physically and verbally at the hands of his father and his father's girlfriend, and he had told his mother about it. The town council had no choice but to intervene and rule that Hendrik was to return the money he had stolen by deception, since Katlijne had "earned it on her own". Thus Katlijne was finally able to reap the rewards of her business in Kortrijk. There is no information, though, about how she managed this money. In any event, her future looked auspicious, having recovered this sizeable sum thanks to the actions of Leuven town council, the support of her friends, and her own enterprising spirit.

Katlijne's story introduces us to a medieval woman who succeeded in setting up and running her own business without her husband's support. Although she let herself be deceived by him, she ended up asserting her rights before the aldermen's court. It is thanks to this trial that we have the exceptional records documenting her life, but such a spirit of enterprise was not unusual in itself. Many a woman in Brabant earned their living as a trader or businesswoman. And women who did not run a business in their own name could still use the financial and property markets to invest or take out loans – some acting out of a necessity, others for profit. How did women manage to run a business, and what setbacks might they face?

Access to capital: Inheritance law in the Low Countries

Women's economic opportunities were bound up with how families handed money and property down to future generations. In places where they were on an equal footing with sons concerning inheritance, daughters had a much stronger starting position in society than if at the mercy of their families' goodwill. In this respect, medieval Brabant was a fine place to be a daughter: in towns and in most rural regions daughters and sons inherited equal shares. Brussels legal texts stipulated that children were to inherit "in equal share, daughters and sons, the youngest and the eldest".[5] The main exception concerned prestigious feudal assets: titles of nobility and seigneuries, such as a duchy, together with the associated political power, could only be inherited by the eldest son. Still, many a noble dynasty waited in vain for the birth of this precious son. In the absence of a male heir, the inheritance passed to the eldest daughter. This explains why the duchy of Brabant was headed by a woman on several occasions, with Joanna of Brabant and Mary of Burgundy attaining this honour in 1355 and 1477, respectively.

As the ordinary families at the heart of this book tended not to have any feudal assets, what they owned was divided between sons and daughters in accordance with Brabant law. This custom was far from self-evident. In some regions of Europe, daughters inherited less than their brothers – or even nothing at all. Such was the case in certain regions in southern Europe where inheritance law was strongly influenced by Roman law (unlike in the southern Low Countries). In these regions, a daughter had to make do with the dowry she received on marrying, meaning that her fortune depended entirely on her relatives' generosity. Most towns in northwestern Europe, on the other hand, had laws similar to Brabant's: in Flanders or Holland, as well as in towns such as Cologne and Basel and various Swedish towns, daughters and sons inherited equal shares. We must not underestimate the impact this egalitarian inheritance law had on women's situations in the southern Low Countries: thanks to it, daughters could likewise acquire valuable family assets. It was thus in their families' interest that daughters be sufficiently educated to manage family wealth with the requisite skills. Additionally, this consideration was not a matter of purely economic concern: to a far greater extent than today, land, houses, and valuable objects represented a family's identity and prestige and, as such, were used to build up profitable networks. It was precisely for this reason that families did not like to see their daughters marrying the first man to come along.

Yet this system of equal inheritance was not without dangers for families. That is why some parents selected a son to receive the majority of the assets. First, to avoid their dispersal, and second, because only sons could perpetuate the lineage and its coveted name. This practice was important in various Brabant cities where political power was linked to the family name. In Leuven and in Brussels, for example, ancestry and belonging to a limited number of families (the so-called lineages) guaranteed access to seats on the aldermen's bench. Thus certain families developed a creative strategy to circumvent egalitarian inheritance law using wills and contracts. In 1449, Jacop Paesdach of Antwerp had it recorded that after his death his daughter Katlijne would inherit an annual income of 80 pounds (about half what a manual labourer earned in one year), on the proviso that she renounced her inheritance rights to her father's property.[6] Yet on occasion such arrangements could benefit women. In 1420, for example, the last wishes of a brewer, Wouter de Backer, gave rise to debate. A group of men had to testify on oath before the Antwerp court that the contents of his will were true: the testator wanted all his goods to go on his death to Liesbeth, his sister Magriete's illegitimate daughter.[7] The bequest was enough to give a sizeable boost to the girl's future. No doubt Wouter had no direct heirs. Childless men and women regularly offered a little additional support to a niece. In many cases we do not know the reasons for these gifts: had the recipient taken care of them? Did they have the skills to manage an asset? Or was it a matter of giving a financial helping hand to help smooth the way to a profitable marriage? In 1438, Beatrice Greven of Lovenjoel bequeathed several valuable assets to her nieces Aleid and Machteld Oeghs.[8] Aleid seemed to be her favourite for she received a large plot of arable land. Yet the largest gift went to the daughters' mother, who inherited all Béatrice's other possessions, and as the latter explained in the document, she was free to manage them as she saw fit. Despite families' attempts to get around the law on inheritance, equal shares remained the rule. This precept meant that inheritance law granted women guaranteed access to a major prerequisite for business: capital and property.

Adult women: Caught between freedom and tutelage

While it was important to have property and capital, it was just as important to be able to control them. It was in precisely this domain that, starting in the fifteenth century, families started putting up ever more barriers to their daughters' and wives' economic activities. The phenomenon may be observed mainly in families who had (or aspired to) a prominent social position and who wished to consolidate their power, or else during economic downturns prompting families to protect assets. This strategy consisted in allowing women to inherit, yet refusing to grant them control over their inheritance. For example, it could be stipulated in a contract or will that a woman was to inherit assets but had to promise not to sell them or use them as collateral. This way the property could be handed down "intact" to the next (male) generation.

In 1449 in Antwerp, Margriet van der Rijt promised her father that she would not sell or mortgage the land and interests she was to inherit from him, but would keep them intact for posterity. Her father granted her a single exception: were she to fall into poverty, she was authorized to sell a single annuity to extricate herself from this predicament.[9] It goes without saying that this arrangement was prejudicial to any future business venture Margriet might have: even if, as a woman, she had inherited significant assets, she was only entitled to profit from them passively.

> **The aldermen's registers: A goldmine for documenting daily life**
> Starting in the fourteenth century, many towns in the southern Low Countries introduced what are known as aldermen's registers. These provided citizens and populations from the surrounding countryside with a way of registering contracts in exchange for a fee. They were often the record of an economic transaction (the sale of a property, a loan, a lease agreement), though also included all other sorts of agreement: a marriage contract, an out-of-court settlement in a murder case, an agreement on using a lavatory shared by two houses. The aldermen's bench thus functioned as a sort of notary's office, offering citizens legal security. The written evidence of this activity makes up a gigantic series of sources: in towns like Leuven and Antwerp, no fewer than 4,000 contracts were registered each year. These registers are obviously a goldmine for historians as they provide a unique

> vantage point on daily life in town. However, their sheer volume is also a stumbling block: they take a long while to analyze, and it is an impossible undertaking for a single researcher. Fortunately, various municipal archives (Leuven, Liège, Antwerp, Ghent, and 's-Hertogenbosch) have set up projects to unlock these sources. With the assistance of a team of volunteers, they are making these precious documents accessible to researchers and the general public.

Family decisions were not the only factor influencing the degree of control women had over their assets. A woman's civil status was at least as important. In nearly all towns in Brabant, an adult woman – if single or a widow – could freely conclude contracts and dispose of her assets. For most of their lives, though, women had the status of wife. And as soon as they wed, they had much less freedom under Brabant law. On marrying, a woman was *en puissance de son mary* (in her husband's power). The Tournai law, which was very similar, stipulated: *elle ne peut contracter, soy obliger ne comparoir en jugement sans l'auctorité et consentement de son mary* (she cannot contract, or oblige, or go to court without her husband's authority and consent).[10] Her husband was henceforth her guardian, her *momboor* in the Dutch of that time. Once married, a woman could not in principle contract agreements without her husband's knowledge nor take a matter to court without his being present or giving his consent. This stipulation was an enormous restriction on women's freedom of movement. They were now forbidden from undertaking any independent legal or economic actions concerning their assets (with a few exceptions, such as drawing up a will).

Yet a married woman was not totally deprived of any possibility of conducting business and making money. There were many exceptions to women's tutelage which eroded its restrictive effect. This was particularly the case in Antwerp, probably because the economy of this commercial town was booming, and so any available labour – including that of married women – was welcome. Still, a similar situation may also be observed in other towns. Under Brussels law, women could conclude transactions necessary for the household without their guardian – a vague formulation enabling women to conduct retail trade. A woman might also obtain her husband's permission to act alone (a letter justifying this consent sufficed) or else represent him in his absence. There were additionally many preserved contracts leaving no doubt that married women regularly conducted transactions entirely independently. In 1492, for example, Margriet van Moelneren of Antwerp, the wife of Peter Truydens, independently registered a contract in which Joos Varent promised her a large sum of money for a batch of cheese he had bought from her.[11] Practice was thus relatively flexible concerning the tutelage of married women, particularly when it came to ordinary monetary transactions or minor business dealings. However, whenever wives wished to commercially exploit the most precious and prestigious assets – namely, those belonging to a family estate such as houses, land, and annuities – the courts strictly monitored their tutelage.

The main exception to this type of situation was mentioned in the introduction to this book. Under Brabant law women could operate as a public tradeswoman (*openbaar koopvrouw*). This specific legal status enabled them to own their own business and conclude contracts independently. Thus if a woman set up her own business and assumed this status, she had no need of her husband's constant consent to conclude contracts. Yet these regulations should not lead us to imagine that the legislators were striving for equality between the sexes. What they were seeking to protect was not women's interests but primarily those of their trading partners and husbands, by creating the transparency married women's commercial partners needed. If we imagine that someone concluded a transaction with a woman at the market without knowing she was married, this person ran the risk of seeing the woman reconsider the agreement and try to pass it off as illegal if her guardian had not given his consent. This risk was genuine, as shown by several legal proceedings. To cite but one example: in 1598 in Antwerp, Martynke Crocx tried to send a creditor packing by stating that she had signed the contract without her husband's consent.[12] The status of trader thus sought primarily to avoid such situations. At the same time, it clearly established the presence of married women in the economy.

Women's possessions: Threats and protections

The law provided legal security for married women's trading partners. Yet did it also protect women and their goods? Legal protection was essential for a woman to have solid negotiating power in her marriage, thus providing a stronger footing for all economic activity. This protection also increased the number of options in the event of marital disputes, and for a woman deciding to leave her spouse, it limited the risk that she might lose her goods. Married women's property was a source of major conflict and potential tension between spouses, especially because the balance of power within a household was far from being equal. Under the law, a couple's property was divided into three parts: the husband's property, the wife's property, and the couple's property. This last category included everything the couple acquired over the course of their union. Unlike the wife, the husband was largely free to act as he pleased: he could exploit his own assets as well as their shared assets without his wife's slightest involvement. He was also authorized to manage his wife's property, though with an important safety mechanism: his wife's authorization was indispensable.

We know, though, that there was a gap between legal requirements and everyday practice. Thus the crucial question is to explore what this safety mechanism implied in concrete terms: did it grant the woman real control over her husband's actions, or was the latter in practice able to act as he saw fit and even take fraudulent advantage of his partner's assets (as in the example of Katlijne and Hendrik of Leuven, discussed at the beginning of this chapter)? A lot depended of course on relations within the couple – something we unfortunately rarely know – as well as on local interpretations of the law which could differ from one town to the next. Additionally, chronology played a role. Over the course of the fifteenth century, the aldermen interpreted spousal tutelage in ever broader terms, with husbands increasingly acting as the legitimate administrators of their wives' assets. Women thus had ever less say in matters. This change was particularly noticeable in Leuven. In 1449, the lawyer Jan Stockelpot presented himself before the court as the heir to Machtelt Mertens, recently deceased, who had been the wife of Hendrik van den Velde. Jan proved that Hendrik had given a part of his wife's inheritance to his brother Wouter van den Velde, without Machtelt's consent. As heir, Jan demanded that this illegal gift, made by Hendrik without his wife's authorization, be returned. The court found in Jan's favour.[13] The aldermen thus intervened in this instance after a complaint by a male heir. Nevertheless, Hendrik had not previously encountered the slightest obstacle when concluding the contract before the very same court. In all likelihood, the aldermen frequently supposed that a woman consented to her husband's actions, paving the way to abuses. The sources show that such practices were current in Leuven: wives had no say in managing their own assets. In that regard, around 1500, the town council explicitly stated that a husband was not authorized to sell his wife's assets without her permission, "even though the contrary is often observed", the aldermen were compelled to admit.[14]

Indeed, provided a husband respected his wife's and their household's interests, it was often admitted that he did so without explicit consent. Still, it would be an exaggeration to say that such usage gave men total freedom in managing their wives' assets. When a husband took decisions that were clearly prejudicial to his wife's interests, the aldermen generally found in her favour, sometimes at the promptings of her family who were distraught to see their precious assets being diminished. Thus having had enough, Zoete of Antwerp went to court in 1427, because her husband Laurens Netensone had farmed out part of her lands at Roosendaal against her wishes. The aldermen's court had to bow to the facts and forced Laurens to cancel his transactions.[15] But Laurens was stubborn: in 1428, the court once again had to oblige him to return various assets to Zoete, with the aldermen adding that he was to allow his wife to "peaceably" manage her own assets without interfering.[16] Zoete and many of her contemporaries needed to be vigilant, for mismanagement by their husbands could have profound repercussions on women's well-being. In 1431, the town council of Leuven was informed that the hatmaker Jan Hovelman had long behaved reprehensibly towards his companion Marie, "both in words and in deeds". Jan had borrowed money from several people by mortgaging Marie's house. By failing to pay off these loans, he had given grounds for Marie's goods to be seized by her creditors, which was his real objective. His intention was in fact to throw Marie out on the street, which the aldermen condemned as an "indecent and unreasonable" practice. They put an end to Jan's machinations, imposing that henceforth he was to conclude no transaction without Marie's explicit acceptance.[17] The town council was even more severe towards Gord Bosschart in 1438. To Gord's mind, he was free to sell and mortgage the properties of his wife Mathilde van Nijvel as he deemed fit. The authorities ruled that such a way of proceeding was quite simply "devoid of nobility", and decided to compel Gord to henceforth sign all contracts in his wife's presence. He was also enjoined to behave better towards his wife, otherwise public punishment would be meted out as an example to other men in Leuven.[18] These examples show that a married woman was not powerless in the face of an ill-intentioned husband. Further still, a man who had voluntarily acted most poorly on several occasions was, in the eyes of the law, a dishonourable family man. A woman whose property rights had been infringed was able to force the court to protect her. Of course, not all women could seek justice with equal facility: those who had no capital, no network, or no knowledge of law encountered more difficulties. Overall, however, a married woman had a relatively valid negotiating power within her marriage.

Yet what happened in the event of divorce? At the moment of a couple's physical separation, jointly owned goods were carefully divided into two shares, a delicate operation in which family members or specially mandated "arbitrators" often acted as mediators. Thus if a couple divorced, the woman did not suffer any financial loss and in this context enjoyed legal protection of her assets. This situation provided her with a valuable means of leaving a marriage should her husband's behaviour go too far. In the event of divorce, the town council ensured that the goods were shared equitably, and that the divorced spouses no longer had any control over the assets of the opposing party. This was also the case even if the husband and wife were not yet officially divorced but were living separately. In 1434, Margriet van Werchter of Leuven asked the aldermen to intervene with her husband Laurens van der Berct, who had long been leading a life of "malevolence". Laurens had left her and no longer had the slightest regard for her or their child. However, they were not yet officially divorced, and Wouter was thus entitled to act as guardian to Margriet and her assets. When he learned that Margriet had received a sizeable inheritance, he thought the time had come to take a chance. According to Margriet's testimony, he was planning on robbing her of her inheritance using a series of contracts. That is why the town stepped in and invalidated all the contracts involving Margriet's assets which Laurens had been planning to conclude[19]

Men who repeatedly mismanaged their wife's assets ran the risk of divorce. This potential outcome is what we may surmise from contracts drawn up by couples when they decided to live together once again. Such a contract often explicitly mentioned the husband's promise not to negotiate his wife's assets without her consent. In the case of Jan Truwants and Petronella, a couple from Leuven, the former's mismanagement probably played a role in their decision to live separately. In 1488, Petronella denounced her husband before the town council for mismanaging not only her personal assets, but also those of the entire household. She accused him of constant bad behaviour: he used her assets to pay off many debts and deprived Petronella of the income from her annuities and from property she rented out. Jan deprived her of so many things – and "without giving anything" – that she feared she would fall into poverty. The town council accepted her request for protection and ruled that whoever owed money to Petronella was henceforth to deal directly with her, no longer with Jan.[20]

Despite the council's mediation, the situation exploded shortly afterwards. In 1491, the couple informed the aldermen of their separation. Before the court they drew up a list of some important sources of income (mainly annuities) which they shared between them. The management of a quarter of the vineyard the couple had bought fell to Jan Truwants, while Petronella received an annual income of two sacks of wheat from a rural property. They promised each other not to sell any of the annuities they possessed – no doubt for the good of the children, though the legal document does not specifically mention them. The aldermen's court also deemed it necessary (or was it Petronella?) to stipulate an additional safety measure – Jan clearly did not inspire much confidence. The divorce contract thus stipulated that all documents and proofs of separate assets were to be conserved in a chest with two locks. Jan and Petronella each received one key, but they could only open the chest in the other's presence. Lastly, Jan undertook not to interfere in Petronella's management of her assets. Her destiny was thus in her own hands, and each could lead their own life.[21] Jan rapidly found a new partner (or perhaps he had been living with her for a lot longer), for the contracts indicate that he had a "girlfriend"" that same year.[22] She was called Katlijne van den Abeele and was a very active trader in Leuven. As a divorced man, Jan was not authorized to remarry for as long as Petronella was alive. Katlijne's assets were thus safe.

Many a woman fell victim to her husband's poor behaviour, but the opposite could also occur. It was less frequent, for the division of powers within a marriage leant in the man's favour. Additionally, it is highly likely that a husband would be too embarrassed to reveal that his wife flouted his authority. When a married man appealed to the aldermen to no longer be held responsible for any of his wife's debts, one may suspect a motive of this kind. By acting thus, he sought to protect his own assets from his wife's creditors. Arnt van der Stegen, an Antwerp trader, testified before the court in 1417. He stated that he disapproved of his wife Liesbeth Bantaerts's lifestyle: according to him, she did "odd" things and lived an "unseemly" life. The allegations remained vague, but his request was clear: Arnt wanted to no longer be financially responsible for her.²³ Liesbeth's debts would henceforth be her own affair. Margriete Alaerts, also from Antwerp, went even further. On fleeing the marital home, she carried off many goods and contracts belonging to husband, thus hindering the latter's management of his personal assets. In 1414, she promised before the court to behave better in future and to return all her husband's property to him.²⁴ Yet even though cases of this sort do exist, they are rare.

Investment and speculation by women

If a woman wished to make the most of her capital or property, or develop a business, it was obviously of key importance to have access to the financial market. Anyone wishing to overcome economic difficulties had to be able to invest and sell assets should an interesting opportunity arise or in the event of financial need. From a formal point of view, everyone had this option, although with the important restriction for married women that for many contracts they had to be assisted by a guardian. Clearly, much of the population was able to participate in the capital and property markets. It was in fact an essential aspect of medieval society, in which, unlike today, there were no banks. Borrowing money thus tended to mean turning to a private individual. There was no possibility of making a return on capital by leaving it in a savings account, for there was no such concept at the time. It was therefore in the interest of anyone with cash capital to lend it to third parties at interest, or to invest in property or annuities.

The capital and property markets attracted mainly men, followed by married couples; single women were present in smaller numbers. Yet the proportion of women on the market was in no way insignificant, even if it varied considerably over time and place. While there are few medieval cities whose sources have been preserved in sufficiently good state to quantify this participation accurately, one important exception is early fourteenth-century Montpellier. Women there accounted for 11% to 14% of the investors on property markets and for 11% of investors on credit markets.²⁵

The figures are sparse for medieval Brabant, but we know that in the mid-fourteenth century about 25% of the transactions concluded in Ghent were by women. In the late fifteenth century, the proportion was lower in

Antwerp and Leuven, where the average was about 10%, even though a rate of 15% to 20% was possible for certain investments. As for men, they accounted for 60% to 70% of market share. The lesser representation of women shows that their economic opportunities diminished towards the late Middle Ages. As mentioned earlier, as the Middle Ages progressed there were ever more obstacles to women working independently. This decrease was due to professional associations, family members, and the law. Especially during economic depressions, trade guilds took protectionist measures, and families reacted by seeking to protect their assets.

How are we to explain the lesser volume of financial transactions by women than men, despite women owning many assets thanks to inheritance law? Various explanations may be imagined. First, there were fewer women than men working independently: they tended to be active within their household, which was represented by their father or husband. Logically, there were thus fewer (single) women on the market. There were many initial factors against them. They possessed on average less property than men, which was an important condition for taking out an advantageous loan. Women also had less social prestige, and fewer suitable networks for concluding private contracts. For instance, most political and economic organizations, such as trade and merchant guilds, excluded women (unless they had connections with a male member). Lastly, all transactions between individuals were preceded by negotiation, and single women were often at a disadvantage in this context: they inspired less confidence and were unable to negotiate the same favourable conditions as other (male or married) businesspeople. Women thus faced many more obstacles than men on the capital and property markets.

Despite these difficulties, a fair number of women became major economic players. They were often widows or wealthy single women who had already accumulated a lot of assets and could dispose of them freely. Investing in annuities and property provided them with a stable income, enabling them to become "a woman of private means". Rich widows even often used what was called an "attorney" to invest in their name. On regular intervals this solicitor had to provide the widow with a summary of her accounts. Widows' capital often benefited not only the economy and themselves, but also members of their family, for they regularly invested in annuities that they left to their relatives on their death. Lijsbeth Scheelkens was a widow from Antwerp who was on her third marriage in 1491, this time with a stonemason. She borrowed a large sum of money from a couple, using her house as security. She did not take out this loan for herself, but to support the business of her son Michiel. He would probably have found it harder to obtain an advantageous loan, whereas his mother, with her wealth and experience, inspired greater confidence among lenders.[26]

Other widows drew income from their property. This was the case of Margriet van Overdile, who in 1449 farmed out to Hendrik d'Ottenburg a property with several pastures in Wavre.[27] This contract brought her a large sum of money each year, enabling her to cover her needs. Such investments in the countryside were clearly a nest egg for widows.[28] Lastly, there were also examples of widows who rented out part of their house to merchants to extract a profit from their property. Participants in the annual fairs at Bergen-op-Zoom often rented out a workshop or empty store from widows. The store and storage space belonging to Geertrui Claus, the widow of a furrier, were located on the market square, and in exchange for a yearly rent were used to store goods belonging to merchants in the German Hanseatic League. A rental agreement from 1495 stipulates that Geertrui also provided guests with meals and a place to sleep with three beds. Two years earlier she had already rented out the basement of the house to a Bruges merchant. In 1499, her neighbour Johanne, the widow of Thomas Hamers, rented out the "De Meersman" store with two rooms and a cellar to traders attending the annual fair. She also provided them with candles, dishes, pots, and jugs.[29] Such arrangements enabled these widows to pocket a tidy sum.

Many women liked to invest their money on the public capital market. This market had been set up by the town authorities. The principal was simple, comparable to a present-day government bond. The town often needed additional money, to finance a war, for example, or for major works in the town. In that case, it raised the necessary capital by selling annuities. The person buying an annuity – the investor – would receive annual interest which, depending on its type, averaged somewhere between 5% and 10%. In many towns women were keen purchasers. In Leuven in 1488, when the town needed vast capital sums to pay for the cost of war during a revolt against Maximilian of Austria, 22% of the lenders were women. In 's-Hertogenbosch in the early sixteenth century, women accounted for an even larger proportion of those who purchased annuities, with no fewer than a third being bought by women.[30] Notably, these figures only include women who bought an annuity independently.

INDUSTRIOUS WOMEN AND THEIR LIFE IN BUSINESS 87

Christine de Pizan works on her book "La cité des dames", while some ladies are building a town outside (Bibliothèque nationale de France, ms. fr. 607, 2r). https://gallica.bnf.fr/ark:/12148/btv1b6000102v/f11.item#

If we add the number of couples investing their capital, the proportion of women is higher still. The profile of these women investors varied significantly for that matter. The largest were widows and a group of very wealthy women. Most of them belonged to the town's political elite. The widow Isabelle Sterckenborchs from Cologne, for example, invested a fortune in annuities. This woman enjoyed high esteem: her son-in-law held an important post at the prince's court. Single women in their 30s were the ones to invest the smallest sums. These young women no doubt saw it as an excellent way of investing a recent inheritance or the fruit of their labour in a fixed income – with young men no doubt motivated by similar concerns. Married women likewise regularly purchased annuities for themselves or else with their husband. Irrespective of the diversity of the group of women investing in public annuities, it is indisputable that towns devised their policies partly thanks to the capital of many women.

Yet it was rare for women to invest in more risky sectors, such as international trade. Such a hazardous undertaking was probably the preserve of very wealthy men with lots of experience and deep financial reserves. Yet we cannot rule out that women took risky bets to make a quick profit. In the fourteenth century, there was a woman named Margriet vanden Grate living in Leuven, whose marital status and family ties are unknown. Between 1360 and 1370, she frequently acted as a tax farmer for excise duties. This activity was wholly comparable to speculating on a risky stock: the town council ceded tax collection to wealthy residents offering the highest bid for excise duty. The purchaser of excise duty was thus working on the hypothesis that this speculation would generate more income than it cost to purchase. Significant financial resources and above all entrepreneurial courage were required to purchase an excise duty. After all, nobody had a crystal ball capable of announcing a war or an epidemic which would disrupt urban trade, resulting in disappointing excise revenues. Most excise farmers came from the wealthiest groups and nearly all were male. Margriet was one of the few women to invest in such a risky venture. In 1360, she received the excise on the bread hall; in 1365, on the bread hall and the fish market; in 1366, the salt tax, the pound tax, and the excise on the fish market and hall; and in 1370, the beer tax.[31] It was doubtless not a matter of chance to see a tax farmer with such an unusual profile in the 1360s and 1370s, for these were years of instability in Leuven due to a craft guild rebellion. In such a situation, less "traditional" purchasers of excise duties managed to acquire a tax farm.

The story of Janne Schuts

For a long while historians thought that only widows were able to be active investors. Recent research has shown, however, that there was a large group of investors made up of young single women and spinsters. The financial markets provided them with an ideal place to invest the money they had accumulated or inherited. In this way, they were potentially able to put together a sizeable marriage gift and thus enhance their attractiveness for a potential partner, or else provide themselves with a stable income. In Antwerp in the fifteenth century, single women accounted for between 7% and 12% of all investors in long-term loans. Given that this group of women represented about 10% of the adult population, they clearly fully realized their potential and were significant lenders within the economy. One of the most remarkable investors in fifteenth-century Antwerp was a woman who remained single throughout her life. She was called Janne Schuts, and the story of her life is a fascinating one: she knew exactly how to seize the (economic) opportunities that the merchant town offered to women. As a single mother – and on top of that – of an illegitimate daughter, her situation was far from easy in a society that disapproved of sexual relations prior to marriage. Nevertheless, between 1421 and 1468, she registered no fewer than 158 contracts before the aldermen's court, a huge number. This total was all the more impressive as these are probably only a fraction of her transactions and business dealings: registering a contract cost money, and so small loans tended not to be officially recorded but just concluded verbally.

Janne Schuts's story starts in the 1420s. At this time she was a young woman, perhaps of middling condition. Like many young women, she worked as a servant in a family. That enabled her to earn an income and acquire important skills. Janne was a house servant to the family of Laureys Hacke, a wealthy man who made his money from fish farming and from property revenues. Laureys was married, but it seems that he was separated from his wife for a fairly long period. It was, in any case, a childless marriage. Several documents attest to the confidence he had in his servant, even designating her at one stage as his representative to appear before the aldermen's court.[32] The fact that an ordinary servant would be entrusted with such a responsibility certainly raises questions. Yet a few contracts further make clear that the relationship between Laureys and his maid strayed from the norm in many ways: when Laureys died in 1430, it turned out that Janne Schuts was the mother of his illegitimate child, Johanne. Since Janne and Laureys had not been officially married, she and her daughter had fundamentally no claim to inherit his property. Shortly before dying, though, Laureys had taken the necessary steps to ensure the two women's well-being: he gifted a large sum of money to Janne and saw to it that she and her daughter could continue to live in a house with a fishpond. This lay just outside the Koepoort, a gateway inside the town walls.[33]

Thus in 1430, Janne found herself in the unenviable position of a single mother deprived of the (economic) security of a marriage. She ended up remaining single all her life, though it does not mean that she was never in a couple or sought to marry. In 1433, she concluded a contract of the type generally preceding a marriage with Jan de Wijze, an Antwerp merchant.[34] The man was no stranger to Janne: she had already concluded several transactions with him and, moreover, he was none other than Laureys's neighbour. She must have met Jan when working as a servant. For reasons that are unclear, however, the marriage never took place. Apparently they either had a dispute or else Jan fell seriously ill shortly after concluding the marriage contract. Nor do we know if Janne was then forced to live singly after 1433 – due difficulty finding a suitable match, given that she had an illegitimate child – or if she deliberately opted for a life without an official partner so as to develop her business without a husband's interference. Whatever the case may be, Janne became an extremely wealthy businesswoman in Antwerp, investing heavily in property and loans at interest. In that regard, she was able to offer a substantial marriage gift both to her daughter Johanne and to her sister Margriete, considerably enhancing their chances of finding an interesting match.[35]

Even before the death of her Laureys Hacke, Janne had taken her first steps on the capital market, where she no doubt found an interesting investment for her wages. Then, especially after 1430, she fully devoted herself to her career in business. For a while she seems to have worked as a fish merchant: in any case, many contracts described her as a merchant, and it is known that she purchased the right to run a herring store at the Antwerp fish market in 1434.[36] She may have relinquished this stall in 1441, when she joined the order of the beguines. Yet it is hard to know whether she really settled down to life as a beguine: she retained her assets until she died, including a building at the fish market.[37] What reasons led Janne to become a beguine? Did this choice provide her with additional security as a single woman, or was she attracted by the movement's pious message? We shall never know. In any case, her brother Wouter made the same choice and lived as a beghard, the masculine counterpart of the beguines.[38] Like many beguines, Janne started teaching: in 1450, she signed a contract with the municipal official Klaas de Broye to teach his daughter and provide her support for two years.[39]

While the beguines cherished the ideal of a austere life, it would seem that Janne did not bother herself with this tenet. Even as a beguine, she kept up her string of economic successes. Her main activity was as a lender, to such an extent that we may suppose she was a professional financier. There are no fewer than 84 contracts documenting loans she granted to clients in the Antwerp region, for a total sum of over 600 Brabant pounds – a colossal sum of money which would have taken a skilled labourer over 40 years to earn. Her record years were indubitably 1456-1457: during this period she registered no fewer than 18 loans (mainly via annuities providing a regular income) and bought a house on the present-day Koolkaai—which, not coincidentally, was the main unloading point for Antwerp's fishermen. No doubt Janne had not forgotten her networks in the fish trade. Among those to whom she granted a loan were very probably people she knew from her life as a merchant: other traders, fish merchants, and people living near the fish market and quaysides. While her business wealth may have received a boost from the support of her former employer, the long series of contracts shows just how much entrepreneurial spirit Janne displayed on her own. She thus managed to amass a considerable fortune. In short, Janne Schuts was a single mother and trader, a beguine and teacher, and above all a major investor on the property and capital markets.

The weight of gender roles and traditional views

Women investors and businesswomen were doubtless not operating on an equal footing with their male counterparts. Various reasons have already been given, but one major aspect has not yet been broached: patterns of social behaviour and ways of thinking. These are partly documented by narrative sources and moral treatises written by clerks and ecclesiastics. Obviously, the ideas conveyed in these texts should not be straightforwardly projected onto daily practices, which often deviated from prevailing stereotypes. Additionally, these behavioural patterns were mainly transmitted via texts written by the clergy and the elite, whose opinions often diverged from ordinary people's. Nevertheless, these ideas circulated and had an impact on how people behaved in daily life. The roles attributed to women thus left less room for independent entrepreneurship than those attributed to men because most authors recognized that a woman was her husband's economic partner, thereby playing a key role in the family's economic activities. Stil, everything had to take place under the authority of the head of family, be that a father or a husband. This idea was also shared by women writers. The French author Christine de Pizan thus advised craftsmen's wives to be closely involved in the family business. They had to make sure they knew everything about the business so as to warn their husbands against poor business agreements or risky loans. It was also important for them to be able to oversee the business when their husband was away, as well as to exert control over the employees.[40] Christine's advice thus attributes a major supporting role to craftswomen, though never imagines any independent activity for them.

> **Christine de Pizan (c. 1364 – 1430)**
> After being widowed at the age of 25, Christine de Pizan made a living as a writer, an unusual activity for a woman not living in a religious order. Christine produced an enormous corpus of work, with 41 well-known titles, ranging from political treatises and love poetry to didactic writings. Various leading figures and influential courtiers read and commissioned her writings. She dedicated her book of advice to women to Princess Margaret, daughter of John the Fearless, duke of Burgundy. Christine's father was a Venetian doctor, Thomas de Pizan, who worked at the French royal court. Though her status as a woman meant she did not study at university, her father provided her with an excellent education. She married when she was 15, which was not unusual for girls from her social circle. After her husband died ten years later, she remained single with her three children. That was when she decided to devote herself entirely to writing.
> Nowadays she is best known for *The Treasure of the City of Ladies*, an allegorical work in which she gives full voice to her disagreement with the misogynistic texts circulating in the late Middle Ages. As

an apologia, she constructs a symbolic "city of women" in which each "constitutive element" corresponds to the history of a famous woman. She thereby sought to valorize women's virtues and their rich contribution to history. Yet Christine was not a feminist in the modern meaning of the word. Not only is this term anachronistic, but at no stage did Christine advocate equality of rights between men and women.

Yet the many samples cited in this chapter show that men and women did not always follow gender stereotypes particularly closely. Foreigners passing through the southern Low Countries were quick to point this feature out. In 1567, for instance, the Italian Lodovico Guicciardini wrote in his travel journal (translated into Dutch) that women "are always very active, both in acts and words, looking after affairs meant to be conducted by men, which affairs they accomplish with such skill and diligence that in many cases the men delegate all decisions to women".[41] Guicciardini also noted the presence of many women traders and businesswomen. A Spaniard who visited the southern Low Countries at more or less the same time told his readers that he had seen women oversee the entire management of their household, along with all contracts.[42] Such accounts should of course be treated with caution. Wishing to regale their local readership with exotic touches, these travellers easily succumbed to exaggeration, especially when describing how women habitually behaved. Even so, their comments indubitably illustrate that these travellers encountered businesswomen in the southern Low Countries, a fact that astounded them.

The strong presence of women in the economy also provoked counterreactions. The theme known as the "henpecked husband" became increasingly popular in art and literature over the course of the fourteenth century, peaking in the first half of the sixteenth. It consisted of caricaturing a household in which the balance of powers had been inverted, with a man living under the yoke of his authoritarian wife. These tales were immensely popular. They depicted cunning women ordering their husbands about and wearing the trousers outside the home, while he remained indoors assuming typically feminine household tasks, including looking after the chickens. Representations of husbands beaten by their wives or women riding their husband as if on horseback were commonplace. The message was clear: beware of women who defy male authority and overthrow the balance of powers within the family. These depictions enable us to observe how women's (economic) activities increasingly came up for criticism, as if they might disrupt relationships within the household and, by extension, the orderly functioning of society (the family being the cornerstone of society). Yet despite these moralizing warnings, ordinary women clearly remained active on the trade, capital, and property markets. Such are the economic facts. They often acted in partnership with their husband, or independently as a young wife or widow, but rarely on an equal footing with men.

Conclusions

Katlijne van Brussele, Janne Schuts, and Margriet vanden Grate were three remarkable businesswomen in medieval Brabant, and they were clearly not the only ones. The advantageous situation for women was linked to the egalitarian inheritance law and the relatively good protection of women's property rights, as guaranteed by the Brabant courts. Women were thus able to set up their own businesses and partake in financial markets, with the most gifted amply demonstrating the extent of their abilities. Other women made effective contributions to developing a family business thanks to their economic experience and by investing their capital, aspects which are unfortunately less visible in the sources. There were however a range of obstacles hindering women's entrepreneurship: cultural perceptions played a significant role, and the exclusion of women from the many craft guilds reduced their access to influential economic networks. Additionally, women's opportunities for partaking in trade declined as the Middle Ages progressed. Amidst a shrinking economy and growing social unease towards women working independently, the trade guilds limited their access to key sectors of the economy. As for families, they made clever use of the law to reduce women's control over their assets. Despite that interference, women continued to be very present in the urban economy – a presence that, once again, astonished travellers passing through the southern Low Countries.

Notes

1. *Met behendicheiden ende scoenen woerden.*
2. *Sij lange bij hem geweest ware ende hem treuwelic gedient hadde.*
3. CAL, 1524, 160v-161r.
4. CAL, 7727, 120v.
5. *Gelijkelijk ende hoofdelijk, zoowel dochters als zonen, de jongste als d'oudste* (De Cuyper, *Coutumes du pays*, I, 180).
6. CAA, SR, 41, 327r.
7. CAA, PK, 90, 69v.
8. SALv, OO, no. 122.
9. CAA, SR, 41, 359v.
10. Godding, *Le droit privé*, 80.
11. CAA, SR, 102, 19v.
12. De Ruysscher, *Handel en recht*, 189.
13. CAL, 8121, 39v-40r.
14. Meijers, *Het West-Brabantsche erfrecht*, 69.
15. CAA, PK, 90, 119v.
16. CAA, PK, 90, 126r.
17. CAL, 1524, 155r.
18. CAL, 7333, 108r.
19. CAL, 7728, 31r.
20. CAL, 7382, 141v.
21. CAL, 7776, 396r.
22. CAL, 7776, 495v.
23. CAA, PK, 90, 32v.
24. CAA, PK, 90, 3r.
25. Reyerson, *Women's networks*, 10.
26. CAA, SR, 97, 205v-206r.
27. CAL, 7344, 220v.
28. Jansen, *Landbouwpacht in Brabant*, 128.
29. Slootmans, *Paas- en koudemarkten*, 308-9 and 364-5.
30. Hanus, "Bossche renteniersters", 18-20.
31. Van Uytven, *Stadsfinanciën en stadsekonomie*, 127-8.
32. CAA, SR, 11, 368r.
33. CAA, SR, 11, 400r; SR, 15, 416r.
34. CAA, SR, 20, 184r.
35. CAA, SR, 38, 142v; SR, 43, 273r.
36. CAA, SR, 21, 456r.
37. CAA, SR, 50, 124v.
38. CAA, SR, 30, 99v.
39. CAA, SR, 43, 84v.
40. De Pizan, *The Treasure*, chapter 47.
41. *Neerstich in de weere [zijn] met hant ende tonghe, in hanteringhen die den mans eyghentlijck aengaen, met alsulcke behendicheyt ende vlyticheydt, dat te veel plaetsen, [...], de mans den vrouwen alle dinghen laten beschicken* (Guicciardini, *Beschrijvinghe*, 29).
42. Vasquez, *Los sucesos de Flandes*, 462.

CHAPTER 4

Pious women: Beguines and their virtuous lives together

Kim Overlaet

> *Around 1207, more and more women in our countries turned away from the things of this world to lead a life of service to God. Large numbers of young and elderly women lived together in ways resembling those in convents, as nuns habitually do.*[1]

So writes Jan de Wilde, a fifteenth-century author of a chronicle about Mechelen. His description of the origins of the beguine community in the southern Low Countries reflected historical reality. In the 1190s, a new informal movement started to emerge in the Liège region, bringing together religious women – *mulieres religiosae* in Latin, as they initially called themselves. These *mulieres* made the conscious decision to renounce material comfort as much as possible and to live a life of chastity devoted to reflection and prayer. Unlike nuns, these pious women did not pronounce eternal vows. Furthermore, on becoming beguines, they did not relinquish their material possessions. At first, the Church looked askance at the rapid expansion of the movement across the southern Low Countries, the Rhineland, and what is nowadays the Hauts-de-France region. Eminent clergymen suspected the first *mulieres* of heresy and mockingly called them "beginae". Recent study has shown that this derisive name probably comes from pre-Indo-European root "begg-", meaning "mumble". Their constant mumbling of prayers was viewed as heretical behaviour. Becoming a beguine was thus not without risk in the early days. The most celebrated victim is no doubt Marguerite Porete (1250-1310), known for her mystical work *The Mirror of Simple Souls*. In 1310, after theologians from the University of Paris declared her work heretical, she ended up being burnt – like her book – at the stake.

While *begina* was originally a pejorative term, over the course of the thirteenth century *mulieres religiosae* increasingly officially referred to themselves as *beginae* or *beguines* (*begijnen* in the Dutch of that era). Their male counterparts became known as *begards* (*bogarden*). Thanks to Pope Gregory IX's (r. 1227-1241) more indulgent attitude towards semi-religious movements, the beguines and begards came to be better accepted by the ecclesiastic community. Yet whereas the begard community remained small in number and eventually merged with the order of St Francis in the fourteenth century, the number of beguines increased dramatically. In that regard, the years 1230-1320 saw the foundation of beguinages (beguine houses) in a handful of towns in the northern Low Countries, such as Amsterdam and Leyden; in a number of regions in northern France, as well as Paris; and in the towns of Münster, Coesfeld, and Bocholt in the Rhineland.[2] It was in the southern Low Countries, however, that the phenomenon was at its strongest. In small towns such as Tongeren, Kortrijk, and Lier more modest beguinages sprang up, with houses grouped around a central courtyard. In large towns such as Antwerp, Mechelen, and Liège, beguines lived in beguinages inside or just outside the town walls, which in size were like little villages inside the town. In the thirteenth century, there were 20 or so beguinages in Brabant, with the main ones being in Leuven (first mentioned in 1232), Nivelles and Vilvoorde (1239), Diest and Mechelen (1245), Antwerp (1246), Brussels (1247), Tienen (1250), Aarschot (1251), Anderlecht (1252), Herentals (1266), Breda (1267), and 's-Hertogenbosch (1274). In addition to houses, convents (communal houses), and a church, most of these sites also had a bakery, a brewery, and a hospital. Financial support from noble women – such as the countesses of Flanders, Joan (1205-1244) and Marguerite of Constantinople (1244-1278) – was of major assistance to beguines during this period. Joan also founded the beguinage in Kortrijk, where the last beguine, Marcelle Pattyn, died in 2013.

Religious sisters
In addition to the order of beguines, other religious movements attracted women, such as the Benedictines, the Cistercians, and the Canonesses. These orders tended to attract noble women who withdrew to a monastic house in the countryside. Yet there were also monastic houses for women in towns. St Michael's Abbey in Antwerp had a section for nuns. Augustinian nuns were also active in Antwerp, running Saint Elisabeth's Hospital where the sick were tended to mainly by servants. The most powerful female monastery

> in Brabant was no doubt Saint Gertrude's Abbey in Nivelles. This was a dual monastery originally dependent on the bishop of Liège and rapidly became a chapter of Canonesses. Remarkably, the abbess carried out important secular tasks. One of her official duties was to name the mayor and town aldermen each year, albeit via the citizens. This privilege only lapsed at the end of the eighteenth century when the French invaded.

Despite the support of secular and ecclesiastical circles, prejudices continued to weigh on the beguines. After initially being associated with heresy by their contemporaries, the *mulieres religiosae* were subsequently criticized especially for their secular activities. To a far greater extent than monasteries, beguinages were buzzing with activity. The beguines were meant to meet their own needs thanks to artisanal activities, teaching, farming, or nursing. Additionally, on becoming beguines, these pious women retained control over all their individual goods, including any they might subsequently acquire (e.g., through inheritance). Their daily life was thus never wholly given over to devotion and was perhaps more similar to the life of single women in town than that of nuns. Furthermore, beguinages' internal rules and ordinances did not always stipulate very precisely how modest their household effects and lifestyle were meant to be. The rules drawn up in 1588 by Archbishop Johannes Hauchinus (1527-1589) of Mechelen for all beguinages in his archdiocese merely forbade expensive beds.[3] Thus in practice beguines were not obliged to renounce the luxury in which they may well have grown up. Kathelijne van Brecht, a beguine in Mechelen, had no fewer than two chambermaids in her household, with enough silver dishes for luxurious meals.

When Rombout van den Dorpe and his wife Elisabeth drew up their will in Mechelen in 1546, they were alert to the major differences between beguines and nuns. As stated in their will, the couple wished above all to ensure "fraternal love and harmony" between their seven children.[4] With this in mind, their daughters Lien and Leen, both of whom were beguines in Mechelen, received the sum of 100 florins. Given that the average yearly salary of a skilled labourer in Mechelen in the second half of the sixteenth century was 108 florins, their parents were clearly being particularly generous to their two daughters. As for Grietken and Beytken, the two nuns in the family, they received far less generous gifts of four florins each.[5]

Furthermore, the parents stipulated that Grietken and Beytken would no longer be entitled to the remainder of their inheritance. These sisters were proactively disinherited. No doubt Rombout and Elisabeth wished to safeguard the family wealth. Unlike a beguine's possessions, a nun's property was transferred to her religious community and could thus never revert to the family. Grietken and Beytken were of course further removed from secular reality, while as beguines the sisters Lien and Leen were allowed to leave their courtyard unaccompanied during the day.

According to Anna Bijns, a sixteenth-century Antwerp poet, beguines were often despised and rejected by their contemporaries and relatives precisely because of their free, secular way of life. According to her, many viewed beguines as hypocritical, perpetually guilty of lust. As one would expect, the reality was far more nuanced. Research on sources left by beguines themselves – such as beguinage rules and beguines' wills – has revealed much about the religious, social, economic, and family life of these pious women. Yet whereas historians have often viewed the beguine movement from the perspective of institutional and ecclesiastical structures, in this chapter we listen to what beguines said themselves. Those from Mechelen will be foregrounded, for many wills by women living at the Great Beguinage in Mechelen have been preserved. Additionally, these documents allow us to establish more general points relating to other beguinages.

The beguine movement in figures

Much of the data about the size and success of the beguine experiment in the southern Low Countries was compiled by the historian Walter Simons, who calculated demographic data for 31 beguinages. His research shows that in the sixteenth century, small beguinages had between 35 and 100 beguines on average (such as in Lier and Turnhout), while there were easily between 100 and 400 in middling-sized beguine courtyards (such as in Brussels and Antwerp). Three beguine sites stand out for their exceptional demographic density: the Great Beguinage in Ghent (which was home to between 600 and 700 women in the thirteenth century), St Christopher's Beguinage in Liège (with about 1,000 beguines in the thirteenth century), and the Great Beguinage in Mechelen (numbering 1,500 to 1,900 beguines in the fifteenth century). This means that in Mechelen the beguine movement comprised no fewer than 5% to 10% of the town's population. The sixteenth century ushered in a period of crisis, however. During the Reformation, nearly all the beguine courtyards in the northern Low Countries disappeared, apart from those in Amsterdam and Breda. In the southern lands, beguinages' chapels and churches did not escape the Iconoclastic Fury of 1566, sparking temporary yet mass migration by beguines from towns which briefly came under Calvinist control, such as Mechelen (1580-1585). Even so, the Counter-Reformation soon breathed new life into the phenomenon in the southern Low Countries, with various beguinages (like the one in Tongeren) peaking as late as the seventeenth century.

From an early stage, medieval chroniclers were fascinated by beguinages. In comparison to ordinary monastic houses, which were rarely home to more than 100 or so women, the beguine enclosures were extraordinarily successful, even during difficult periods. Gerardus Dominicus de Azevedo, an eighteenth-century Mechelen historian and canon, describes in his chronicle (*Korte chronycke* – 1769-1776) how "nearly all the 900 beguines" of the Great Beguinage welcomed Charles the Bold, duke of Burgundy, when he visited the town in 1466.[6] The four grand mistresses, elected by the beguine community to oversee the observation of their beguine courtyard ordinances, gave the duke fine linen.[7] The Great Beguinage in Mechelen peaked nearly one century later, around the mid-sixteenth century. In a letter to the governor of the Habsburg Netherlands, Margaret of Parma, the vicar general of the archdiocese of Mechelen, Maximilien Morillon, declared that no fewer than 1,600 inhabitants of the Mechelen beguinage took communion at Easter.[8] Even allowing for the fact that many non-religious people (such as servants, maids, and other laypeople) sought refuge in beguinages, the community in Mechelen was far larger than all the other beguinages and convents in the southern Low Countries.

In his 1563 description of the southern Low Countries (*Descrittione di tutti i Paesi Bassi*), Lodovico Guicciardini of Florence enthusiastically portrayed the Mechelen beguinage as a "dignified and exquisite beguine courtyard, fortified like a castle", as indeed it was at this period. Inside the beguinage itself, he admired the fine church dedicated to Saint Alexis, together with the "many houses and fine dwellings", as he writes, noting the large number of beguines.[9] Guicciardini was also well informed about how beguinages actually functioned. For instance, he explained that the community was governed by four beguines elected by the community, the grand mistresses, who oversaw religious orthodoxy in their beguinage. Nor was Guicciardini ignorant of how they differed from nuns, noting that beguines were authorized to dispose of their goods wholly independently and were even free to leave the beguinage (to marry, for example). In other words, unlike nuns, beguines were allowed to change their minds after entering, apparently without any risk of gossip or slander.[10]

Beguinage ordinances were very clear on this matter: a beguine did not pronounce eternal vows.[11] Even if Archbishop Johannes Hauchinus's ordinances mentioned above emphasize the miserable lot of those deciding to leave the community, beguines were able to leave the Mechelen beguinage to marry. Beguine Leneke van Brecht thus turned her back on a life of religion to marry Gerrit van Ymmersele.[12] Nevertheless, research indicates that, in practice, only a minority chose to marry – whether under pressure from their family or not. No doubt the opposite was more frequent, with women who had been widowed choosing to enter the beguine community. Yet such a decision was not without risk: in 1460, the grand mistresses of the Aalst beguinage brought a lawsuit against a certain Egied de Drivere for having kidnapped a wealthy widowed beguine one night with the (unfulfilled) aim of forcing her to marry him. The preserved statements even give the impression that widowed beguines were frequently kidnapped for just this motive (especially wealthy ones). So, contrary to what one might expect, the walls of the beguinage did not always offer sufficient protection against abduction.

The foundation and development of beguinages

Beguines were also part of the town from a spatial point of view. Like elsewhere, the first Mechelen beguines were not an organized community but lived scattered across the town. During the first informal phase of the movement, they aspired to a life modelled on that of famous hermits, such as the Brabant mystic Marie of Oignies, originally from Nivelles (1177-1213). As of the early thirteenth century, beguines increasingly started living together in communal houses. These were located in the district of the hospice for retired priests, in Melaan on the right bank of the River Dyle (phase 1 on the map). After a while these women acquired a plot of land together where the current Kanunnik De Deckerstraat lies and built a chapel there in honour of Saint Catherine. The first official community in Mechelen gradually took shape in the vicinity of these streets (phase 2). Seeking a calmer place to live and work, the beguines successfully petitioned the bishop of Cambrai in the second half of the thirteenth century to be allowed to choose a place to "live together very virtuously".[13] Then they moved to a new and far larger beguine courtyard outside the Kathelijnepoort, between the Antwerpse Poort and the Dyle (phase 3).

In 1578, the town council had the beguinage demolished to prevent enemy armies using it as a military base. Before and during the short Calvinist regime (1581-1585), most beguines were forced to take refuge in beguinages in neighbouring towns, such as Brussels, Antwerp, and Leuven. In 1585, after the duke of Parma's Spanish armies' victory over the Calvinists, a large majority of these refugee beguines returned to Mechelen where they set up home in a new beguinage in and around the Keizershof. This settlement complied with Council of Trent (1545-1563) regulations stipulating that new beguinages were to be founded within city walls. During the 1590s, the Mechelen beguines acquired the "Fontes" house on the Nonnestraat, together with its orchards, stables, and well. Shortly afterwards, other buildings were purchased or built on the Kromme Elleboogstraat and other streets in the sparsely populated area around the Nonnestraat (see map).[14] Lastly, in 1595, the beguine community received permission from Philip II of Spain to establish a boundary between the beguinage and the town centre by building a perimeter wall with two gateways. Two years later, Archbishop Matthias Hovius inaugurated the beguinage's new church. In the wake of the Council of Trent and the spread of Calvinism, the great beguinages in other towns in the southern Low Countries, such as Antwerp, were progressively replaced by smaller beguine complexes within the city walls.

Devout women refusing any other union?

While it is true that as of the thirteenth century devout texts traditionally described beguine life as the ultimate external manifestation of the apostolic virtues of poverty and chastity, historians now agree that the experience was also a demographic and socio-economic phenomenon. In the early days, beguinages offered an attractive alternative for women from socially inferior classes wishing to lead a religious life, but without the means to pay the fixed entry cost to join a convent. Other historians, considering that late medieval towns were confronted with a systematic surplus of women due to the higher mortality rate among men, have linked the success of beguinages to their offering a refuge to women who, for various reasons, could not (or did not wish to) find a husband. However, recent studies have shown that the number of surplus women never reached sufficient levels to explain the popularity of beguinages, and any cost difference between entering a beguinage or a monastery also needs to be strongly qualified. Additionally, this line of reasoning might lead us to view becoming a beguine as a default plan for women who would have preferred marriage or a monastic life. Yet novices in beguinages tended to be older than their sisters in convents. This difference suggests that they were not motivated solely by religious grounds. That is why the latest research emphasizes characteristics specific to beguine life, which could be more attractive for single women independently of costly convents or any surplus of women. Walter Simons thus argues that the success of beguinages may probably be explained by the opportunities this religious practice offered to single women aspiring to a relatively independent life in a safe environment. The example of Janne Schuts from Antwerp, discussed in the previous chapter, provides a remarkable illustration of this situation. According to many historians, marrying late and loosening family ties seem to have created conditions favourable to the emergence of the beguine movement. The Middle Ages were characterized by the emergence of associations of people based on grounds other than ties of blood, like guilds – and beguinages, too.

Yet the link between loosening family ties and women's increased freedom of individual choice with regard to their families has not been conclusively proven. The condition Rombout and Elisabeth Van den Dorpe attached to the inheritance they left to their two beguine daughters even suggests that one's immediate family may have been a major influence on single women's individual choices. With this context in mind, it is conceivable that opting to be a beguine may have been an interesting strategy to preserve a family's wealth. What was it about becoming a beguine that women (and their relatives) found attractive? To answer this question, it is important to take individual factors into account, such as a beguine's social status, wealth, and the size of her family. Even if it is tempting for today's secularized society to suspect the beguines of being motivated by economic rather than religious reasons, we cannot necessarily exclude the latter. Research into material possessions shows the extent to which religion played a leading role in their lives. Barbele Cnobbaert of Mechelen was the owner not only of silver dishes, but also of several precious rosaries and pictures of St John the Baptist and of the Last Supper.[15] It therefore seems mistaken to suspect Barbele of feigned piety on the sole grounds of her possessions. Religious considerations no doubt also entered into the equation when she decided to join the beguine community. After all, she had still possessed the means to lead a secular life as a single woman.

In towns there was a relatively large number of single women who could meet their own needs in various ways. In this respect, the poet Anna Bijns of Antwerp was firmly convinced that women who preferred to marry must be mad. She addressed the following warning to young people: "think well before marrying hastily: it is not some sort of amusement, but possibly eternal torment".[16] To her mind, though, this possibility did not mean that celibacy was the next logical step: she earned a living outside the Antwerp beguinage as a teacher and poet. In other words, not all single women were necessarily attracted by the religious obligations and restrictions of living as a beguine. It also remains to be seen to what extent beguinage walls protected their residents against abduction, for example. To better protect these women against criminality, the Leuven authorities decreed in 1444 that the only legitimate access to the town's beguinage was via the gateway, not by climbing its walls.[17] Especially during the troubled sixteenth century, life in a beguinage was not always safer than life in town. The beguines at the "Hof Sion" beguinage – at some distance outside Antwerp's city walls – had to leave their residence in 1542, during a siege by troops from Guelders. As for the Mechelen beguinage, it was pillaged twice – during the Iconoclastic Fury in 1566, and by the duke of Alba's soldiers in 1572 – before being demolished.

Lastly, the strict entry conditions influenced young single women's freedom of choice. From the outset, most beguinages pursued a policy to curb the number of impoverished women able to join. Under most statutes and ordinances drawn up from about 1400 onwards, beguine aspirants had to prove they could meet their own needs for at least three years. Women wishing to obtain this status were therefore obliged to have all the requisite resources and/or skills before being eligible. Most beguines therefore worked throughout their life to meet their needs. Additionally, prior to joining, they had to possess at least one bed, adequate clothing, and the necessary household items. It was only after three years without

Some beguines were able to afford a rich tomb, as was the case with the Leuven beguine Catharina van Neten. She was buried in 1460 under a magnificent tombstone in the Great Beguinage of Leuven. (Leuven, Sint-Jan-de-Doperkerk).

support that poor or impoverished beguines could call on the charity organized by the community and move into one of the communal houses. In her will dated 1575, Anneke Stockvis of Mechelen expressed her affection and compassion for the indigent beguines with whom she lived.[18] It is thus highly likely that many beguines came from the upper classes. Such was certainly the case for the grand mistresses. Equally, many administrators of monasteries in Leuven had ties to leading families in the town. The 1412 will of Grand Mistress Catherine Van Oppendorp, a descendant of one of the oldest families in Leuven, shows that she had lands and sizeable interests.[19] What about the beguines in her entourage, though? Were they too from rich families? A 1526 census indicates that large percentages of beguines were not rich enough to pay a new tax. In Aarschot and the Great Beguinage in Leuven, this figure amounted to half the residents, while in the beguine complex "Ter Wijngaard" in Brussels and the beguinage at Saint Catherine's in Diest the figure stood at between 30% and 40%.[20] While there is no doubt that people often claim to be poorer when it is a matter of taxes, the figures are nevertheless surprising.

Of good repute and good family?

Clearly, opting for life as a beguine was in any case not the simplest choice for women who wished to remain single or were incapable of finding a husband. This circumstance raises the following question: how and thanks to whom did beguines already own, prior to arrival, a bed, adequate clothing, and the requisite household items? These women additionally had to pay rent for their room or house in the beguinage. The will drawn up by Adriane van Hanswijck in 1546 clearly shows how important it could be to have support from one's relatives. To express her gratitude, she left her father the large sum of 150 florins, the equivalent of what he had lent her to buy a house in the beguinage where she had lived all her life.[21] Adriane's example is probably not exceptional. It was only thanks to the support of family members and the right to manage their assets themselves (including any inheritances) that wealthy beguines were able to build new houses or rent existing houses of fitting status. On their death, these new houses passed into the hands of the beguinage and were converted into convents or rented out to other beguines, in accordance with the last wishes of their former occupants. In the archdiocese of

Mechelen, beguines were additionally encouraged to invest in repairing and renovating older houses to prevent the beguinage from deteriorating.[22] A will was the ideal means to respond to this call. In 1546, the wealthy Barbele Cnobbaert left to the convent a modest annuity of three florins to maintain the house where she lived.[23]

In conjunction with the priest, the grand mistresses elected by the community saw to it that all women admitted were of impeccable repute, in good physical and mental health, and free of contagious disease. To prove not only that they could meet their needs but also lived a virtuous life, beguine aspirants had to have at least one person vouch for them. This person guaranteed their good repute and promised to support them if initially necessary. It was better to be vouched for by a beguine or ecclesiastic, possibly a layperson such as a relative, who promised, in the worst-case scenario, to pay for their upkeep for three years.[24] A sixteenth-century list from Mechelen of the names of all the beguines and their guarantors for the period 1553-1600 shows that this function tended to be fulfilled by next of kin.[25] In 1558, Catharina Tsrycken's brothers vouched for her capacity to meet her needs for three years. Three years later, she in turn vouched for her niece Liesbeth. As for Anne Pester, her mother and aunt supported her ambition to become a beguine in 1560, while Margriet van Heyst's parents vouched for their daughter when she wished to join in 1567.

There were several ways in which a family could influence a pious young woman's options and freedom of choice. The beguine costume that Heilwijch Ansens gave to her niece Anneke was worthless unless Anneke, too, became a beguine.[26] Beguines even attached this condition to gifts to young women in their family. Among the things Marieke, niece of Kathelijne van Brecht, was to inherit after her aunt's death was the bed in which she had apparently been sleeping for some while already. If Marieke became a beguine, as her aunt had been, she would also inherit her finest beguine habit.[27] In 1558, all Liesken Jans's nieces were bequeathed various valuable pieces of furniture, together with a hereditary annuity, provided they continued to live in the beguinage. Should any of them leave, they would immediately lose this inheritance.[28] Similarly, Appollone de Soricke declared in her will of 1553 that her niece Klara would inherit a hereditary annuity of six florins if she became a beguine. Were Klara not to do so, she would only inherit the modest annuity of three florins. Appollone additionally made provision for a hereditary annuity of four florins for any of her other nieces who became beguines.[29] In her will of 1548, Johanne de Bruyne was more explicit in her support for beguines in her family entourage, making provisions for bequests to all women in her family who wished to become a beguine.[30]

The question is to what extent these women still felt free to choose in cases where they risked being disinherited should they not join the beguine community. Their relatives' support was in any case most useful for beguine candidates, both inside and outside the complex. The importance of family support may also be seen in the fact that many beguines shared a household with a female relative. In Mechelen, the sisters Liesbeth and Dympne Tsermertens shared a house in the Great Beguinage, and in their 1551 will they designated whichever of the two survived as heir to the other's property.[31] The wealthy Kathelijne van Brecht shared her last house not only with her sister Leneke but also with Marieke. It even seems very likely that Kathelijne was able to offer them a luxurious life. Her capacity to choose her own tomb within the beguinage church is only one aspect reflecting her wealth. Her vast collection of silver dishes and valuable furniture for her house, including various beds, probably reduced the entrance costs for Leneke and Marieke, who no longer needed to acquire a bed or household items.[32] The same was true of Katharina Van den Brande's sisters who, according to her will dated 1589, lived with her for many years at the Mechelen beguinage.[33] Similarly, members of the same family sometimes lived in the same beguinage convent. Barbara Smets, who was still a minor on arriving in the beguine world, joined her elder sisters Cecilia and Martine who had been living together in a convent for several years.[34] These examples are no doubt representative of the situation in many beguinages in the southern Low Countries. Research has shown that the situation was similar in Leuven, where beguines also often lived with younger female relatives who, voluntarily or not, had followed the example of their sister or aunt.

The walls of a beguinage, unlike those of an ordinary monastic house, did not necessarily entail a separation between beguines and their families, as borne out by the observation that beguines were sometimes a great support to their relatives in town. In her will of 1546, Dorothea Scaellye of Mechelen left all her real estate assets to her sister Anna's two needy children: the first, Rombout, was one-eyed; the other, Cornelis, simple-minded.[35] As beguines retained control of their assets, they were able to provide financial support for their relatives over the course of their life.

In her will of 1588, Katharina van Buscom cancelled the debts her brother Willem owed to her.[36] Clara Triapyn, one of the four grand mistresses at the Great Beguinage, no doubt got on well with most of the beguines. Yet when she drew up her will in 1546, her thoughts went mainly to her relatives inside and outside the beguine courtyard. Her last wishes illustrate beguines could manage their assets strategically (even after their death). She left a large plot of land to her cousin Charles on the proviso that, in accepting this bequest, he give his two nieces one and a half florins per year throughout their lives. The close relations beguines could have with their relatives in neighbouring towns has also been demonstrated for other Brabant towns and periods. Wills of beguines in Leuven thus show that as potential heirs and testators, they retained an important position within their family network.

Craftswomen: Survival or business?

Apart from a few very wealthy beguines able to live from a large inheritance, most had to work for a living. The options were relatively varied. From the beginning, most beguinages included at least one school where some beguines taught mainly girls from the town. During the period 1286-1300, at least two teachers were active at the Great Beguinage of Saint Catherine's. It is unclear to what extent they were remunerated for their work, but the beguinage's oldest statutes indicate that they were entitled to their own house. In the early sixteenth century, 34 girls attended the Diest beguinage, while 57 girls were taught at the Great Beguinage in Antwerp.[37] Kathelijne van Brecht of Mechelen, mentioned above, was also probably teaching. In any case, in her will she expressed the wish that the pupils be her pallbearers at her funeral.[38] Bedridden Anna van Acxele bequeathed Anna van Schotteputte the fine sum of 50 florins (amounting to six months' wages for an unskilled labourer) as a token of her gratitude for her help teaching pupils, for which she had apparently only received meagre compensation until then.[39] However, the quality of the education varied considerably. The public education provided in beguinages probably went no further than learning how to read and write and acquiring a skilled trade. The teaching provided specifically for beguine aspirants tended to be significantly better. *Scholae* that only admitted beguine aspirants are known to have existed, where these pious women studied Latin, French, and music.

Otherwise beguines could earn a modest revenue as nurses in hospitals, leper houses, or private homes. Others worked in the field or in farms surrounding the beguine courtyard to provide the community with enough vegetables and dairy products. Until well into the twentieth century, the vast majority worked in the textile industry as spinners, weavers, or bobbin lacemakers. Given that beguinages traditionally had large green spaces and often were located near a waterway, they were the ideal environment for large-scale textile work. Water was required to process the wool and to eliminate waste. Many beguinages, such as Saint-Trond, had what was known as a washing meadow to launder linen. Of course, such work also had an important religious purpose. When working together on the land or in textile workshops, beguines recited prayers and pious texts together. Some wills nevertheless indicate that beguines could become wealthy businesswomen, despite the ideal of a sober and godly life. Conversely, as seen in the previous chapter, certain clearly successful businesswoman deliberately chose the beguine world at a particular moment in their life. Already back in 1314, a beguine at Turnhout made gifts in her will to no fewer than 40 sisters she employed as weavers.[40] A few centuries later, in 1558, the Mechelen beguine Lysken Jans set down in her will her hope that there would not be any disputes over her estate after her death. That is why all the spinners who worked for her received new clothing, and she even set aside a budget for the mourning garments her weavers and spinners were to wear at her funeral.[41] This type of practice was far from specific to Brabant, or even to the southern Low Countries. The phenomenon of beguine businesswoman was just as prevalent in medieval Paris, where there were several workshops where beguines worked as spinners or weavers for a wealthy beguine businesswoman.

Beguine nurses
From the earliest days of the beguine movement, beguine sisters tended to the sick. Those living in beguine courtyards provided their services to hospitals in town. Other communities (such as the "Hof Sion" community in Antwerp and the Great Beguinage in Mechelen) took in women needing medical care. The small and great beguinages in Leuven both had an infirmary and their own table to feed the poor, mainly intended, it must be admitted, for their own community.

> Beguines also looked after the elderly, particularly widows. Maternity care was rarely within their scope, however: in Mechelen and Hoogstraten, beguines were not allowed to dispense maternity care, while the statutes of the Herentals beguinage stipulated that a beguine could not attend childbirth unless it was their mother or sister-in-law giving birth (childbirth being the domain of urban midwives). Lastly, various beguinages also provided funeral services, such as wakes or prayers for the salvation of the deceased's soul.

Beguines' tasks also involved charity work. From the first years of the movement, many indigents lived in beguine complexes. In response to this need, "poor tables" – or "Tables of the Holy Spirit" as they were called – were set up in most beguine courtyards to provide the community's poorest members with the requisite assistance. The oldest Tables of the Holy Spirit were those at the Great Beguinage of Saint Catherine's (in Mechelen, 1269), the Great Beguinage "Ter Wijngaard" (in Brussels, 1273), and the beguinage of Saint Elisabeth's (in Valenciennes, 1273). Gifts to these Tables of the Holy Spirit were almost exclusively destined for members of the beguine community, certainly at first. In 1258 Margareta, the widow of Willem Cassart, gave one bunder of land to the poorest beguines at the Great Beguinage "Ter Wijngaard" in Brussels, on condition that the revenue from this land be destined exclusively for the 30 poorest women. We are especially well informed about the poor table at the Great Beguinage in Leuven, whose accounts have been preserved since 1395. This rich institution mainly looked after impoverished members residing in a separate building. As was also the case for other poor tables in Leuven managed by laypeople, most of the revenue was in kind (71% on average). However, expenditures on charity increased over the course of the fifteenth century. On average, one third of total expenditures went to cash distributions and one half to material gifts.[42] Each Sunday the table organized a distribution, and on feast days indigent beguines could queue up for a festive meal. Distributions were mainly of rye, meat, and fine cloth. It has not yet been ascertained how much support also reached poor people living outside the community. No information was preserved concerning those receiving assistance, but the content of distributions suggests in any case that these were mainly for beguines themselves. For example, there were no gifts of bread but of rye, with which beguines could make their own bread. Fine cloth was also a raw material that the women could make into clothing. The accounts often explicitly indicate that any shoes bought were women's shoes. Of course, these could also be given to women who were not part of the community, or to sick women in the infirmary.

Through their work as textile workers and businesswomen, beguines were directly active in the town's economy. Although nuns could also spend their days transforming wool and flax, the clothes and cloth they produced were almost exclusively intended for their own community. Beguines, however, sold their merchandise on the local market to generate necessary income. As they were in principle not allowed to make large profits, they invariably sold their products at below market prices. The judicial archives that have come down to us show that textile workers regularly perceived the beguines' activity as direct (and disloyal) competition. This perception was the basis for a major conflict in Brussels in 1296, which sprang up between the clothmakers' trade guild, which was active in manufacturing and selling cloth, and the beguines from thebeguinage "Ter Wijngaard". In protest over the accusations brought by guild members, certain beguines ceased their activity and left the beguinage. This action had little impact, though, for the conflict led to salary agreements (in fact, restrictions) with which beguines henceforth had to comply. The head of the association, whose members included the main Brussels cloth merchants, was in charge of monitoring these salary agreements and could inflict heavy fines on the beguines should they fail to comply.[43] Other sources document similar (and almost inevitable) conflicts for other Brabant towns, such as Antwerp and Mechelen. There, too, the textile industry, pursuing the greatest profit, was opposed to the members of religious movements, such as beguines and nuns compelled to make a smaller profit.

From the outset beguines were aware of their delicate business position and often took initiatives to avoid conflict and disputes. The ordinances of most beguinages thus included many clauses concerning their competitive position. To avoid conflict with the textile processing trades, beguines were only authorized to provide semifinished products such as grey cloth, and there were generally also restrictions on the number of articles they could produce in a given time. The oldest statutes of the Great Beguinage at Saint Catherine's (in Mechelen, circa 1295) included stipulations that no beguine was authorized to produce more than ten bolts of white cloth, on pain of a fine. The money thus generated was used for the upkeep of the streets, walls, and moats around the beguinage. If a beguine was caught red-handed selling (unprocessed) English wool, she lost this wool to the Church of Saint Rumbold and to the beguinage church. Other fines also went to the community: any beguine violating the ban on offering their wares in cloth markets, however small the piece of cloth in question, had to pay a modest sum to the institution's poor box. The presence of such clauses in most beguinages' ordinances has led historians to associate the success of the beguine phenomenon with the relatively independent life these religious sisters led thanks to their financial autonomy. Beguinages were even regularly designated as female trade guilds – professional associations constituted exclusively of women. We shall explore this comparison in more detail in the following chapter, but the great similarity between trade guilds and beguine convents already provides a key to understanding the conflicts between the two.

Beguines' words and deeds

In religious matters beguines were under the authority of the bishop, represented by a priest in larger beguine structures. In practice, it was the grand mistresses who ensured that pious women lived a life worthy of the order. The statutes of the Herentals beguinage – drawn up in 1461 (and supplemented through to 1489) – spell out exactly what this meant. Inhabitants were bound to respect their vows and live chastely: it was forbidden to frequent the company of men or to write love letters.[44] An additional clause stated that beguines were not allowed to get love letters written by anyone else, either, nor to send them via somebody else. The penalty was a fast of bread and water for three Fridays. Should such illicit behaviour nevertheless result in relations, the offending beguine was to leave the community and marry virtuously. She would only be allowed to return as a widow. There were also statutes regulating contact between sisters: those who quarrelled or were recalcitrant were subject to disciplinary sanctions. Furthermore, the women were not allowed to mislead anybody, only allowed to talk of religious matters at church, and had to ensure that the beguinage remained free of rumour.[45] The penalties were mainly fines and, in the worst cases, exclusion from the order. Lastly, the principles of obedience and austerity guided the regulations, together with practices such as confession and fasting.

What did beguines' religious life consist of? Among other things, they celebrated mass daily and organized the Liturgy of the Hours into seven offices. On Sundays and feast days, they held a special service in their own church. They were also obliged to attend all sermons preached in the church or elsewhere in the beguinage, as indicated in the statutes for Mechelen.[46] Pupils in beguine schools also took an active part in religious life, singing during masses. In addition to daily prayers, each beguine had to go to confession with the parish priest at least once a month, plus once during Lent and once during Advent. It would seem that beguines' religious activities still came in for questioning at this period. That is why no beguine was allowed to read religious books without the parish priest's express authorization. The 1588 uniform ordinances also stipulated in what order beguines were to parade during religious processions and public prayers. These probably confirmed a practice which by the sixteenth century already dated back several centuries, with beguines having played a part in public religious life since the beginning of the movement. In any case the ordinances were very clear: beguines were to walk behind the cross and in front of the grand mistresses and beguinage priest(s), with intendants and any other active beguinage officers bringing up the rear.

A beguine's habit

When beguines went to town, they were easily recognizable from their typically austere dress. Under the 1588 ordinances of Archbishop Johannes Hauchinus of Mechelen, beguines had to have short hair and, like nuns, cover their head with a simple wimple (known as a "chaperon"). They were not allowed to use any starched or particularly special fabrics for these headdresses, for their costume had to be without any ornamentation. Beguines habitually wore grey or black outer clothes, a headdress, and light underclothing. The statutes for the Herentals beguinage stipulated that the garment worn beneath the habit could not be coloured, with only a white shift or nightdress being authorized. Shoes were of cowhide or sheep's leather and could not have any form of ornamentation. While their secular activities sometimes aroused distrust from society (and particularly from textile workers), their austere clothing meant there was no way of mistaking beguines for other women from the town.

Beguines' level of piety and education may be seen from the books they possessed and their talent for plainsong. Of the 1,100 manuscripts known today to have been indisputably produced by religious communities in the southern Low Countries before 1600, 7% come from the beguine movement. While this might not seem a lot, given the pitiful preservation conditions it is a sizeable testament to the bookish possessions of these educate women. This percentage includes Latin treatises and works in the vernacular on the religious life of saints, psalms with commentary, and accounts of pilgrimages. The Brussels beguine Yde tSrademakers bequeathed a devout work, *Den dissipel ende de sierheit* [The disciple and beauty] to two other beguines for use in teaching poor children and to make it available to anyone who wished to read it.[47] The text *Die volmaectheijt der zielen* [The perfection of souls] circulated among the inhabitants of Saint Catherine's convent in Diest in the sixteenth century. These texts emphasizing the piety of religious life were popular among adepts of mysticism, a religious movement whose prescriptions included virtuous behaviour. Given beguines' educational activities, it seems entirely normal that they should have nurtured an active culture of reading (aloud).

It is harder to ascertain to what extent they also wrote texts. Only the beguinage "Ter Wijngaard" in Brussels is known to have had a scriptorium. Conversely, we know the names of two beguine authors: Hadewijch and Marguerite Porete. These two thirteenth-century writers are known for their edifying works and poetry, although it is not certain that Hadewijch actually joined the beguine world. Nevertheless, her mystical texts circulated in beguinages. Marguerite Porete ended up burnt at the stake due to the heretical nature attributed to certain of her writings. What her fate primarily expressed, though, was the Church's uncertainty about the emerging beguine community. Be that as it may, her work remained popular after her death, especially among beguines. Lastly, mention must be made of beguine plainsong, even though this area is unfortunately very poorly documented. Hadewijch's work is one illustration, containing several plainsongs; another is a 1437 document in which the Saint Gommaire chapter of Lier gave the beguines permission to brighten up masses with their plainsongs (including during funeral services and celebrations of feast days), "as in the churches of the Mechelen and Brussels beguinages".[48] Beguines thus not only had a remarkable reading culture, but also a plainchant culture, about which unfortunately little is known.

Wills are another source documenting beguine piety. First, it is striking that among other religious belongings, beguines bequeathed devout writings to one another, as illustrated by the example just cited. In her will of 1431, Ide Olivier of Tienen gave her missal and rosary to another sister.[49] Second, it is clear from will clauses that beguines made many gifts to the beguinage itself (to convents and to clerics), as well as to other religious institutions, even if they chose their main heirs from among their family circle. In 1482, another beguine in Tienen, Johanna Mijs, bequeathed a large plot of land in Niel to Montenaken parish, land in Houtem to third orders at the Tienen convent, and an annuity to the Saint Lambert chapter in Liège and to her own beguine institution.[50] Third, as death drew near, many beguines set aside money for commemorative masses, or gifts in exchange for prayers for the salvation of their soul. In her 1558 will, Lysken Jans of Mechelen bequeathed enough money to purchase five loaves for the convent where she lived, with the explicit request to pray for her soul's salvation.[51] When Agnete Claes, sick and bedridden, felt her end approaching in 1579, she provided in her will for a gift for commemorative masses.[52] Fourth, data about beguine funerary culture indicates that they were at least as concerned about the effect a glorious funeral service would produce on their community as they were about the salvation of their soul. In her will, Kathelijne van Brecht expressed the wish that ten wax candles be lit in the beguinage church on the day of her funeral. Like many other town dwellers, she adhered to the memorial culture typical of the medieval and pre-modern period, consisting in building a public commemorative cult around her own death. Of course, it should be noted that such measures were mainly the preserve of the wealthiest people in society. Few were able to follow Kathelijne's example and fund a magnificent tombstone inside the beguine church.[53] Once again, her will confirms the extent to which secular and spiritual matters were hard to separate. Yet this aspect of religiosity applied equally for many citizens in town.

Conclusions

The source documents left by beguines themselves tell us that these pious women, unlike nuns, continued to be at the heart of urban society. Most beguine spaces had at least one school attended by pupils from the town, while a hospital often took in other town dwellers. Those working in the textile trade were in regular contact – and often conflict – with the large group of beguines likewise working in the textile industry. Though some sisters were wealthy businesswoman, the vast majority produced relatively cheap textiles which were sold on the local market at a low profit margin. Beguines rarely became wealthy from their work. Due to the ban on making a profit, only single women with a sizeable inheritance were able to lead a luxurious life. The socio-economic composition of beguinages thus broadly reflected that of urban society. Just like single women and widows of modest origin, beguines often lived at the poverty line. However, beguines were able to call on beguine charity and were thus better protected against economic setbacks than their lay counterparts.

Given that entering the beguine world depended on personal factors such as social status, devotion, and family support, it is hard to make general statements about the beguine community's immense power of attraction. It is certain that any decision to go and live in a beguinage was an individual (and/or family) assessment of both religious and socio-economic needs. Life as a beguine guaranteed fixed moments of prayer, religious education, and a communal mode of life very similar to that of nuns.[54] At the same time, it also offered the opportunity to generate one's own revenue and to lead a free and independent existence in a safe environment. Women for whom the beguines' free and secular way of life was too far removed from the spirit of God set their sights on monastic houses, while less pious women wishing to remain single – or finding no marriage partner – instead chose to live in town, for example as an independent trader. To what extent were single women and widows free to choose? That option depended of course on their capacity to meet their needs, either through manual work or thanks to their savings. As we begin to learn more about what life was actually like for beguines, it becomes clear that various factors need to be taken into consideration to fully understand the appeal of beguine life for single women – and for their family circle.

Notes

1. *Ontrent den iaere MCCVII begonsten de vrauwen in desen landen die werlt te laten, en god te dienen en vergaderden met grooten hoopen, out en jonck, bij een wonende op die maniere als die cloesters* (De Wilde, *Die cronike van die scone en heerlijke stadt*, 20v).
2. Typical beguinage sites were granted UNESCO World Heritage listing in 1998.
3. CAM, OCMW, 9436 (ordinances for beguinages by Johannes Hauchinus, 1588), first chapter.
4. *Bruederlijke en susterlijcke liefde, minne en eendrachtigheyt.*
5. Will of Rombout and Elisabeth Vanden Dorpe (CAM, OCMW, 9445).
6. *Alle beggynen van den Grooten Hove, ontrent negenhondert in getal.*
7. De Azevedo, *Korte chronyke*, D, 4r-v.
8. Van Gelder, *Correspondance française*, 102.
9. *Seer veel huyskens en ander goede wooninghen.*
10. Guicciardini, *Beschrijvinghe*, 134.
11. CAM, OCMW, 9436, first chapter.
12. *Ibidem*, no. 8; Will of Kathelijne van Brecht (CAM, OCMW, 9445).
13. De Ridder, "De oorsprong", 58 (*int ghemeyn seer deuchdelick*).
14. De Ridder, "Mechelen's groot begijnhof", 28.
15. Will of Barbele Cnobbaert (CAM, Wills, no. 10, 47r-49r).
16. *Peijnst, jongers, die om houwen loopt soo snel: 't en es geen vrij spel, maer een eewich gequel* (Pleij, *Meer zuurs dan zoets*, 109).
17. CAL, 1523, 115v.
18. Will of Anneke Stockvis (CAM, OCMW, 9445).
19. Gigliotti, *Over begijnen*, 38.
20. Simons, *Cities of ladies*, 103.
21. Will of Adriane van Hanswijck (CAM, Wills no. 10, 73r-v).
22. CAM, OCMW, 9436, 9th chapter, no. 1.
23. Will of Barbele Cnobbaert (CAM, Wills no. 10, 47r-49r).
24. CAM, OCMW, 9436, first chapiter, no. 7.
25. *Den boeck van de professie en overleden begijnkens*, 1553-1600 (CAM, OCMW, 9437).
26. Will of Heilwych Ansens (CAM, OCMW, 9445).
27. Will of Kathelijne van Brecht (CAM, OCMW, 9445).
28. Will of Lieskens Jans (CAM, OCMW, 9445).
29. Will of Appollone van Soricke (CAM, Wills no. 11, 74r).
30. Will of Johanna de Bruyne (CAM, OCMW, 9445).
31. Will of Liesbeth et Dympne Tsermertens (CAM, Wills no. 11, 52v).
32. Will of Kathelijne van Brecht (CAM, OCMW, 9445).
33. Will of Katharina Van den Brande (CAM, OCMW, 9445).
34. Will of Cecilia, Martine et Barbara Smets (CAM, OCMW, 9445).
35. Will of Dorothea Scaellye (CAM, Wills no. 11, 13r-v).
36. Will of Katharina van Buscom (CAM, Wills no. 17, 71r-v).
37. De Ridder, "De oudste statuten", 22-25; Simons, *Cities of ladies*, 80.
38. Will of Kathelijne van Brecht (CAM, OCMW, 9445).
39. Will of Anna van Schotteputte (CAM, OCMW, 9445).
40. Simons, *Cities of Ladies*, 86.
41. Will of Lysken Jans (CAM, OCMW, 9445).

42 Peeters, *De tafel*, 74-6.
43 Pirenne, "Note sur un cartulaire", 54.
44 Verellen, "De oudste", 215.
45 *Ibidem*, 217.
46 CAM, OCMW, 9436, fourth chapter, no. 1-7.
47 Simons, "Staining the speech", 104.
48 Goetschalckx, "Het Begijnhof", 48.
49 Moulaert, "Quatre testaments", 343.
50 *Ibidem*, 347.
51 Will of Lysken Jans (CAM, OCMW, 9445).
52 Will of Agneet Claes (CAM, OCMW, 9445).
53 Will of Kathelijne van Brecht (CAM, OCMW, 9445).
54 De Wilde, *Die cronike van die scone en heerlijke stadt*, 20v.

CHAPTER 5

Working women: women's professional activities in and outside craft guilds

Nena Vandeweerdt & Jelle Haemers

In August 1461, a butcher from Leuven, Hendrik Michiels, defended his wife Katelijne before the town council in a dispute between her and the butchers' guild, with which one had to be affiliated to work as a butcher. Given that married women were not allowed to join, however, Katelijne was not a member. The corporation had demanded that Katelijne cease producing and selling tripe, roasts, and salted meats. Hendrik, for his part, argued that he was a "true son of a butcher", something that he claimed entitled his wife to sell tripe, just as she had always done.[1] The guild's case was thrown out, and the town ordered it not to bother Katelijne. No doubt the butchers' conflict with her stemmed from fears of seeing their privileges affected. In medieval towns, economic life was highly regulated: privileges and statuses determined who could sell what, what finished products should be like, and what rules members had to comply with. As recognized professional associations, craft guilds had more rights than other workers in the same sector. It was thus essential to belong to an association to develop an advantageous market position. Katelijne fell victim to the rigour with which the craft guilds monitored respect for their rules, but she managed to take advantage of a chink in the system: as a wife, she could continue to work in the sector.

This conflict shows the extent to which guilds were able to hinder women's activity, as well as how women managed to work within trades. Their work, along with the subsequent tensions which could arise, are the topic of this chapter. Women's tasks were not just those of a housewife, looking after the children while the husband saw to the family's income. On the contrary, women's work was extremely important to households, whether they worked alone or, as was often the case, alongside their husband. Katelijne's experience is a perfect illustration: whether at home or in the meat market, she assisted her husband in producing sausages that she then sold. There were also other options enabling women to claim their place in the job market. While craft guilds regularly provided the framework, women (and men) could also propose products and services on the "informal" market, that is, outside corporations. In craft guilds, women often acted as their husbands' associates or else as independent traders. Tradesmen's widows also sometimes enjoyed exceptional privileges. In each and every case, women played an essential role in the urban economy.

Craft guilds in town

In many Brabant towns during the twelfth century, associations emerged amongst rich merchants mainly involved in long-distance trade in textile products. Though often referred to as guilds (*gilden* in the Dutch of that era), these were not the same as the craft or trade guilds of the late Middle Ages. Indeed, these older associations did not admit workers in charge of production. Archers' guilds were also present in towns, but – in Brabant at least – these were exclusively male associations with a military or cultural function. Workers were also underrepresented in these guilds whose members were mainly wealthy townsfolk. Since the thirteenth century, however, these workers had set up other types of associations with charitable or religious objectives – craft guilds, or *ambachten* in Dutch. The oldest known craft guild in Brabant is that of the Mechelen blacksmiths. Although this was a religious society, helping members in need doubtless figured among its goals. During the thirteenth century, guilds evolved into bodies that – increasingly – regulated their members' behaviour. Additionally, they put pressure on merchant guilds to establish better working conditions. Artisans paid an entrance fee to the worker's association, in exchange for which they had access to all the facilities the guild offered. In addition to finished textile products, guilds gradually came to manufacture everything available in town and sold their goods and foodstuffs in open-air or covered markets. These groups were thus well-oiled machines that extensively controlled production and sale in towns. This character explains the term "corporation", by which they were also known, coming from the Latin *corpus*, meaning "body". A craft guild formed a little autonomous "body" in the town. Since the second half of the fourteenth century, they had also become a major political voice, for as of 1360 an increasing number of craft guilds in Brabant towns obtained the right to elect several aldermen to the town council. This role meant they were able to influence policies and seek to get legislation passed on working conditions.

Candidates for the town council were designated by leaders of guilds, which were very hierarchical. At the bottom of the ladder were apprentices training with a master craftsman. After their apprenticeship, apprentices could seek to become masters themselves. This training entailed making a product demonstrating they were worthy of practising the trade independently and of starting their own business. If they succeeded – though few did – they could use the title "master". Above apprentices but below masters were journeymen. These were "qualified" apprentices who had not yet obtained the title of master, either because they did not have the requisite capital to start their own workshop, or else due to restrictions on the number of masters within the association. A guild was directed by a "dean" who was usually elected by members, although internal election rules differed from one association to the next. Apprentices and journeymen tended to have little impact, with the decisive role being reserved for masters.

Lastly, in social, cultural, and religious terms, craft guilds held a central place in their members' lives. For instance, they staged annual processions which were attended by many tradesmen. In addition to their undeniable religious character, guilds also sought to enhance the corporation's reputation. Furthermore, each association had its own chapel or altar in a church, where they worshipped their patron saint and had masses celebrated for deceased members. This religious component gave rise in turn to charity within guilds. The association would help members unable to work due to ill health. In exchange for security, each member paid a monthly contribution into what was known as the "guild box" or "chest" – *(ambachts)bus* – which was thus based on the principle of solidarity. Support included covering any funeral expenses, distributing food in case of need, and so on. The richest guilds even created houses to take in needy members, including women. The Saint-Hubert Hospice in Brussels provided medical treatment to bakers' widows, while the Crispin Hospice in Antwerp was able to take in between 12 and 16 tanners' widows. A guild did not just provide services to its members, it also monitored their behaviour. Guildsmen who insulted one another could be sure to face penalties, and guilds even regulated relations between men and women. The weavers of Vilvoorde, for example, were not allowed to invite an unmarried woman into their house or to consort with prostitutes. Additionally, any weaver who behaved badly in public in the presence of prostitutes could be expelled from his guild.[2] Fullers in Brussels were forbidden from "keeping brothels", insulting one another, and playing dice games.[3] In Leuven, male and female sellers in the covered markets (where all sorts of trade products were on sale) were forbidden from "mingling", that is, entering into adulterous or sexual relations with one another.[4] The reputation of its members affected on that of the association as a whole, potentially compromising sales in the event of bad behaviour. A craft guild was meant to be a respectable institution.

These regulations also pertained to the proper functioning of the main unit of trade production, namely, the family. Guildsmen worked mainly in small businesses, generally in their own home. The home thus functioned both as main residence and place of public production. It is where goods were finished, while also serving as a sales outlet, in a space set aside for this purpose or through a window giving onto the street. The nuclear family thus formed a "family business". Since the thirteenth century, the production of goods had increasingly become a collective domestic activity. The couple and their children were jointly responsible for running the business and thus guaranteeing an income. The children carried out more modest tasks, which were nevertheless important, and from an early age learned the trade from their parents. Married women were thus active components in the urban economy through their considerable role in family businesses. They were involved in producing and selling goods from home, on the street, or at markets. Admittedly, the business was run by the man, who as husband (and father) was legally responsible for his family. From this point of view, it is easier to appreciate why it was so important to prevent men from having extramarital relations, and why they could expect to be punished in the event of (persistent) adultery or fornication, for such behaviour compromised the proper functioning of their household, the fundamental cornerstone of guild life.

As head of the family, only the man was a member of the craft guild, at least in theory. In practice he shared membership with his wife, with the two of them carrying out the economic tasks required of their trade. Whereas in the twelfth and thirteenth centuries women often had a separate income (often from poorly paid tasks), the institutionalization of trade production in the fourteenth century meant they became increasingly active within the household (generating the family income just like their husbands). We may deduce that women were also part of craft guilds from the poor box regulations produced by these associations. Although wives tended not to be guild members, they could receive an allowance should their husband die. The mother organization also looked after the husband's funeral costs. Initially, the "solidarity fund" was also for journeymen and apprentices, but over the course of the fifteenth century craft guilds increasingly restricted assistance to members of the nuclear family. In 1473, Brussels mercers (that is, retailers selling at markets) created a new "box" reserved exclusively for masters, their wives, and their widows. This function had long been carried out by the guild's chapel, which also assisted journeymen, but it had gradually lost its importance and ended up being abolished. What this example illustrates above all is the general tendency towards oligarchization within craft guilds: important families increasingly formed a closed circle. This evolution did not fail to trigger tension between journeymen and the women in their families, as we shall see.

The "informal" market

Before turning to the guild market, it is worth briefly describing the "informal market", given that it was often in conflict with the guilds and that many women were active in it. The informal circuit, which varied considerably in size, included all open sale of goods not organized by the guilds. The guilds worked with the town to create rules to rationalize such "informal sales" and to avoid competition with their main products. For the informal market was very popular. Inhabitants from inside and outside the town could buy or sell goods cheaply. It is hard to calculate the total value of goods sold in this market, for it was obviously not recorded by guild administrations. In any case, research into violations of all sorts of rules on the informal trade circuit in Bruges have shown that it was really very large. One striking fact is that women accounted for one third of all violations committed in this market.

On occasion, guildsmen themselves turned to the informal market for it enabled them to avoid taxes and any extra costs exacted by the corporation. The Leuven town council regularly forbade guild members from selling products in the streets behind the covered market. In 1467, for example, the town no longer authorized butchers, their wives, or other relatives to go around taverns or inns offering unsold goods more than three days old. In this way the town council prevented the sale of meat of inferior quality at knockdown prices, as a measure to safeguard public health conditions in the town. At the same time, it regulated the informal market which was thus accessible to women, for the ordinance explicitly states that it applies equally to butchers' wives. The range of professional sectors operating on the sidelines of the guild economy was for that matter very diverse. Nearly everything was available for sale, but products were generally of lower quality given that the associations focused on specialized goods. Throughout the town, people could thus buy unfinished textile products, homemade food, or fruit and vegetables sold by farmers. Others also offered services on this informal circuit: porters transporting all sorts of goods, handymen, and domestic staff, for instance.

It goes without saying that conflicts could arise between guildsmen and people offering products or services on the informal circuit. In 1403, the Leuven town council was informed by the glovemakers' and bagmakers' guild that women were making bags "both secretly and in public", and that they were teaching one another to sew gloves without having completed the officially established apprenticeship. As these women paid no admission fee to the corporation, the guild argued that they should not be authorized to exercise this trade.[5] Glovemakers and bagmakers were entitled to provide high quality products, and cheaper or "counterfeit" variants were a real nuisance for them. Various aspects of glovemaking and bagmaking were considered "women's work", as we shall see later, and it is probable that many women were active in the Leuven corporation. It could thus not tolerate "unofficial" production, which jeopardized its members' income. The guild won its case in this instance, which is not surprising given that the guildsmen could rely on the support of their representatives on the town council.

The fishermen's guild likewise often found itself competing with the informal market. Many people sold (freshwater) fish caught on their own land or in a fishing pond rented out by its owner. In Leuven itself, fish caught in the well-stocked River Dyle was on unofficial sale. Arguing that the catch was its by right, the fishermen's corporation sought to oppose this trade, though in vain. Each inhabitant retained the right to fish in the stretch of the Dyle running through the town. The corporation thus had very few means to counter competition from the informal market, in which women were certainly active, selling, among other products, "women's fish". The town council knowingly created a space for this sector of the informal market, obliging fish peddlers to offer their produce for sale on the fish market itself – and nowhere else, and necessarily after ten in the morning. Furthermore, in 1424, it was explicitly forbidden to start sales on the streets around the market.[6] In this way the town council created a controllable framework for providing one of the main foodstuffs in town.

> "Women's fish"
> Fish sold independently of the guild – often carp, eel, and herring – were sometimes called "women's fish". Peddling fish was a mainly female activity and took place in a distinct part of the fish market. In Leuven, members of the butchers' guild were also authorized to sell fish at the place where "women habitually peddle this type of fish". Additionally, in 1400, the corporation complained that its members were becoming poorer due to the many women selling fish who were not guild members. These women were not entitled to set up stalls. They generally offered their goods in baskets, an activity depicted on a sixteenth-century painting probably depicting the Antwerp fish market. In the same town, "fishermen's wives" (*vischcoeperswive*) were also authorized to sell their goods outside the fish market.

Of course, women in markets not regulated by craft guilds were not always acting on their own. In late January 1442, the couple Willem de Bruyne and Katelijne Dierix were brought before the Antwerp town council. Willem and Katelijne sold fish together in the *Cradewyck*. In the evening, after they had been selling for the day, the street stank with a "strong and unusual smell". To limit the inconvenience caused by unpleasant smells from processing fish oil, the town decided that the couple was to move their activity to Slijkpoort to the north of the town, outside the walls.[7] One week later, however, the couple were back before the aldermen's court. Transporting their goods every day to the designated point of sale was causing complications for their business. That is why the aldermen gave them permission to transport their goods to the town centre by barge without having to pay the tax at *Sluisvliet* lock. This case is a clear illustration of a couple developing an activity on the informal market together.

Women in craft guilds

What was the position of women working within a craft guild? In answering this question, it is preferable to distinguish between married women working as part of the family, on the one hand, and, on the other, single women and widows. Their respective rights and activities could differ considerably. Initially, in the twelfth century, when guilds were virtually non-existent, men and women offered their services to textile merchants, both individually and as a family. Merchants subcontracted out the various stages in producing cloth and linen and thus turned to individuals and families wishing to make a bit of money. In the textile industry, for instance, there were many female workers. An ordinance about woolworkers in Diest, dating from 1333, mentions various branches of the cloth industry in which women worked, such as spinning and combing wool, hanging it on drying racks, and so on.[8] These activities progressively came under the control of guilds, with families starting to carry out tasks collectively. One of the practical consequences of this change was that women were no longer separately mentioned in corporation statutes. This observation led many historians to wrongly conclude that women were scarcely present in craft guilds. This was not the case, because henceforth they were quite simply working within their families, which belonged, as entities, to associations.

Yet up until the late Middle Ages, one category of women – those carrying out a different trade to their husband – could be full, independent guild members. Nevertheless, there was enormous variation here between trades and between towns. There were guilds, such as the Mechelen surgeons' guild, which women were not authorized to join despite carrying out the same tasks. For example, women carried out minor medical interventions, such as bleedings, an activity that was explicitly forbidden to women in the guild's 1421 statutes. Surgeons were, however, allowed to call on women to carry out more subaltern tasks, such as taking blood. To do this, *laterssen* – those who "make blood flow", in the words of the ordinance – used a lancet, then carried the blood out of town.[9] In Mechelen, in short, women could only be involved in the surgical trade as assistants. In other associations they were fully fledged members, but once again there were major differences between craft guilds. Between 1516 and 1555, 233 women joined the Antwerp mercers' guild, amounting to just 6% of the total number of members. However, between 1466 and 1471, 97 out of the 325 new members of the

A couple makes bread – another woman waits to buy it. Such artisanal activities were mainly a family affair, whether inside a craft guild or outside it (Bibliothèque Nationale de France, ms. lat. 1173, 6v). Zie https://gallica.bnf.fr/ark:/12148/btv1b52502694t/f22.item.zoom

Brussels drapers' guild were women, amounting to about 30%. These were mainly married women and widows (as well as six beguines) in charge of selling cloth.[10] In 's-Hertogenbosch, the list of bakers who pledged an oath concerning a new measure affecting the guild's organization includes 11 women out of a total of 83 (13%).[11] Most of the time we have to deduce the proportions from indirect references in guild statues stipulating that measures apply to both men and women. "Guild sisters" (*guldsusters*) also figure in the 's-Hertogenbosch tanners' guild regulations in 1407, as do "mistresses" (*meestersse*) – female members who had acquired the title of master – in those of blacksmiths dating from 1463.

It was unusual for a guild to be composed mainly of female members. There were however a few "women's guilds" in the silk industry in Lyon and Paris, as well as in the spinning industry in Cologne and Rouen. Men could also join, but most members were women. Furthermore, the dean of these guilds could be a woman, something that was normally ruled out in the southern Low Countries. This title, though, was probably only accessible to widows of deceased (male) deans. As for their functioning, these guilds differed little from those in the Low Countries. There was no real freedom of action for these women. Conflicts regularly arose concerning the sale of goods outside the association's control by the poorest female members. Women with the title of master thus reacted severely to safeguard their own position. This general policy characterized all guilds in a town: internal competition was forbidden. Men and women had to follow the rules, and women administrators of these corporations did not think any differently.

There were no specifically female guilds in the southern Low Countries, but various associations functioned like guilds. This was true of religious movements, on the one hand, and very specific professions, on the other, such as midwives and female porters. Textile production by beguines was formidable competition for the weaving guilds, as already noted in the previous chapter. Conflicts also regularly broke out with other similarly structured religious orders likewise producing goods for market. There were often quarrels between textile guilds and sisters from the so-called Third Order (*Derde Orde*) or else their male counterparts, the begards (*bogarden*). The two non-consecrated orders followed the rule of Saint Francis, often producing textiles to meet their own needs. This activity displeased guildsmen, mainly because the price agreements weavers imposed on their members did not apply to these competitors. In 1461, the deans of the Antwerp weavers' guilds declared that Third Order sisters were weaving various types of cloth despite this being forbidden to those who were not guild members. The mistress of the religious order defended the sisters, invoking a privilege over 100 years old which stipulated that sisters had to be able to provide an income for themselves. The town council finally ruled in favour of the religious congregation. The sisters obtained authorization to spin and weave as much as they wished in their convent, in addition to selling any surplus.[12] The congregation thus behaved as if it were a guild: the sisters established rules and sold finished products. So from this point of view, the southern Low Countries did indeed have guilds in women's hands.

In towns there were also a whole range of non-religious women's associations involved in various economic activities, though without amounting to officially recognized guilds. In Leuven, an aldermen's ruling of 1478 shows that some women, known as *uutdragerssen* (second-hand clothes women), lodged a complaint against the guild for purchasers of old clothes.[13] The clothes purchasers in question apparently obliged the women to pay a sum of money because they competed with the association. The clothes women's business of buying and selling household articles included reselling used clothing. The town recognized that they were thereby encroaching on the guild's domain and thus obliged the women to pay a sum. We do not have any further information about the organization of the Leuven clothes women, for as they did not leave any officially recognized statutes, they remain under the radar of historians. Nevertheless, the fact that these women went as a group to the aldermen's court to lodge a (failed) complaint concerning this obligation shows that, all in all, they did form an association.

A slightly more regulated activity was midwifery. There were some accredited midwives active in Leuven, and in Brussels the town council founded a midwives' guild in 1424. The town observed that several midwives were not carrying out their work properly. The council said it was concerned that the intervention of incompetent midwives rendered pregnant women "sterile and made some of them suffer from permanent illnesses". Additionally, the council wanted to avoid midwives "treating the vulnerable foetus so brutally that it no longer emerges alive". It was thus to make up for this lack of expertise that the town council founded a specialized professional association. As of 1424, the number of active midwives was capped at five. Should one of them be unable or unwilling to work, she could designate a replacement. If one of the certified midwives died, the others were to take care of finding a replacement. The new recruit, though, was not allowed to receive a salary for her profession until the Brussels master of medicine gave his assent. In this case, the female guild was not created to bolster midwives' rights, but rather to oversee their delicate profession. Indeed, it is wrong to speak of a fully fledged guild given that the internal regulations were limited and no "master's level" was established.[14] In 1424, nevertheless, Brussels joined the many towns where midwives formed a distinct female association, for their job remained exclusively female throughout the Middle Ages. During the same period, the town also regulated the "professional branch" of "praying women" (*bidderessen*) – another exclusively female activity.

> **"Praying women"**
> For weddings, baptisms, and funerals, people could employ praying women whose job was to pray for the salvation of those being celebrated. Although these women had to be eminently honourable, in 1424 the Brussels town council heard that several of them had swindled people. As a solution, the town capped the number of official praying women to eight. Henceforth, they would receive an equivalent salary and would in no case be allowed to receive any property having belonged to the deceased. The introduction of this rule seems

> to indicate prior dysfunctions. One of the eight women was henceforth to be designated dean, in charge of managing the "profession" and its proper functioning. Yet this was not a real female guild, for the women did not produce anything and did not provide tangible services. Nevertheless, once again the council created a professional branch resolved solely for women.

Married women within the nuclear family

What economic functions did women perform within the family? Legally speaking, married women ceded a considerable share of business responsibilities to their husbands. The meticulous organization of the craft guilds left little scope to married women as "free" members. In 1463, for example, the Brussels embroiderers' guild decreed that on marriage a woman was to lose her title as master. She then became the "master's wife" and was no longer authorized to run her own workshop.[15] However, there were countless ordinances that apparently accepted that the man and wife each could be affiliated with a different guild, or which at least did not prohibit such situations. Be that as it may, apparently only a limited number of married women were independent members of such organizations. Still, that does not therefore mean that wives' field of action was limited to household tasks. On the contrary, they played an active part in work, though they did not have their own income. Wives certainly played an important role in sales, while also contributing usefully to production. On occasion a married couple jointly ran a business outside any guild. One only has to think of the many inns and taverns in towns which were often run by a married couple and provided lodging to merchants and other regional or international travellers. In Lier, the sources mention female master brewers and the daughters or wives of brewers (either male or female) who inherited the business along with guild membership. Mechelen fishermen, for their part, had difficulty keeping their members' wives away from the fish markets, as illustrated by many rulings in the fishermen's guild register. Additionally, even after marriage, a (new) husband could take his wife's profession should he so wish.

The guilds and the town council both recognized that wives had their own responsibilities. The Leuven tailors' guild, for instance, stipulated that on marrying, women were to leave the guild and the profession to their husband. In this way, craft guilds limited the number of members, wishing to keep the organization as exclusive as possible, especially in times of economic hardship. However, as these married women had long mastered the trade, they could profit from their vast knowledge and carry on working in the profession. A conflict between Leuven mercers and a married couple in 1454 illustrates the important place married women could hold in the association. The mercers filed a complaint against Andries De Meyer and Machteld Van Winge because Andries performed the trade without having paid membership fees. Before their marriage Machteld had been a guild member, probably as a descendant from a family of mercers. This membership is suggested by the fact that she was called by her full name, whereas women were generally identified by reference to their husband or a (deceased) relative. Given that Machteld worked alongside her husband, the mercers argued that he should pay membership to become an official member. The town council found in their favour and obliged Andries to pay the necessary sum. Nevertheless, it added that Andries was only entitled to buy membership to the corporation on the grounds that his wife was prepared to teach him the trade. It thus seems that Machteld was a guild mistress, or in any case considered as capable of initiating her husband into the association's traditions.[16]

If, however, a woman became too active in a trade other than her own, she could run into resistance on the grounds of disloyal competition. In 1435, the Antwerp used clothing merchants took action against Liesbet Maes before the aldermen's court. The leaders of this corporation voiced their disagreement that Liesbet had remained a member of the association after having recently married a tanner. The plaintiffs declared that women should give up their membership after marriage: they were henceforth meant to serve their husband in whatever his professional activities were. Liesbet responded that she had herself "acquired her membership to the guild", arguing that she was entitled to continue working within the association since she had paid all the membership fees. For her there was no question of allowing her marriage to interfere with her own economic activities. Given that the statutes of the used clothing merchants' guild did not provide any grounds for precise arguments against, the aldermen decided that she could continue to be a member. For his part, her husband was authorized to help her, though solely for the transport of any clothes she repaired. He was not allowed to play any part in sales, for this capacity was strictly reserved for used clothing merchants.[17] Liesbet and her husband were thus each able to continue to exercise their own profession, and the family continued to work in both sectors. Provided there was no flagrant distortion of competition, the aldermen allowed women to pursue their own business activity.

Nevertheless, certain associations had stricter rules: wives lost their membership if they married a member of another association. That may explain why many women sought a partner within their trade. Furthermore, marrying a guild member enabled a wife to gain access to activities denied to other women. A butcher's son inherited a stall in the meat market from his father, so that it remained in the same family, given that there were a limited number of available stalls. As for a wife, when her husband was away, she was allowed to direct sales from such a stall. The sales themselves were carried out by a journeyman, but the wife oversaw proceedings.[18] For the husband, marrying a tradesman's daughter did not always secure a function within the trade. In 1429, the Antwerp butchers entered into conflict with the tanner Andries De Meyer, who had married Liesbet Alouts, a butcher's daughter. It might be the same person who a few years later clashed with the mercers, but it is also wholly possible that he was somebody else with the same name. Andries reckoned that his marriage entitled him to manage a "bench" in the meat market. The butchers disagreed, arguing before the aldermen that women were not allowed to manage such a stall, hence by extension nor could their husband. The Antwerp aldermen took the step of consulting with their colleagues in Leuven, Brussels, and Ghent about how the meat trade was organized there so as to help ground their ruling. Women, other than butchers' widows, were not allowed to manage their own stall in the meat market in any of these towns. Andries thus had to back down, especially after testimony by Liesbet's father who stated that he had told his son-in-law prior to the wedding that Liesbet did not manage a stall in the meat market. The couple were thus obliged to leave the guild. However, Liesbet's sister, who also worked in the meat market, was able to pursue her father's trade unhindered.[19] The aldermen's manner of proceeding and their wish to align their ruling with practice in other towns may indicate that the organization of meat markets was largely identical outside the town's boundaries. Newcomers to a craft guild, whether men or women, always ran into difficulties whenever they confronted the power of its established members.

Married women created their own businesses distinct from those of their husbands. In general, these women worked in the same informal sectors as single women, or else they regularly clashed with the guilds. In 1504, three women entered into conflict with the Leuven fishmongers. Joanna de Cuypere, the wife of Michiel van den Vekene; Joanna van Zallaken, a married woman; and the widow of Gielis in Inghelant all lived at the fish market. They made good use of their residences by selling sea fish, along with other goods. Obviously, this displeased the guild. Selling saltwater fish was a privilege reserved for members of their association, for it was the only type of fish that the inhabitants of Leuven could not catch themselves. Without denying this restriction, the women simply declared that they were taking advantage of the location of their houses to sell their goods. Yet the town council did not find in their favour. It ruled that the fishmongers were in the right, and so the women were no longer authorized to sell fish given that they were not guild members.[20]

Artistic women
The production and sale of art was also controlled by guilds, and women were members of those relating to art. Women accounted for one in four of those listed as members of the Bruges booksellers', printers' and miniaturists' guild. Likewise, women were active partners in the leading families of Antwerp printers. There is evidence of women painters as early as the fourteenth century. The Saint Luke Guild in Antwerp was composed of sculptors, tapestry makers, and painters whose work was on sale in a building near the Church of Our Lady (on present-day Place Verte). In 1551, Elisabeth Borremans bought eight paintings there that she transported by boat from Antwerp to Middelburg. In exchange for payment, the widows of master craftsmen produced art, thus continuing the tasks they had carried out in the workshop as wives. In this sector there were also women who were independent traders in art objects. In 1502, Heilwijch Swandeleere, as a "merchant", paid the sculptor Jan Baruzeel for a reredos. Her husband (the painter Jan de Pape) was to finish the work, though Heilwijch was clearly responsible for the sale. As was the case in the production chain for many types of goods, women thus played a crucial role in running the family business. Even if works of art were often signed by men, that did not mean that they were not produced by a woman.

Single women

For single women it was harder to operate on the job market, for unless they worked as servants, they did not benefit from the protection of a household. They thus sought to secure other sources of support, by joining an association of some kind, for instance, such as the beguines or Third Order sisters. Even women without a religious vocation found openings on the job market, though. Outside the world of guilds, girls sometimes joined a family as a maid, or else worked under a master or mistress to learn a trade. The example of Janne Schuts in Antwerp (see chapter 3), who started out as a servant before going on to a successful career, shows that domestic staff could work in close cooperation with their employer. Their remuneration included food and lodging, together with a meagre salary. On leaving a household, a maid generally received a sizeable bonus and even a marriage bonus. Still, disputes could flare up between a servant and the family. In 1479, the Antwerp silversmith Jan Hart had to swear that neither he nor his friends and relatives would physically or verbally attack his former chambermaid. We do not know exactly what had happened, but it would seem that he had mistreated her. The incident probably related to a sexual assault in the house.[21] For their part, chambermaids were also capable of causing injury to their employer. Such an occurrence may be illustrated by the legal action initiated in 1403 by the Antwerp fishmonger Jan van Bruesel against his chambermaid Alijt. Jan declared he had lost money after Alijt had spread rumours about him. For merchants, their reputation was crucial. Hence calumny was severely punished in all market sectors, and Alijt was sentenced to a pilgrimage to Cologne. Were she to return before having carried it out, she was to lose an ear. The town council also punished Jan, however, sentencing him to a pilgrimage to Rocamadour because he had taken revenge on the girl (without it being stated what he had done).[22]

Many families took in a girl apprentice, in the same way as boys were trained for an independent business or perhaps with an eye to marrying. Many of these girls and boys were probably children of guild members. Likewise, apprenticed girls were actively involved in production and commerce. In 1403, as already stated, the Leuven aldermen forbade women not affiliated with the glovemakers' and bagmakers' guild from offering their products for sale on the informal market. Yet they made an exception for women living with a master, that is, for wives and daughters, as well as any girls apprenticed to them.[23] Furriers' sons and daughters were also entitled to training from the association, for which they paid only half the membership fee.[24] As for the wives and children of master tailors, they carried out the trade with the assistance of a paid apprentice without paying any fees.[25] To prevent abuses, the regulations of the Leuven cobblers imposed the restriction that a master could only take one apprentice per year.[26] They thereby sought to prevent tradesmen from using apprenticed boys and girls as cheap labour instead of giving them the appropriate training. Of course, conflicts could arise between apprentices and their employers. In 1461, Katelijne Guldemans, a girl apprenticed to a Mechelen butcher, insulted her master's wife at work. She was sentenced to publicly begging her pardon in the meat market with a lit candle in her hand.[27] The public nature of this sentence suggests that Katelijne had mocked her in public, a humiliation deemed unacceptable.

In addition to young maids and apprenticed girls, tradesmen also employed women for the day, who offered their services temporarily in exchange for a modest sum. They were not necessarily single, but it was no doubt an interesting option enabling single women to generate an income. Master craftsmen employed them as labour, which gave them "non-free" guild membership in the terminology of the period. In such cases, they did not pay any inscription fees, nor did they enjoy the advantages conferred by membership. They did, however, receive a daily wage which varied with the seasons. For example, women working on large building projects in Antwerp were paid to finish polished stone.[28] They earned the same amount as their male colleagues for this task, which amounted to a little over half the salary of an assistant mason. In the mid-fifteenth century, such a daily salary in the summer months amounted to about seven groats (the local currency), worth about three to four grammes of silver; the winter salary was sometimes half this amount since building work stopped once the sun went down. Of course, not every day of the year was a working day, and day labourers also had to pay a (small) amount (called "candle money", *kaarsgeld*) to the guild. The real salary of an assistant mason was thus a little less than five groats. An assistant mason's salary was enough to buy on average a little under six kilos of wheat bread, although major fluctuations in the price of bread need to be factored in. As for day labourers, they only earned half this sum and were generally only active when there was enough work. It is thus understandable that most female day labourers worked to generate supplementary income.

They could be active in various sectors, or else top up their main revenue by work of this kind.

Once again, women sometimes encountered opposition from professional associations. In 1474, for example, a conflict arose between masters belonging to the Antwerp guild of glovemakers and bagmakers. One group of masters accused their colleagues of employing several women and apprentices to sew bags and gloves for them, a practice which was forbidden. It amounted to disloyal competition for any masters unable to pay for additional labour. The defendants argued, however, that the women were only assembling and lining gloves or bags, which they claimed was "women's work".[29] Their opponents countered that the association was a men's guild. The town council opted for a middle-of-the-road ruling: a master craftsman was henceforth allowed to employ only two apprentices and to benefit from the additional help of people living with him (his wife, children, and grandchildren). On top of that, they were allowed to employ one woman who was to live with the family. These women were allowed to sew bags and closed gloves but nothing further. The aldermen were thus clearly protecting the family economy by limiting the work of unaffiliated female workers. Women workers were thus not all treated equally: a guild might offer women protection, while imposing severe restrictions on female workers who did not belong to it.

Various guilds accepted single women as full members, as was the case for the Leuven tailors' guild, for instance. In 1450, the corporation introduced a system of payouts, should its members fall ill. In exchange for a monthly contribution, guildsmen who were unable to work for several days due to a work accident or professional illness were entitled to an indemnity. It is interesting to note that the rules applied both to men and to unmarried women.[30] Additionally, the decision was reformulated several times in similar terms, suggesting that the presence of single women was now a regular occurrence in the tailors' guild. Single women belonging to the guild were thus entitled to the same payouts as men, unlike wives who could only claim half. The Leuven butchers likewise applied ordinances giving single women a place in the guild. These provisions would appear to make Leuven atypical in comparison to other towns, where women had but little access to this profession. In Leuven, butchers' eldest daughters could join the guild provided they paid half the admission fee. The first condition, that they be the eldest daughter in a family of butchers, was no doubt to guarantee that the trade remained in the hands of butchers' families. If the trade could only be handed down from father to son, the exclusive group ran the risk of seeing its numbers diminish. And if a butcher's daughter married, her husband could become a member, and she had to cede her position to him. Thus the situation in Leuven was finally less exceptional than it might at first appear. It illustrates the fact that guild leaders admitted women provided they did not constitute a threat to the income of the leading families. Single women were only entitled to carry out less profitable tasks marginal to the prestigious meat trade managed by the established families. Nevertheless, these women were very visible in the streets around the meat market, and, as was often the case among butchers, skirmishes regularly broke out at the place where tripe was sold. In 1593, the town council thus issued an ordinance addressed to butchers and their wives (*pensvrouwen*, "tripe women") because it had received complaints about the manifest misconduct in the meat market and surrounding streets. Apparently stones and bones were frequently used as projectiles. The document also mentions shouting and attacks on stalls belonging to third parties.[31] This type of disorder on places of work was attributable both to men and to women.

Single women were not welcome in all guilds. In 1492, the Antwerp town council decided that single women would no longer be authorized to join the market gardeners' guild (who mainly looked after the fields within the city walls). One exception was tolerated: gardeners' daughters after their parents had died. The decision came in the wake of a complaint by market gardeners about violations to a long-established custom, which stipulated that the guild could only accept married women. Yet the number of single women belonging to the guild was such that its younger members feared "all would drown", as they put it. Additionally, they protested, the presence of women would indirectly harm the entire town.[32] These complaints were heard, and the town council decided that single women would no longer be accepted. In this way it hoped to safeguard the privileges of the market gardeners and protect the eminent position of recognized master guildsmen from "disloyal" competition. This conflict clearly shows how, at the end the day, a guild was a patriarchal institution despite the many women belonging to it. Of course, the implementation of this ban could be challenged. After all, old customs had been neglected in the past. For single women, the ban on joining the guild probably did not mean the end of their business life. They could always opt for the informal market or marry a man belonging to the association.

Widows and work

Widows suddenly found themselves alone. The death of a family member caused great problems, for it meant the workshop lost a worker. If it was the mother who had died, the children, including the daughters, could replace her. In Antwerp, for example, the spouses Liesbet Van Den Oever and Jan Van Den Zande, who were in the cloth trade, had agreed in their wills that the surviving member was authorized to use the work equipment to carry on with their trade. However, when Liesbet died, her family disputed this arrangement after Jan had transferred these tools to Katheline, a daughter from a previous or extramarital relationship. Yet the family failed: in 1433, the aldermen gave their backing to the transfer of the tools to Katheline, who was henceforth to occupy the place left vacant by Liesbet.[33] When the father of the family died, the widow was entitled to carry on with the business due to what was referred to as "widows' right". This privilege enabled widows to retain their husband's title of master or journeyman (together with any stall in the market). Should they remarry, widows generally lost this right. Either they left the profession, or else their new husband took over from them. In most cases, guildsmen's widows remarried, for it was no easy task running a business single-handedly.

In various corporations, widows were the only women admitted, as was the practice with the Leuven barbers' guild. In several other guilds, such as the cobblers' guild and the bakers' guild, widows had the option of continuing to pay the monthly contribution into the solidarity fund after their husband died. In cases of need, they only received half the payout during their marriage, but as widows they often received the full sum. In this instance, the widow replaced her deceased husband. On occasion colleagues complained about widows who continued to perform the trade without paying guild fees, and who maintained this situation by not remarrying. In Leuven in 1417, the widow of a man named Goossen entered into conflict with the guild of merchants of "fatty products" (such as wax and animal fats). Since Goossen's death, she had carried out the trade without paying any fees, as she had been "authorized to do when her husband was alive" as she declared to the aldermen's court.[34] The guild council objected and demanded that the widow pay membership fees. The town council finally decided that the widow should pay the sum in question, six months after her husband's death. On this condition she was allowed to remain active independently within the corporation. Here the conflict did not arise from jealousy of a working widow, but rather from the desire that each pay their fees. Each member had to be equal before the law, the guild declared.

Women were excluded from a guild especially in cases of disloyal competition. Should they so wish, widows took the place of their deceased husband in the Leuven blacksmiths' guild, which claimed to be the oldest guild in town (and thus endowed with undisputed prestige). Even should they remarry, they retained, if they wished, the right to payouts from the guild fund.[35] Historians suppose that guild membership did not necessarily mean that widows carried out the work themselves. While inheriting the title of master, they could employ a journeyman or apprentice. Yet it would seem that women were also active in the Leuven blacksmiths' guild. A 1433 ordinance stipulates that blacksmiths, "whether man or woman", were not authorized to work on Sundays, the day of rest.[36] The term "woman" may here refer to wives helping their husbands, but even in that event the ordinance shows that women were not wholly external to the blacksmiths' guild, a practice which was also well established in other regions. Single guildsmen considered blacksmiths' widows an attractive possible match, for marrying one provided access to the corporation.

Yet criticisms of widows' rights intensified over the course of the sixteenth century, for they could damage guilds' economic interests. This phenomenon may be illustrated by the rules for joining the Leuven butchers' guild, which feared that widows' rights might significantly reduce the income of young journeymen. In 1566, the town council decided that widows would no longer be allowed to manage a stall in the meat market. In pleading for this legislation, the powerful butchers had argued for overturning old customs, under which widows were allowed to take up their husband's trade, including his market stall. Their worries were motivated by the fear that widows subsequently transfer their position to adult sons. Widows marrying outside the guild might introduce a large number of new arrivals into the association. New young guild members further complained that widows' established businesses were a drag on their own income. The town council was receptive to this complaint and ruled in favour of the butchers: it considerably reduced the possibilities for widows within the corporation.[37] Yet it was aware of the impact of such a decision. Shortly afterwards, two widows were thus allowed to circumvent the 1566 ruling.[38] Hence the new rule did not remain long in effect. In 1550, there was a relaxation, with widows once again being authorized to sell certain preparations in the meat market, and this stricter legislation was finally abolished in 1655.[39] it is possible that in 1566 – the year of the Iconoclastic Fury – guildsmen were facing a difficult economic period, and that it was widows in the association who paid the price. The decision shows in any case that women were tolerated within craft guilds provided they did not harm the interests of other groups. It will be noted that wealthy families did not fail to protect their own women. The position of a woman thus varied considerably depending on her origins. Furthermore, when times were good prospects were better for women, whereas in times of hardship protectionist tendencies came to the fore.

In cases where a widow had obtained her place in a guild via a male relative, certain members managed to maintain themselves independently, provided they had the means to do so. Widows were not obliged to remarry, as shown by the episode concerning Jan Venijn in Antwerp. In 1440, the ropemakers took legal action against Jan Venijn, a single man. Custom stipulated that practising this trade required prior apprenticeship of three years and enrolment with the corporation. Widows were allowed to carry on with their husband's trade with the assistance of an apprentice, but on remarrying they had to leave the guild and, if they wished, their position passed to their new husband. Jan Venijn did not belong to the guild, but worked with the widow of ropemaker Jan Van Eeleghem. The town council allowed him to continue with this profession, provided he marry the widow.[40] This finding did not take the widow's wishes into account. Three years later, the town council once again heard from the ropemakers about the same conflict – Jan Venijn was still working as a ropemaker but had not married the widow. The defendant firmly maintained he had moved heaven and earth, but had met with no success, stating he was not the one to blame. The aldermen reacted with moderation: they authorized Jan to continue working in the guild provided he pay the – in his case increased – enrolment fees. Jan duly paid the sum and remained a member of the guild until his death in 1454. The widow had turned him down, but he ended up establishing a family with another woman, Liesbeth Engels.[41]

Conclusions

After a visit to the southern Low Countries between 1577 and 1592, the Spanish captain Alonso Vasquez wrote as follows about the women in Brabant towns:

> The women act like men. In most transactions concluded by their husbands, the couple speak with a single voice. Not only do women partake in trade and running their business, their house, and their family, but they also work as barbers in barbers' shops. Their help with shaving is so clean, precise, and controlled that one would willingly believe they had been invented for the trade, especially as their husbands are generally in the taverns, and they thus solve their own problems with more patience and tact than their spouses.[42]

This chapter has shown that Brabant wives carried out a range of tasks that went beyond simply helping their husband with his economic activity. Vasquez's words thus contain an element of truth. Admittedly, it is hard to ascertain whether the men were indeed out getting drunk, but on the other hand we have observed that women were very active on the job market. They did not act entirely freely, but the context of the nuclear family in particular provided a number of opportunities enabling them to work in trade. The butcher Hendrik Michiels and his wife Katelijne – referred to at the beginning of this chapter – were only one couple in a larger network of married couples, trade families, and widows trying to find their place on the job market. Yet that does not mean that only men occupied the guild world. As explained above, Hendrik's complaint against his fellow butchers produced the hoped-for result, as they were later reminded of on various instances. When 16 years later their son came into conflict with guild members (the family had a reputation, after all), he proudly declared that his mother had continued selling salted and roasted meat and tripe until she had died.[43] Hendrik and Katelijne's family business thus functioned following a setup characterizing the work market more broadly. This aspect of Alonso Vasquez's depiction is therefore accurate.

Indeed, the economic context of a late medieval town provided a relatively large number of opportunities for women, enabling them to work professionally and independently, despite the many barriers that guilds erected to safeguard their business and retain it within their closed circle. They thus limited the field of action for independent women (as they also did for journeymen and new entrants), so as to control any competition with households belonging to the guild. Rules were on occasion relative, however: as long as "abuses" did not exceed accepted limits, a fair degree of tolerance was the rule. Within families, women were certainly considered capable of running a business. Daughters, wives, and widows thus worked in – or even ran – a male relative's trade. Of course, a sizeable number of women did not belong to this wealthy group and nevertheless managed to generate an income for themselves and their families. When young, such women worked as servants; later they sought salaried employment. Others opted for the informal market, in which they sold everyday products in small quantities or else provided their services. While all working women on the Brabant market clearly did not always enjoy the same opportunities, they were nevertheless omnipresent.

Notes

[1] CAL, 1528, 123v (17 August 1461).
[2] In the event of a weaver "behaving in relation to prostitutes" (Peeters, *Bloei en verval*, 115).
[3] Favresse, "Règlements inédits", 215.
[4] CAL, 1523, 65r.
[5] CAL, 1523, 207r-210v.
[6] CAL, 1528, 37v.
[7] *Zwader locht ende ongewoenlike roeke* (Bisschops, "Het 2de Oudt Register (2)", 41-2).
[8] *Kemmerssen, spinnerssen, nopperssen, setterssen, vleigherssen* (Vannérus, "De keure der wollewevers", 33).
[9] Born, *De meesters in wording*, 38-9.
[10] Des Marez, *L'organisation du travail*, 112.
[11] Van den Heuvel, *De ambachtsgilden*, 169-71.
[12] Génard, "Het Register vanden dachvaerden (1)", 145-6.
[13] CAL, 1524, 9r.
[14] CAB, CA, 15, 389v-391r (See these same documents for praying women).
[15] In Dutch: *meesterswijf* (Des Marez, *L'organisation du travail*, 114).
[16] CAL, 4648, 397r-v.
[17] Van den Branden, "Oudt Register (4)", 3-4.
[18] CAL, 4748 (20 October 1566).
[19] Van den Branden, "Oudt register (3)", 104-5.
[20] CAL, 4659, 10v-11v.
[21] Génard, "Het Register vanden dachvaerden (3)", 157.
[22] Van den Branden, "Clementynboeck", 404-5.
[23] CAL, 1523, 207r-210v.
[24] CAL, 1523, 61r (1424).
[25] CAL, 1523, 69r-v (1426).

[26] CAL, 1526, 291r-292r.
[27] CAM, CB, 1, 99r.
[28] Scholliers, *Loonarbeid en honger*, 79.
[29] *Women's work* and *women are supposed to do it* (*Vrouwenwerc* and *vrouwen betaemt te doene*); Génard, "Het Register vanden dachvaerden (2)", 400.
[30] CAL, 1523, 73r-74v (1471). For what follows, see: Vandeweerdt, "Van den vleeschouweren", 17-8.
[31] CAL, 1527 (1593).
[32] CAA, GA, 4001, 64v.
[33] Van den Branden, "Oudt register (3)", 371-2.
[34] *Vrij souden moegen doen als hij dede in zijn levene* (CAL, 4648, 3r-4v).
[35] CAL, 1523, 202r-204r.
[36] CAL, 4648, 12v-13r.
[37] CAL, 4748, 1566.
[38] CAL, 4748, 1567.
[39] Meulemans, "Leuvense ambachten", 296-7.
[40] Bisschops, "Het 2de Oudt Register (1)", 405.
[41] Bisschops, "Het 2de Oudt Register (2)", 98-100.
[42] Vázquez, *Los sucesos de Flandes*, 462-3.
[43] CAL, 4648, 174r-v.

CHAPTER 6

"Bad women": Violence, crime, and rebellion

Jelle Haemers

"This book acts as a lesson and example to all men, young and old, so that they know the extent to which all women are unstable, sly, and deceitful." This unequivocal statement is the opening line of *Dat bedroch der vrouwen* ["The deceit of women"], probably by Jan van Doesborch of Antwerp.[1] In its day this book was popular, known especially through a reprint produced in Utrecht around 1532. Its author concludes that women, irrespective of age and circumstance, are the greatest danger for men. They thus need to be kept on a very short leash. The author spares no effort in warning men against bad women (*quade wijven*, as they were called in that period in Dutch). Drawing on a battery of quotations – from famous philosophers and Church fathers to classical authors and the Bible – the book provides a plentiful harvest of eloquent examples showing how female cunning and violence have laid low the most illustrious of men. The author thus cites Secundus of Athens, the second-century Greek philosopher, who (he states) wrote that "a good woman, like a good house, is built on a shithouse":[2] that is, though beautiful in appearance, she in fact conceals abject filth. Still, there is hope: if a woman "adorns herself with virtues", then a path of salvation is open to her. Honourable conduct, such as obeying her husband, may lead a woman to become a "precious gold vase" overflowing with "faith, hope, and love".

Nonetheless, this "treatise" takes a special pleasure in listing the many examples illustrating women's supposedly negative aspects: lying, prattling, thieving, and so on are, according to the author, typically female vices. It considers adulterous women, fornicating nuns, and impure virgins, debauchery certainly being the worst sin of which women are guilty. The author thus teaches his readers that woman's untrustworthy behaviour requires a strong husband. Yet the husband must take care too, for, as another literary work teaches us: "a good man becomes bad under the influence of a bad woman (*een quay vrouwe*)".[3] This line, taken from *De Stove* [The stove] – a story printed in 1528 by Jan van den Dale

Yael murders captain Sisera (a story from the Old Testament's Book of Judges). The image on the title page of the book entitled *Dat bedroch der Vrouwen* ["The deceit of women"] sets the tone (Braekman, *Dat bedroch der vrouwen*, 19). http://volkoomenoudeherbariaenmedisch.nl/dat%20bedroch%20der%20vrouwen.htm

in Brussels – seeks primarily to warn men about their choice of a future spouse. It was a very sensitive topic in the early sixteenth century. As we have seen in chapter 3, a wife's role within the family was changing during this period, and men increasingly expected their wives to play the part of ideal partner. In this context, literary works admonished men to think carefully before taking a wife. Erasmus thought no differently. In his 1526 treatise on marriage, with biblical quotations to back up his case, he wrote that a man is the "head" of a woman: *Vir est caput mulieris*. While wives allow themselves to be guided by their emotions, such as revenge, husbands need to maintain order in the household.[4] Yet moralist literature did not spare men, either. In another book circulating in the southern Low Countries since 1543 – *Bedroch der mannen* [The deceit of men] – the opposite sex came in for sharp criticism, too: men are sometimes just as untrustworthy, and, without a life partner to domesticate them, both sexes give in to debauchery. Despite singing the praises of marriage, these books give a far from commendable image of a humanity that seems intrinsically prone to deceit, covetousness, and insubordination. These works thus give pride of place to humankind's alleged wickedness.

One frequently reads that medieval society was more violent than ours. Images of the sombre Middle Ages conjure up ideas of towns as crime-riddled places of filth and depravity. Yet were towns really more dangerous than they are today? Any meaningful comparison is hard to conduct due to a lack of demographic data and the loss of sources that might tell us about anti-authority behaviour. Most of the available sources only tell us about acts of violence that were punished, giving an incomplete picture of real (unpunished) violations of the norms of the day, including domestic violence. Quarrels, physical injury, and fights within the family are hard to detect, as is still the case today. The sources have nothing to say about such matters, for courts privileged public offences and paid scant attention to domestic violence. Leaders intervened mainly when public order was under threat or when administrators' authority was compromised. After all, punishment often had a political purpose. The prince, the church, the town, and other authorities such as guild administrations condemned and imposed fines primarily for offences undermining their dignity. Obviously, offences against physical integrity (such as assault and battery) or against the property of others (such as theft) called for punishment, given that they ran counter to the fundamental values of urban society. Still, a series of offences were clearly "criminalized". In this chapter we shall encounter townspeople who, after casting slurs, received harsher sentences than those meted out to thieves: their behaviour was perceived as more harmful to the town council's authority than ordinary theft.

In any case, all insults, physical confrontations, acts of pillage and plunder, and certainly all murders called for punishment. Misdeeds such as a quarrel between two families were, however, resolved through mediation without the authorities getting involved. Violence was also curbed by social control, by all sorts of implicit rules and self-discipline. A tense situation could escalate, but it was just as likely that the altercating parties could be reconciled and reach an amicable agreement. In towns as densely populated as those in Brabant, inhabitants were all too aware that quarrels were in nobody's interest, and that an initial physical attack often degenerated into more serious violence. To defuse such situations, urban society had put together a model of values targeting deep-rooted pacification. One result of this goal was frequent warnings in the literature of the period against women's "bad nature" and men's explosive character. These morality lessons exaggerated and distorted reality in the hope of channelling townspeople's behaviour. Living together required people to control their emotions together with any behaviour likely to disturb the public order. This discipline was certainly a valuable truth for both sexes. Yet were men and women punished in the same manner?

The figures

The figures are stark. Most punishments were of men. In the second half of the fifteenth century, only 7% of the crimes punished in Mechelen were committed by women. The figures are even clearer for Lier: between 1402 and 1429 and between 1477 and 1484 – periods for which the sources have been preserved – only 5% of the sentences concerned women. The proportion stood at 6% in Nivelles between 1449 and 1459. While these are only three examples, they are part of a broader trend. By way of comparison, in the late Middle Ages, 5% of those sentenced in Namur were women, 14% in Mons, and similar figures were recorded in France.[5] In the fifteenth century, the number of punishments inflicted on women was thus far lower than that for men.

Let us now look at the figures for Brussels: of the 41 murderers sentenced over the course of the fifteenth century, four were women. Of the

351 cases of violent crime resulting in death, only one was committed by a woman. Likewise, in other categories of crime the percentage of women was lower than that of men: 17.5% of punished thefts were committed by women, 11% of cases of assault and battery – a figure which applies on average to other forms of criminality. Women thus accounted for only one tenth of those sentenced for violence. Lastly, categorizing figures for Mechelen, women were sentenced mainly for physical violence, crimes against property (theft, possession of stolen goods, etc.), and "inappropriate behaviour".[6] This latter category, also referred to as "uselessness" (*onnutscape* in Dutch), covered a plethora of phenomena ranging from various forms of fornication and indecency to insults and street brawls. The three main offences committed by men were different: though physical violence came first, verbal violence (insults, disputes, etc.) came second, followed by the opaque category of "inappropriate behaviour". Even though it seems natural to believe that women used words as a weapon more frequently than men, more men were sentenced for insults or other challenges to authority. The idea that men fought while women hurled abuse is thus totally false. Both groups committed the same sort of crimes, but men were punished more. Unstable, sly, and deceitful behaviour – in the words of both titles discussed above – was not tolerated.

The figures are thus lower for women, but that does not mean that the tolerance threshold was higher for them: as shown by many examples in this chapter, they, too, were liable to prosecution for murder, theft, or assault and battery. Still, the percentage of women to stand trial never reached that of men. Do these figures thus conclusively prove that men were more violent than women? It is hard to answer this question. First, as stated, we only have data about crimes which were punished, not about real violence. It is possible that men were more frequently in conflict with the courts because their acts of violence were more disruptive to the public order. As a rule, men were better at handling weapons and punched harder. Consequently, clashes between men in the grip of anger degenerated more often. On occasion the man, as the representative of the family, paid for crimes committed by his partner, but women tend to be less visible in registers of adjudication rulings. Lastly, we need to take into account that men simply had more impact in the public space than women. Given that crimes that disrupted the public order were especially sanctioned, men were more firmly in the judges' sights. In a society in which women had no public power, their subversive behaviour was less of a threat to the authorities. Conversely, the rebellious behaviour of men, who could potentially take or claim power, was far more damaging from this point of view.

Fighting, thieving, and punishing

What sorts of rebellious behaviour are we talking about? Theft, of course, was a very common crime. Poverty and sharp inequalities in town regularly resulted in theft, particularly when times were hard. In general, the sentence consisted in returning the stolen goods together with a fine, sometimes accompanied by public humiliation or exile in the event of major theft. In 1482, the Mechelen aldermen sentenced Katelijn van den Broecke to public humiliation for having stolen something in the beguinage. Katelijn had to stand in the stocks from 10 to 12 in the morning.[7] Not only did the judge thereby diminish her honour, but he also confirmed his own authority. Town authorities were entitled to imprison and dishonour a person if they had wronged the community or an individual. For Katelijn, the sentence was prolonged by exile for two years. Anyone infringing town rules was (temporarily) no longer welcome in town.

The prince's servants also had the power to pass judgment for theft. In each town there was a bailiff who had the power to punish crimes. The name of the officer varied from one town to the next (the *amman* in Brussels, the *meier* in Leuven, and the *bailli* in Nivelles). Their powers were often set out in privileges, but there could be some overlap with the town authorities, and on occasion the two intervened in concert. The situation differed from town to town. The duke retained jurisdiction over "high justice", including punishment for murder. Lesser acts of criminality were mainly punished by the town, while offences such as rape, insults, and fornication were often handled by both parties. Both the central and local authorities had the power to inflict corporal punishment, which was carried out by a *beul* (executioner). In Brussels in 1430, the executioner carried out punishment on Liesken Sbien after she stole a purse of the silver from a careless passer-by.[8] The bailiff paid the executioner to cut off one of her ears. Corporal punishment was thought of as a correction, which was literally the case here: she who would not hear must be made to feel. At the same time, this type of punishment was also a public humiliation, for it was carried out on a platform on the market square. The visible mutilation was to subsequently act as a reminder of the serious misdeed, not solely for the person being punished but for their entourage, too. Judges habitually reserved corporal punishment for cases of reoffending or serious theft. The death sentence was rare in such cases. There are only two known cases of women being executed in Mechelen in the fifteenth century. Anna Stroeprot and Lisa van der Bele were both sentenced to death, in 1405 and 1419, respectively, for repeated theft after previous convictions.

Judges were also generally less severe for one-off offences, taking extenuating circumstances into account. In 1459, the Antwerp bailiff passed judgment on Willeke Nulant of 's-Hertogenbosch, who was "well known for the ease with which she got into people's purses and stole their money".[9] She had thus reoffended on several occasions. The bailiff had had her put in gaol and wished to "examine her", as the expression went. That meant an interrogation often accompanied by torture. A conviction was only valid if preceded by a confession, and there were many legal means for obtaining it, such as imprisonment, placing in chains, thumb-screws, red-hot pokers, and so on. Sometimes the mere threat of torture was sufficient to get the "guilty" to confess – or should one rather than say the "victim"? Willeke, though, escaped torture thanks to "the request of many women and other people". The women's pleas apparently bore fruit for in Willeke's case the bailiff settled for a *compositie*. This ruling was an amicable settlement between the bailiff and the alleged offender, who paid a sum of money to avoid conviction and, in this case, interrogation. Lijsken paid a large fine and was released. It goes without saying that the "*compositie* right" of the prince's servants led to abuses on occasion. Such cases could be sanctioned, however: town councils and sometimes even the duke himself intervened, should a bailiff overstep his functions.

Yet let us return to offences committed by ordinary citizens. It is striking that men and women received fairly similar types of punishment. Both were sentenced to public humiliations, fines, or exile if found guilty of theft. The incomplete nature of the sources means it is hard to make an exact comparison. In general, only the final sentence has been preserved, not the witness reports or the reasons for the verdict. This summation means that any attenuating circumstances remain out of sight. The legislation sometimes provided for different punishments depending on sex, but the sentencing of women was not intrinsically more severe. A punishment which was largely specific to women, though men could also be sentenced to it, was "carrying the stone". In Breda, this public humiliation was reserved for "women guilty of defamation of men or women".[10] Likewise, in Bergen-op-Zoom, women unable to pay the fine for having uttered "forbidden words" were punished in this manner. The punishment consisted in going around the town on a fixed route carrying a (heavy) stone, which was often placed around the person's neck on a chain. This humiliating experience symbolized atonement for the suffering inflicted on the victims and for the damage caused to the community. For slandering a person affected society, and if the culprit was not solvent then the community suffered a financial loss. In Turnhout, the stone of humiliation that the culprit carried around the cemetery, normally on a Sunday, the Lord's Day, was hung in the town hall (where it is still kept today).[11] In Brussels, women who came to blows had to publicly carry the stone of humiliation along a fixed route running from the gate of the Steenpoort to the gate of the Sint-Katelijnepoort. In 1426, the aldermen sentenced a total of 17 women to this punishment. These included Lien van Haasdonk, who had given Kateline Sconinx a beating.[12] Spectators, learning that Lien had behaved badly, could choose to cast looks of anger or compassion her way.

Another very common – if more drastic and equally symbolic – punishment was punitive pilgrimage. Under this procedure, the person sentenced to obligatory pilgrimage had to go to a predetermined place. The authorities made frequent use of this punishment, which enabled the defendant to repent and also removed hotheads from the town. With the forced departure of the perpetrator, the aldermen prevented any escalation and the victims coming to blows or wreaking personal vengeance. To avoid the logic of "an eye for an eye, a tooth for tooth" and prevent violence spiralling out of control, the judges preferred to chase offenders out of town. Pilgrimage destinations were thus often places where convicted citizens gathered.

On pilgrimage

During a pilgrimage it was not unusual to encounter criminals, many of whom were undertaking such a journey in compensation for a crime. Compostela was a favoured destination, but the obligatory place of pilgrimage could be anywhere in Europe. Local legislation in Leuven made provision for Vendôme, between Le Mans and Orléans in France, as a place of pilgrimage to punish those who had drawn their sword or knife. Those who failed to comply with a summons were sentenced to a trip to Cologne Cathedral. Insulting or contradicting a judge was to be atoned for by a pilgrimage to Canterbury, and so on. These punishments applied to both men and women. On returning to the town of origin, the pilgrim had to provide proof in the form of a banner, medallion, or certificate, clearly establishing that they had indeed gone to the imposed destination. Sometimes a fixed fine could be paid in lieu of a pilgrimage, based on the distance to be travelled. A list of tariffs for Leuven shows that a trip to Strasbourg cost half that of a trip to Milan. In such cases the town council thus made do with a fine. In Nivelles, nearly two thirds of those sentenced to pilgrimage chose to pay the equivalent fine.

Pilgrimages were used especially often as punishment for theft, insult, and brawling. When in August 1453 Willem Verenbrunen approached the Leuven aldermen's court because his daughter Geertrui had been beaten until she bled by Margriete, the wife of Willem De Mey, the aldermen brandished the threat of a pilgrimage to Strasbourg, should the accusation turn out to be true. Margriete admitted that she had slapped Geertrui, but without this act resulting in any bloodshed.[13] The aldermen replied that a punitive pilgrimage would be inevitable, should investigations prove the contrary. If the offence was not too outrageous, the parties could nevertheless agree on reconciliation and compensation. Private disputes generally ended thus, with mediators negotiating a "kiss" or a "peace", a sort of amicable settlement. In such cases the aldermen's court scarcely intervened or only recorded the dispute. The *ad hoc* term in use in Antwerp in the fifteenth century was *oorvrede* (a kind of peace settlement), of which 113 were recorded for the period 1450-1490. A contract of this sort – such as the promise made in 1473 by Anthonis de Backer de Roosendaal to Ruisse, Gillis Claus's daughter – stipulated that the perpetrator "would do no further harm" to his victim, "neither in word nor in deed, neither secretly nor in public".[14] With raised hand Anthonis swore by God that he would respect his oath. Although compensation was frequently required, the aldermen did not pass judgment. In this way, the parties could settle their fights, altercations, and other conflicts themselves. Nevertheless, should one of the parties break the "peace" (*peisbreke* or *zoenbreke*, that is, "breaking the peace" or "breaking the kiss"), then the town intervened and imposed severe punishments, such as imprisonment, a fine, or an obligatory pilgrimage.

Many people who infringed a town's rules were sentenced to pilgrimages of this sort: it was a popular way to modify citizens' behaviour. The town of Leuven even kept a "pilgrimage register", in which it recorded the names of those sentenced to a pilgrimage and who had indeed carried it out. It lists a total of 803 pilgrimages for the period 1398-1422, meaning that, on average, the town sent 33 persons on a pilgrimage every year. Only 3% of them were women.[15] The 9,000 sentences issued in Nivelles between 1378 and 1550 include a total of 1,400 punitive pilgrimages. There are four times as many men as women among those sentenced.[16] Similarly, the town of Diest carefully recorded sentences handed down between 1426 and 1503. These records tell us that of the 229 sentences concerning women, 70% of them consisted of a pilgrimage. Two women were even sentenced to a double pilgrimage: Noykene Basteels had to go both to Ferrare (between Venice and Bologna) and to Rome, while the aldermen obliged Katelijne van Bekkevoort to go to Cologne and to Nizelles Abbey (between Brussels and Nivelles). Noykene, who was probably a prostitute, had to atone thus for her "immoral behaviour" in the vicinity of the beguinage, as well as for an injury she had inflicted on a man.[17] Women thus went on obligatory punitive pilgrimages, but except for more serious offences the aldermen generally sent them to places less distant than those used for men.

Of course, there could also be false accusations, as shown by the case of Willem Verenbrunen mentioned above. Citizens might approach the aldermen with the aim of discrediting someone. Should an accusation be ungrounded, however, the accuser could be punished for acting in bad faith. Medieval legislation included many measures against false declarations, calumny, and perjury. One of the crimes that was hard to judge was rape, to which we shall return in the following chapter. It was sometimes a case of word against word when seeking to determine whether a woman had consented or not. In 1427, the town of Brussels issued an ordinance obliging women to report rape within three days, failing which their complaint would not be received. According to the town, many men lived "in great fear and great alarm" because they had to unfairly "bear the burden and shame" of having committed rape. While the town authorities were doubtless not exempt from exaggeration, it is not inconceivable that a wave of false accusations of rape had been directed against notables. Two years later, the town sentenced Katelijne Sconinx to the stocks for having wrongly accused Heynen de Bocq of Mechelen of rape.[18] Of course, the question remains of whether such provisions did not make it even more difficult for women to take legal action against men.

There were few female murderers. A woman could be punished for infanticide or held responsible for deliberately murdering somebody else, but any such cases were exceptional. In 1467, the Leuven executioner went to take a woman from her bed in the middle of the night, because an investigation had shown that she had "let her child die through negligence".[19] The facts are not clearly stated, but the town accused this mother of having neglected her unfortunate child. Since the (anonymous) woman got away with a public humiliation, it would seem this was not a case of voluntary homicide. Conversely, three cases in Antwerp in the fifteenth century concern women who had clearly instigated murder. One of them had had her husband assassinated and then had intimate relations with the murderer, another had stabbed a man to death, and the third had mortally wounded someone. In Nivelles, the only woman found guilty of murder in the fifteenth century was in fact sentenced for her assistance in the horrible deed. Named Jeanne, she was not the murderer but was sentenced to be burnt at the stake for having "aidiet a faire mourdere" (helped to do murder).[20] Female murderers tended to opt for poison. In Brussels in the fifteenth century, one of the rare cases of murder involving a woman, in 1427, was murder by poisoning. In what would appear to have been a crime of passion, Bate Mostinx and the miller Thiel de Scempere had bought rat poison (i.e., arsenic) from a doctor.[21] Bate had mixed it with food for her husband Willem De Mol, who died shortly afterwards. Then Thiel in turn had administered the same substance to his own wife, mixing it with milk and fish, with equally fatal consequences. In accordance with the law, the judges sentenced Bate to be burnt at the stake and Thiel to public execution. Thus on the Grand-Place in Brussels, the executioner beheaded Thiel and then cut his corpse into four pieces, each of which was hung on a gibbet at one of the city gates. Given the seriousness of the offence, Bate's punishment was carried out just as inexorably (and publicly). An annotation in the accounts of the Brussels bailiff tells us that the members of her family, together with her children, subsequently bought the confiscated inheritance from the bailiff. The crime was inexcusable, and so the punishment could not be changed. The town authorities subsequently announced in a council decision that nobody, on pain of death, was henceforth to sell arsenic without authorization from the authorities.

On suicide, witchcraft, and adultery

In addition to the crimes discussed until now, and which are just as reprehensible today, various acts were punishable in the Middle Ages which are no longer deemed to be "criminal". Yet misconceptions circulate about the criminalization of behaviour deemed immoral on religious grounds, such as adultery, suicide, abortion, and "witchcraft". A persistent cliché about the Middle Ages is that witches were frequently burned at the stake. This view is incorrect on several counts. First, there were virtually no trials for witchcraft, for there was no witch hunt in the southern Low Countries at this time. It was only in the sixteenth century that casting around for female scapegoats to blame for all sorts of misfortunes really took off. Second, it is striking that the few sentences for "witchcraft" to be issued involved men as much as women. Third, the accusation of witchcraft rarely resulted in the culprit being sentenced to the stake. There were but few cases of the "crime of witchcraft" given how marginal it was in medieval towns. Yet the notable absence of mass criminalization for witchcraft does not imply that superstition and magic did not exist at the time. As in our societies today, superstition was omnipresent, as was blasphemy, but that did not mean that people openly abjured their faith. A fundamental change took place over the course of the sixteenth century. In a 1486 treatise called *The Hammer of witches* [*Malleus Maleficarum*], two ecclesiastics from the Rhineland declared that the devil found most of his acolytes among single women. Their work inspired subsequent generations of persecutors of witches, but condemnations for witchcraft were an exception in Brabant in their day.

From time to time, the authorities punished a woman or a man for "witchcraft". There are five known cases in Lier in the fifteenth century. In 1417, Heyne van Roesbroec was sentenced for having practised "witchcraft" (*toverien* in Dutch) with his mother.[22] Unfortunately, it is impossible to establish what the mother and son did exactly, but at the time of the judgment Heyne had fled and his mother had already been gaoled. The town sentenced Heyne in absentia to five years of exile and a hefty fine. The habitual punishment for such offences was a fine and public humiliation. Likewise, Marie Haveloes – known as "Bad Marie" (*Quade Marie*) – was sentenced to one year of exile for having insulted a priest in 1414, both inside and outside the church. When she "reoffended" in 1423, the town sentenced her to exile once again, this time for a period of three years. Her townsman Roel Costens had to undertake a pilgrimage to

Milan in 1426, for having committed an "act of magic" (*wonderlicheyt*). He was able to redeem his sentence, though, by repairing a section of the city walls. This punishment was a contemporaneous disciplinary measure in compensation for damage done to the community. Additionally, Roel was not allowed to enter the town for two years and had to pay a small fine. In short, the town used traditional punishments to remind inhabitants that public blasphemy was unacceptable.

A remarkable case in Antwerp tells us a little more about what such an "act of magic" might consist of. An entry in the aldermen's court register dated 14 May 1491 records that three ladies – Liesbet Gielis, a certain Aagje, and Liesbet Tessels – were sentenced to pilgrimage to Einsiedeln (in present-day Switzerland) for having cut off the head and hands of a hanged thief and done strange things with these trophies. They had hidden the head under the doorstep to their house and hung one of the hands in the chimney after having soaked it in vinegar. They had then used it to sprinkle their house. Liesbets and Aagje had cut off four fingers from the other hand, which they had then taken to altars in the Church of Our Lady "in order to read masses in their presence". Had the thief robbed their house, and were these ladies hoping to thus frighten away future villains? We may only conjecture, for the registers tell us nothing about this topic. Given the laws of the day, such examples of superstition should have led to the culprits being sentenced to death. Yet the ruling teaches us that the – merciful – bishop of Cambrai pardoned the women and spared their bodies and appendages. After the confiscation of their goods, they were let off with a punitive pilgrimage.[23] This strange case shows that mercy was an important aspect of the legal practice of the day, which always took extenuating circumstances into account. It was only in the sixteenth century that such forms of superstition took on a new dimension, when the associated religious tension and political conflict considerably lowered the threshold of tolerance for "magic". Even so, in Antwerp in the fifteenth century, "witches" often got off with just a pilgrimage.

Still, the law was less merciful towards suicide and abortion. The Church held taking one's life or the life of an unborn child to be an act of blasphemy. Women who aborted could thus expect severe sanctions. Proof had to be provided, though, that a pregnancy had been deliberately terminated. In 1392, the Mechelen bailiff sentenced Jan van den Hoene for having sold medicinal plants to a pregnant women with the goal of terminating her pregnancy.[24] The bailiff's account does not enable us to ascertain if Jan had acted at the woman's request, but the text states that he was not sentenced, for the bailiff was unable to prove that the plants in question had produced the expected effect. As it was equally impossible to ascertain whether the woman had indeed taken the initiative to put a premature end to her pregnancy, she was not sentenced, either. Despite normative texts since the thirteenth century declaring that women risked exile or the death sentence should they abort, such sentences were rare in practice. It is thus virtually impossible to estimate the frequency with which women sought to terminate undesired pregnancies. Given the scandalous nature of the act, it is highly likely that it tended to take place at home, often resulting in permanent consequences. Yet families kept it secret due to the severe legislation.

This observation no doubt also applied to suicide. It is true that there are larger numbers of recorded suicides than of abortion. Gathering evidence in this area was equally difficult, however. In any case, suicide was strictly forbidden and from a religious point of view considered as a more serious crime than murder even, for it amounted to killing not only one's body but also one's soul. For the mentally disabled, mutilated, or the depressed, such a desperate act was often viewed with a degree of indulgence. In this case, the body was buried in consecrated ground. Others, however, were refused this right and lost all honour. As a rule, the authorities displayed suicides' corpses and then staged a public humiliation or an "execution". In such cases, the corpse was posthumously hanged from the gibbet. In 1453, for example, Peter Smyters of Oostmalle had hanged himself in a forest far from home. When his devoured and half decomposed body was finally found, the Antwerp bailiff had the remains placed in a coffin which was suspended from a tree.[25] Nevertheless, once again judges sometimes draped themselves in leniency. Thus in 1474, the wife of Jacob Eysterlinc of Mechelen committed suicide by drowning. The incident is recorded in the usual terms: *noyee par desperacion*, drowned out of despair.[26] Contrary to custom, the bailiff granted the husband's request that his wife's body be spared public humiliation, without the reasons for this clemency being specified. Conversely, in the same town in 1462, the bailiff sentenced Jan van der Hagen to a fine for culpable negligence: his wife Kateline Smetins had taken his life without his intervening. What exactly happened? It is hard to know.

Public humiliation was thus the main reason suicides were concealed. The same applies to another "crime" that is no longer punished by the courts, adultery. Similar sentences such as fines and public humiliations were used to punish this offence, which once again pertained to the moral sphere. As marriage was contracted before God, extramarital relations were, from a religious point of view, reprehensible. In 1452, the town of Antwerp issued an ordinance according to which, for some time, "the sin of adultery is committed in public, to the shame and dishonour of God and the Church, and likewise to the shame and dishonour of the town".[27] Married women living adulterously with another man were to attach a piece of red cloth to their clothing so that they would be publicly recognizable as shameful and indecent. It is stated that they were to do this "for the example of others and in honour of all good women", suggesting that the main objective of this law was to discourage women from committing adultery.[28] Additionally, unfaithful women lost all right to their husband's possessions and to any inheritance from their new partner, should the latter leave them something in his will; for their part, unfaithful men were barred from holding public office, whether for the town or in a guild. The fact that this ordinance was repeatedly reissued – in 1472, 1482, and 1517 – shows, first, that it was hard to control adultery, and second, that the aldermen were constantly preoccupied with reminding spouses of the vows they had made. Extramarital relations signified great dishonour for families, as observed earlier. They disrupted relations within and between families, while adultery could lead to quarrels and public disorder. Hence, not only the Church sought to curb husbands' dissolute conduct, but the secular authorities were also involved in strictly monitoring marital morality.

Nevertheless, in Antwerp, the number of convictions for adultery was not such as to alarm the civil authorities: 36 between 1392 and 1496. This tally suggests that the aldermen only intervened when the situation degenerated too far, or at least when the adultery was public. Logically, the Church took more action. In the period from 1438 to 1453, the registers of the ecclesiastical judges of the diocese of Cambrai (which included Antwerp) record 150 instances of Antwerp residents being fined for having broken their marriage vows. Thus whereas the town punished on average one case of adultery every three years, the Church punished ten per year. Once again, the difference between the sexes is noteworthy. The vast majority of punishments handed down by the town involved women, whereas the Church mainly moved against adulterous husbands. In three quarters of the cases punished by ecclesiastical judges, the man had to pay a fine. It is hard to explain this difference, for the situation diverged in many other places. Might it be because the Antwerp ecclesiastical court tended to hold the man to be the instigator of adultery, whereas the town was seeking primarily to denounce women's poor public conduct? In 1392, the Antwerp aldermen thus obliged Kateline Scoenbaerts, the wife of "Potterkens", to make a pilgrimage to Notre-Dame in Paris. The reason for the punishment was that "she had no shame" about living with a married man "in a public situation of adultery".[29] As for Marie Bochoot, she was sentenced to a pilgrimage to 's-Hertogenbosch in 1491, because she had caused "shame, grief, and a breach of the peace" within a couple, by seeking each day to draw the husband away from his wife, according to the register.[30] Of course, the Church also targeted women who sought to get men to leave their wives. In 1450, Katrien Laille was judged for having had relations not only with an ecclesiastic, but also with her relative Jan de Wever and another married man. It is stated that she held gatherings where married men had sexual relations with other women. Lastly, the diocese accused her of witchcraft because she possessed a book on the forbidden arts, as well as a pony used for practising magic. It is not stated exactly what role Katrien got this animal to perform during her ceremonies, but her punishment is duly recorded. She was excommunicated and hence expelled from the religious community, in addition to having to pay a hefty fine.[31] This punishment is clearly an extreme example, in which the combination of different charges led to a severe sentence, but it is also possible that her crimes were in fact a form of organized prostitution.

Insults and disputes

Just as for many of the crimes discussed above, in cases of insults the main source of irritation was public dishonour. Why did honour have such importance? Towns were characterized by an unequal society in which lineage and social position determined a citizen's privileges. While a series of rights were accorded to all citizens – such as the right to property – other, supplementary privileges stemmed from social position. In this way, a family's reputation determined its prestige and influence; the privileges of nobles were based on their lineage and good conduct; and the authority of judges was grounded in the position they held. Therefore, if somebody publicly called one of these elements into question through public insult, it amounted – metaphorically speaking – to sawing off the legs of the comfortable chair on which the victim was sitting. When, for example, someone called a nobleman a *hoerezoon* (literally, "son of a whore" – one of the most popular insults), the assailant was questioning his victim's noble origins. This act was dangerous because the influence of the insulted figure, once torn down from his pedestal, might suffer. It explains medieval society's extreme sensitivity to slights to reputation or honour.

How frequently were people punished for making insults? In Antwerp, there were 260 cases in 100 years, between 1414 and 1513. A little under 15% of them concerned disputes between residents. In 60% of cases, the victim was an official. Lastly, other cases concerned a person publicly spreading dishonourable comments about others (25%).[32] These figures show that the town mainly intervened when the public order was compromised. Other cases generally led to a "peace" or a "kiss" being arranged by the families. Both men and women defied the ban on insults, but it was mostly men who were sentenced. In Antwerp, the proportion stood at 87% men, 13% women; likewise, in Lier, only a tenth of cases concerned a woman accused of hurtful comments. In Mechelen, the proportion of women was slightly higher (21%). These figures refer both to verbal violence between individuals, as well as to public humiliations involving officials. The distinction between the two types of insult was sometimes a fine line, and there was likewise considerable overlap in the insults used by men and by women.

> **Popular insults used by women, and those used against them**
> The list of insults is long and colourful. Hoodlum, traitor, adulterer, braggart, donkey, sucker (or licker), sissy, and so on were used to humiliate the adversary. Scatological insults were also sometimes used: *ic bescyt u* (I shit on you) and a whole range of variants were frequently hurled during bitter quarrels. Such a declaration reduced the victim to the level of an animal, living, like them, in his or her own excrement. Sexual allusions were also very frequent, for they conveyed moral discrimination. That was certainly true for a range of typical invectives against women. "Priest's whore" and "priest's woman" referred to a woman living dishonourably with an unmarried cleric. "Priest's whore" or else just "whore" were doubtless the most common insults used against women, for they stated that the woman sought to sell her body. Men were also sometimes associated with prostitutes: "son of a whore" referred to the illegitimate origins of the offended person, while "whore chaser" criticized his sexual morality, and "pimp" accused him of trafficking women.

"A sharp tongue may break a leg, and it takes long to heal" was a popular saying in the southern Low Countries in the late Middle Ages.[33] Words could strike harder than the sword: although not causing physical harm, public humiliation or a stinging insult could generate severe psychological damage or loss of reputation. Additionally, rumours and accusations, whether founded or not, could acquire a life of their own. That is why the authorities took severe steps against "bad words" as they were called. Other terms to describe words that caused suffering were "terrible", "villainous", "dirty", and so on. Punishments were severe, but varied from one case to another: public humiliation, pilgrimage, exile, a fine, and, in exceptional cases, corporal punishment, such as piercing the culprit's tongue with a hot iron. In Nivelles, a 1438 ducal ordinance stipulates that *parollez injurieuses ne diffamatoires* (hurtful and defamatory words) were to be punished by pilgrimage: men to Santiago, women to Rocamadour – though the destination remained at the judge's discretion.[34] In 1464, the town punished Margriete, wife of Aard De Vriese, for having insulted the wife of Willem Bertenscamp in her home. Because of the *skandal et blasme* (scandal and opprobrium) thus provoked, as the record puts it, Margriete had to leave the town within six days on a punitive pilgrimage to St Peter's in Rome.[35] Before departing, and in front of the abbess of St Gertrude's (the main abbey in town), the highest-ranking bailiff publicly handed her a pilgrim's staff, and then she left.

A public ceremony not only served to convince spectators, it also enabled the aldermen to re-establish public order as the masters of such a ceremony. Women not sent on pilgrimage were sentenced to an equivalent humiliation, such as ritual begging for pardon. In 1443, Katelijne, wife of Jan Moens of Mechelen, had called the wife of Jan Bruekers a "ferocious whore".[36] Katelijne was sentenced to begging her victim's pardon within three days, in the presence of a town officer and some neighbours, while holding a lit candle in her hand. The aldermen in person decided on the wording: Katelijne had to say that she had used "bad and shameful words" to "dishonour" her victim. She was then to add that these words were false, deceitful, and had been spoken "with heated blood" (*uut heeten bloede* in the Dutch of that time). She thus indicated that the discussion had been animated and emotions had run high, before going on to say that "she had never known her other than virtuous and honourable", and openly asking pardon from the adverse party. Katelijne was then to go to the Church of Our Lady holding the lit candle as an offering to the Virgin

Mary. Finally, she was to pay a fine within six weeks, half of which was to go to the duke and the other half to the town. All public humiliations thus received fitting response.

The need for the town authorities to re-establish order – or rather to prevent a conflict from escalating – transpires clearly in accounts of brawls sparked by insults. Shortly after the promulgation of the above-mentioned ordinance in Nivelles in 1438, an entry in the aldermen's court register shows how an exchange of insults could degenerate.[37] Two women had insulted each other, and each was sentenced to a pilgrimage to Rocamadour. Two men who had wanted to defend one of the women were sentenced to go to Compostela. One of these two men had insulted a third man, who was defending the other woman, and was sentenced to a second pilgrimage to Compostela. In the meantime, tempers had flared to such an extent that one of the women attacked the other, though without drawing blood, according to the ruling. For that she had to pay a fine on top of her sentence. The aldermen sought to intervene rapidly to prevent the town from becoming the theatre of clan warfare. In this case, it is true, they were only partly successful. Still, had they not intervened, there would have been the risk of violence escalating and the situation spinning out of control.

For the aldermen, public insults against a man of rank were an even greater menace. To avoid such conflicts there was the threat of harsher sentences, heftier fines, prison sentences, or long periods spent standing in the stocks. In Leuven, insulting a fellow towns(wo)man could cost up to five shillings. Apparently, though, this measure was not dissuasive. More men than women insulted aldermen or royal officials, but women also lashed out at important men. In 1486, the widow Liesbet van Nec used "coarse" words in the presence of the rector of Leuven University. Unfortunately, we do not know the exact terms she used, but the rector felt humiliated, according to the record, and appealed to the bailiff. The investigations the latter carried out showed that the widow had indeed made coarse insults, and Liesbet was sentenced to a hefty fine.[38] No doubt the rector could count himself lucky in comparison to what the Antwerp judge Wouter van Hove had to endure at the hands of an even more aggressive woman in 1471. Kateline Piermans insulted her victim by hurling many "bad and vulgar words" at him, before then setting about him with her hands and feet.[39] The record indicates that Kateline then "celebrated" her actions – that is, she probably boasted about them. She was sentenced to a pilgrimage to Maastricht and a hefty fine, which could be converted into corporal punishment (having fingers cut off) should she fail to pay. The aldermen could not tolerate such behaviour, and the same applied to dishonourable activities in holy places. In 1466, the Mechelen aldermen exiled Louise van Moerkerke because she had poured a "pot of impurities" (probably a full chamber pot) on another woman in the Carmelite church.[40] For that she had to undertake a pilgrimage to St Peter's in Rome, where, it is hoped, she did not reoffend.

Political protest and riots by women

Slandering a figure of authority could easily shade into political protest. Officeholders considered personal criticism directed against them to be a political crime, because it amounted to questioning their authority, by a citizen who, to their mind, had little grounds for doing so. As for judges and administrators, they viewed words of protest, just like acts of physical violence, as a dangerous precedent which could destabilize the community as a whole. Such situations were no doubt damaging primarily to their personal standing. It is in any case striking that "bad words" about the authorities in medieval towns often resulted in hefty fines. Many uprisings and political conflicts may be traced back to accusations, whether false or not, or "calls to arms" as they were termed in the sources. The name of an uprising could even refer to the verbal resistance that had sparked it, such as the "criers' revolt" that rocked 's-Hertogenbosch in 1525. The phrase refers to those who had chanted slogans openly criticizing the town council's policies in public places where the population gathered, such as various cemeteries around the town. Insurgents also made themselves heard elsewhere. Rather than the clash of arms, gossip, outcries, and rumblings of discontent were the most frequent forms of resistance. Words were enemies to be feared by all those embodying authority: ecclesiastics, judges, and aldermen were terribly afraid of insults and political protest.

Verbal rebellion was the work of both men and women. Men no doubt used it more, though: in the decade from 1420 to 1430, the Leuven bailiff sentenced 78 men for having insulted a figure of authority, as against only four women (amounting to 5%). For the decade between 1475 and 1485, the proportion changed slightly: 52 men as against 10 women (i.e., 84% against 16%).[41] Yet women were no less sharp-tongued when they felt they had been wronged. This observation runs counter to the received idea that political protest in the Middle Ages was a matter of exclusively male revolts. Women clearly did not refrain from expressing their discontent. Public criticism of administrators – though no longer punishable today (except in the event of serious forms of discrimination or defamation) – used to be an offence. Records about these offences provide exceptional insight into how ordinary people expressed themselves and what their points of view were. While a literary source may depict a woman disputing a judge's decision, it is never more than a fiction. Looking at the court documents enables us to ascertain what women actually said.

Of course, we do not always learn the exact words these women used, let alone the precise circumstances in which the events took place. When Margriete Brants told a Brussels priest to his face that he "read letters in a way unlike that of before", what exactly did she mean?[42] No doubt it was a personal conflict, but the invective had been delivered in public in the presence of other people, so the aldermen considered it to be a political offence. This case is reminiscent of that of Katelijne Goblijns of Mechelen, sentenced to one year's exile in 1452, because she had "publicly sang songs" targeting some Franciscans.[43] Was the woman angry because she felt wronged by certain members of the mendicant order? Had she clashed with a Friar Minor or criticized their privileges? We do not know, but the severity of the sentence shows in any case that the aldermen did not consider it to be a run-of-the-mill offence. Men, women, and sometimes couples frequently sang songs poking fun at the authorities. Against this backdrop, the Mechelen aldermen did not tolerate a bitter tone and direct insults targeting the town council. In 1539, it sentenced a couple from Hasselt for having sung songs in the town and having distributed texts printed in Mechelen, Dendermonde, and elsewhere.[44] 1539 was an eventful year, with revolts against Emperor Charles V at Ghent, Oudenaarde, and Kortrijk. Doubtless to nip in the bud any rebellion like that in Mechelen, the man was put in the stocks. The pamphlets were burnt, and the woman (Digne Paget) got off with a symbolic pilgrimage to Hanswijk. Though we do not know exactly what the couple sang, it was clearly felt to be offensive in both form and content.

A more transparent case is that of Goeris van Piermont's girlfriend, who was punished in 1478, after having told the Asse aldermen that they would be "better off keeping pigs rather than dispensing justice as they did".[45] This (anonymous) woman paid a sum of money for a wax candle, which she probably had to light in a church as atonement. This woman was no doubt in the grip of emotion after being handed a sentence by the aldermen, which she deemed to be unfair, leading her to criticize their skill so openly and facetiously recommend a change of career. Such skirmishes generally occurred at work. In 1436, for example, a certain Perinne spat in the face of the Antwerp dean of mercers when he visited the workshop where she was casting pewter pots with her two brothers. They had been summoned by the dean on three occasions, but Perinne and her brothers had not appreciated this interference in their business. This affair was not a political protest, but an open attack on the dean's authority. Perinne was thus sent on pilgrimage to 's-Hertogenbosch.[46] In 1423, Machtilde Poerloecx was likewise involved in a conflict in Leuven, telling the inspectors of the fishmonger's guild that they had wrongly rejected the plaice she was selling, and that "they stank", as the record reads – probably in reference to the inspectors rather than her fish.[47] She was sentenced to a pilgrimage to Milan. In this case once again, a woman mocked the authorities after clashing with them. Nevertheless, it raises the question whether something more was not at stake. The public nature of the attack of course bore the seeds of a possible uprising on a far larger scale, but criticism from women perhaps simply resembled open acts of resistance often committed by men. Indeed, historians have often noted that much of men's rebellious discourse sought not only to personally denounce the aldermen's incompetence, but also to criticize the unequal division of power. Threats made by women seem to partake in this critical attitude.

Jacomine Claus in Antwerp in 1496, and the wife of Michiel Speelbouts in Mechelen in 1441, were even more vehement: the first labelled certain "important people" as "traitors" in the presence of a lot of people, while the other insulted some town officials at the market, calling them "dirty thieves".[48] For her part, Lien Lenaerts of Diest had to undertake a pilgrimage to Milan after having insultingly called the authorities swindlers, thieves, and traitors.[49] The circumstances of these incidents are uncertain, other than that in Mechelen the affair had to do with a ban on selling certain products. In using such violent language, women were clearly seeking to attack their victims, but at the same time they were also seeking to denounce what they saw as injustices. They thus sought to turn the tables: they took the risk of being punished for flouting a ban and publicly accused their opponents of lacking integrity. Barbara van Steynmolen did not hold back in 1517, when she accused the mayor of Mechelen of being both incompetent and corrupt. The imperial charter recording the judgment – for even Charles V became involved after a trial before the Great Council – states that she had publicly declared to the mayor's face that "he did not dispense justice but only used brute force", and that "he only dispensed justice as he saw fit". The fact that the emperor was involved arose no doubt because the imperial court was in town, and it is also highly likely that a court official used imperial power to stiffen the sentence handed down to Barbara.[50] Be that as it may, rather than being random insults, Barbara's accusations went straight to the heart of the problem. Making the accusation that justice was arbitrary and dishonest seriously challenged the aldermen's judicial power in general and the mayor's authority in particular. They were thus criminal offences. Like many other women, Barbara was seeking to turn the tables. Instead of being judged, she was putting the mayor in the dock. Regardless of whether she was right or wrong, such allegations were tantamount to political opposition to perceived mismanagement. The fact that power was in men's hands was never denounced, but their abusing this power was unacceptable.

> *Urban uprisings*
> Although chroniclers often attribute political resistance to the impulsive behaviour of the turbulent poor, the reality was very different. Most of the time, it was wealthy citizens who headed political protest, and they were the first to take up their pen or speak out to voice their discontent. Strikes, occupying the market square, or mass departures from town were frequent occurrences, should the authorities remain deaf to complaints about their policies. Women certainly supported such collective actions, as illustrated by an ordinance issued in Mechelen in 1361. The town forbade male and female members of the fullers' guild from continuing with their rebellion, whether "by word or by deed". Women were thus clearly involved in protest actions, though it was mainly men who assumed this task due to the authorities' frequently strong-armed reactions. If fighting broke out, men were better able to withstand the blows. And in the meantime, women could continue propagating the fire of rebellion through their words.

The next stage in – rightly or wrongly – denouncing injustices visited by the authorities on citizens was collective protest in the form of letters of complaint or, at a subsequent stage, by acts of violence. It was a regular occurrence for rebels to chase the aldermen out of town, to lock them up, or to express their demands in a vehement manner. On occasion, such an accumulation of violence might result in armed conflict. Women then mostly stepped back. As already stated, arms were a male preserve; mercenaries were men (with Joan of Arc truly being the exception). Nevertheless, women operated as spies in times of war, or they carried letters through enemy lines for cities. For example, a woman from Zoutleeuw was injured during the 1489 revolt against Maximilian of Austria, while carrying a secret message to the town of Hasselt and running into soldiers along the way.[51] Similarly, in Leuven in 1363, women were expelled for having taken part in the weavers' guild revolt. In the early sixteenth century, there were some well-known "women's riots". Later on, in the early modern period – and certainly in the seventeenth century – women rebelled on several occasions against an increase in the price of wheat, or else headed hunger riots. Actions of this type are not known for the earlier period, probably because there were practically no protests against famine. That does not mean that the Middle Ages were exempt from famine, not to mention poor harvests and grain shortages, but towns in the southern Low Countries were fairly successful in securing food supplies and controlling prices. Their policy in times of famine consisted of taking many measures to ensure smooth supply, explaining why there were few protests in this context.

As of the sixteenth century, women start appearing in contexts of organized rebellion, but it is no longer clear what the issues involved were. In 1531, for example, the Mechelen town council sentenced 17 women to permanent exile, having found them guilty of "unauthorized gatherings, riots, and rebellion".[52] There is no way of ascertaining the cause of this unrest, but they were probably protesting against increases in the price of grain. A second case concerns a major revolt by "bad women" (*quade wijffs*) in Antwerp in 1522, when, according to a chronicler, angry women sprang a preacher from gaol.[53] The chronicle states that no fewer than 300 women managed to snatch the cleric from the hands of the bailiff. The town's registers state, however, that only one woman was condemned. Margriete Boonams of Mechelen was sentenced to a pilgrimage to Nicosia in Cyprus because of what she had yelled out at the entrance to the Augustinian monastery.[54] While the chronicle may perhaps exaggerate the incident, it would not be surprising that the town only punished the most agitated of the agitators.

For his part, another chronicler explains that the protests emanated from the entire population, mainly denouncing the high cost of grain. He compares the event to the "great riots" also in Mechelen and in Leuven, that women staged at the same period to denounce grain merchants, but does not breathe a word about a similar and massive women's uprising in Antwerp. He does, however, mention the boatmen who, with "certain bad women", sought to influence the price of grain, provoking "uproar and tumult" among those present.[55] It was not a coincidence that the town issued an ordinance shortly after forbidding its inhabitants, particularly women and children, from stealing wheat.[56] From this point of view, this type of collective protest is to be considered as a form of crime organized by the least fortunate, a factor that was also present in the Middle Ages. Be that as it may, in the 1520s and 1530s, protests against wheat shortages, price increases, and the advent of Protestantism may be observed among many strata of the Brabant population, and women clearly took part, too. Just as, in the Middle Ages, they used to sing to defy authority. Women in subsequent centuries knew how to react when they felt they had been treated unfairly. Their "bad words" addressed to the aldermen show they were capable of defending themselves and openly criticizing the authorities. They presumably did not fail either to voice their discontent at injustices to their families and at their place of work, or to share their vision of what "fair government" would look like, just as men did. This conduct is reminiscent of what a chronicler writes about the role mothers played in religious conflicts in Arras in 1577: he says that they told their children how and why their medieval ancestors had opposed the authority of the king of France. In this way, he states, "mothers suckled their children not just on milk, but also on implacable hatred of France".[57] It is thus probable that women's role in communicating political ideas was greater than historians have tended to suspect.

Conclusions

When the authors of medieval fiction stated that women, irrespective of age and circumstance, were the greatest danger for a man, the message was primarily moral in nature. Some stated, for instance, that without their husband's reins, women were unguided missiles threatening to disrupt society, given their penchant for indomitable lust on top of their weakness of mind. Yet the proportions of court sentences clearly show that it was above all the foolish conduct of men that led to problematic situations. Did it mean that women could go about their business with impunity? No, for female criminals came up against royal representatives, or else the wise old men at the town hall. Men's greater weight in the public sphere, combined with the tendency of lay and ecclesiastical authorities to target public forms of criminality, meant that male offenders predominate in court records. Behaviour disturbing the public order was criminalized, whether such offences were committed by men or by women. Assuredly, bad women (*Quade wijven*) lived in town, but the authorities sanctioned "bad men" a lot more.

There is a specific group of women operating on the margins of society that we have not yet discussed. They were not punishable as such, but were in closer contact with criminality than others. We are speaking of prostitutes. The following chapter shows that they were not considered as "bad women", their activity instead being viewed as a "necessary evil".

Notes

[1] *Tot een onderwijs ende exempel van allen mannen ionck ende out / omdat si sullen weten hoe bruesch/ hoe valsch/ hoe bedriechlijck dat die vrouwen zijn* (Franssen, "Dat bedroch der vrouwen", 274).

[2] *Een schoon vrouwe is een schoon huys getimmert op een schijthuys* (quoted in Pleij, *Anna Bijns*, 235; see too the critical edition by W. Kuiper).

[3] *Een goet man wort quaet doer een quay vrouwe* (Degroote, *Jan van den Dale*, 142).

[4] Taken from: Erasmus, *Christiani Matrimonii Institutio* (ed. Weiler, 218). See too Rummel, *Erasmus on women*, 10.

[5] Bourguignon & Dauven, "Une justice", 217.

[6] Aernouts, *Dwijf es van naturen loes*, 10. For Brussels: Vanhemelryck, *De criminaliteit*, 307-10.

[7] Maes, *Vijf eeuwen*, 618.

[8] GSAB, CC, 12701, 245r.

[9] *Zeere befaemt was in den luden borse te gane ende den luden haer gelt alsoe te nemen* (GSAB, CC, 12903, 345v).

[10] *Wive die quaet sprake tot wive ofte manne* (Bezemer, *Oude rechtsbronnen*, 4). See Van Rompaey, "Rechtsbronnen", 216 (for what follows).

[11] Peeters, "De keuren", 106.

[12] GSAB, CC, 12701, 124r.

[13] *Eenen tets* (CAL, 7747, 39r).

[14] Génard, "Het Register vanden dachvaerden (2)", 332.

[15] Dewilder, *Boete of zoen*, 57.

[16] Rousseaux, "Religion", 63.

[17] *Onzedeleicheden* (Lintermans, *Ter beternisse*, 54).

18 GSAB, CC, 12701, 198r, and CAB, CA, 15, 399v.
19 *Van ghebreke hadde laten sterven* (CAL, 5094, 84v).
20 Bourguignon & Dauven, "Une justice", 220.
21 *Rattecruut dat men heet arsenick* (GSAB, CC, 12701, 144r-v).
22 Stockmans, *Het correctieboek*, nos. 54, 80, 139, and 174.
23 Van Herwaarden, *Opgelegde bedevaarten* 212-3; Vanhemelryck, *Het gevecht*, 31; CAA, VS, 234, 158r.
24 Maes, *Vijf eeuwen*, 267.
25 GSAB, CC, 12903, 46v.
26 GSAB, CC, 15665, 3v.
27 CAA, PK, 913, 23r.
28 *Ten exempelen van anderen [...] ende ten eeren van alle goeden vrouwen.*
29 *In openbaren overspele* (Van den Branden, "Clementynboeck", 257).
30 CAA, VS, 234, 158v.
31 Vleeschouwers & Van Melkebeek, *Liber sententiarum*, 725.
32 Haemers & Delameillieure, "Women and contentious speech", 329.
33 Veldhuizen, *De ongetemde tong*, 9.
34 Godding, *Ordonnances de Philippe*, 177.
35 Rousseaux, "Religion", 76.
36 *Felle hoere* (CAM, CB, 1, 58r).
37 Van Herwaarden, *Opgelegde bedevaarten*, 252.
38 GSAB, CC, 12659, 116r.
39 *Quaden ende dorpeliken woerde* (CAA, VS, 234, 117v).
40 *Eenen pot met onreynicheden* (CAM, CB, 1, 112v).
41 Haemers & Delameillieure, "Women and contentious speech", 331.
42 CAB, CA, 16, 41r.
43 *Openbaerlic liedekens gesonghen* (CAM, CB, 1, 70v).
44 Haemers, "Commotie in Mechelen", 89.
45 GSAB, CC, 12694, 9v: *dat beter waere dat sij die vercken ghingen hueden dan dat sij trecht daden dat sij doen.*
46 Van den Branden, "Oudt register (4)", 99.
47 *Dat sij stoncken* (GSAB, CC, 12654, 344v).
48 See respectively CAA, VS, 234, 180v, and CAM, CB, 1, 33r.
49 Lintermans, *Ter beternisse te doen*, 55.
50 CAM, PC, 335: *Voires, vous ne faictes droit synon a ceulx que vous voulez.*
51 SALv, SG, 3590, 6, 35r. See also Haemers, "Women and war".
52 *Quaede ende ontamelijcke vergaderingen, commotien ende muterien* (CAM, CB, 1, 175r).
53 Bertijn, *Chronijck der stadt Antwerpen*, 73-4.
54 CAA, VS, 235, 20r.
55 *Sommighe quade wiven ... groot remoer ende ghetier* (*Dits die Excellente Chronijcke*, aanhangsel, 13v).
56 CAA, PK, 914, 102v.
57 *Affin de leur faire sucher avecq le laict une haine irréconciliable contre la nation franchoise* (*Mémoires de Pontus Payen*, II, 76).

CHAPTER 7

Eros and women: Sexuality, consent, and prostitution

Chanelle Delameillieure & Jelle Haemers

In 1419, the prostitute Griet van Boxelaer paid a large sum of money to the Antwerp bailiff to be released on bail. Shortly beforehand, she had been surprised at St Bernard's Monastery with a monk who, according to the record, had "become mad" about her to the point of no longer attending collective prayers. The abbot filed a complaint with the bailiff against Griet for having committed "idle things" inside the monastery.[1] Additionally, he suspected her of having purloined a key to the kitchens, for several of the cook's items were missing. The investigations revealed, however, that the only key in Griet's possession was to the monk's cell, which she had received from her smitten lover. No doubt the abbot saw to the monk's punishment himself, hoping that lodging an official complaint might also set an example for any other female visitors to the monastery. After careful consideration, in which even the mayor was involved, all the parties reached an agreement, with the woman paying the bailiff and obtaining her release.

Even though the monastery walls will remain forever silent about what exactly happened there, the dalliance of the Saint Bernard's monk magnificently illustrates the gap between actual practice and the idea of sexual abstinence many authors – particularly clergymen – wished to promote. Opinions on sex differed. Whereas certain ecclesiastical as well as lay authors presented sexual relations as a sin justified solely within the framework of marriage, others celebrated the sexual pleasures of men – and of women too. Certain manuscripts contain explicit images of genitalia and of couples making love, while there were absurd folktales about, for example, knights capable of speaking with vaginas. Sex was scarcely taboo, and, like today, often gave rise to lascivious laughter. Not only was there commerce in bodily pleasures, but within love itself erotic play was deemed a high point. Even in the story of Griet and her smitten monk, the two aspects seem intertwined, given that the two were clearly in a relationship. The fact that the monk had given her the key to his cell suggests in any case that she came there regularly.

Furthermore, the story of Griet and her monk can tell us something about the general attitude towards paid sex. For example, Griet was not sentenced for prostitution, or for having slept with a cleric. Both points are fairly striking. In itself, prostitution was not deemed an offence, and as no force had been deployed to elicit sexual relations there was nothing condemnable. What this story shows, however, is that Griet's situation was a delicate one. Due to their shameful and often clandestine activities, prostitutes were easy prey for money-hungry bailiffs, and so have often been assimilated to the criminal sphere. Yet it would be wrong to believe that prostitutes were ineluctably victims of arbitrary decisions: in Griet's case, as in others, the bailiff was obliged to respect her rights. As a citizen, Griet had civil rights. Hence the officer could not confiscate her goods. Yet her unauthorized visits to the monastery deserved punishment. Even though the bailiff let her off lightly, Griet lost out in this case. At times a prostitute had little means of defending herself. It was in any case not unusual for women to have run-ins with the law once their involvement in embarrassing situations relating to sex had been proven. Since the court cultivated a discourse that held women to be passive partners in sexual matters, it was, for example, very difficult to lodge a complaint for rape or to prove this type of assault. Throughout history, sex has been one of the most sensitive themes and taboos, for it is a matter of a direct physical relation between a man and woman. There have often been power struggles over controlling such relations within societies dominated by men. How did men view women's bodies? And what was women's point of view?

Women and sexuality

Many ecclesiastical authors had a very negative view of sexual pleasure. They often drew their inspiration from the earliest Christian texts: the letters of St Paul, in which he wrote that Christians should avoid sexual relations as much as possible, or the work of St Augustine, who urges his readers to lead a life of chastity and abstinence. Of course, the Church Fathers were aware of the importance of procreation to maintain the Christian community. That is why marriage came to be considered as the sole path for a man and woman to have honourable sexual relations. Even within this framework, sex had to be intended primarily for procreation, and fervent passion was to be avoided. From this viewpoint, all sexual contact unrelated to reproduction, such as anal or oral sex, became "culpable" and counted as a criminal offence of sodomy or unnatural sexual relations more generally. The church thus had a panoply of rules to ensure sexual relations between spouses remained within the limits of the acceptable. These included curious provisions on authorized positions, in addition to a ban on sexual relations on Fridays, Sundays, feast days, and during menstruation.

Yet several ecclesiastical texts adopt a more indulgent attitude towards marriage and having a family. From this point of view, the latter was a worthy alternative to celibacy, provided it was celebrated under the auspices of the church. Sexual pleasure was nonetheless condemned, and not just by ecclesiastical authors. Jan Van Boendale, the Antwerp town clerk, stated that *this play* was only to be tolerated within marriage, and furthermore was only justified insofar as it served reproduction.[2] Even so, other less rigid approaches also existed at this period. Certain authors emphasized pleasure rather than sin and procreation. The Bruges town poet, Anthonis de Roovere, even gave his readers instructions on how to enjoy their time in bed: men were to be tender, discreet, and skilful so that both partners could derive the greatest pleasure. He too held "this play" to be reserved solely for spouses.[3] Men of medical science likewise emphasized physical pleasure, albeit because it was believed to promote procreation. And while some thought that only men ejaculated, others stated that both the man and woman had to "ejaculate" for fertilization to occur. Supporters of this theory therefore held orgasm – and hence sexual pleasure – to be necessary for both men and women. In this respect, certain medical treatises were diametrically opposed to ecclesiastical texts vilifying sexual enjoyment.

There were also many stories about sex that were poles apart from the Church's prudishness, or else which broached deviant forms of sexuality. Medieval people were fond of street comedies that provoked much hilarity. Other stories told of the impossible love between two people from different social backgrounds. A sad story in the *Cent nouvelles nouvelles*, compiled in the 1460s at the request of Duke Philip the Good, describes a young couple in love who, though bound by "a deep and sincere passion which inflamed their hearts", were not allowed to marry. While fleeing together towards more clement lands, they encountered a gang of ruffians. The lover dies in the ensuing fight and the girl ends up committing suicide.[4] While it is true that such stories tell of impossible loves, they nevertheless depict men who love women, or they show how sorrow may lead to a desperate act. Such stories were far from being the preserve of the court and also circulated in towns. In the early sixteenth century, the Brussels poet Collijn Van Rijsele wrote a play set in a town, called *De Spiegel der minnen* [Love's mirror], in which a rich Middelburg merchant is in a relationship with a seamstress. The couple cannot stay together because of resistance from their friends and family, and both end up dying of sorrow. The history was intended as a warning against the potential danger of forbidden loves and passions, or as Van Rijsele wrote: "Love in moderation" (*mint bi mate*, in the Dutch of that time).

As such stories obviously present caricatures, they cannot tell us much about men's and women's actual sexual experiences. They do show, however, that the theme of sexuality, cloaked in numerous taboos by the Church, was not always treated as seriously as it may have wished. We thus need to avoid projecting onto the Middle Ages the vision of a limited group of clerics and concluding that medieval society was characterized by extreme prudery. Additionally, most ecclesiastical and folk tales, like most medical treatises, were produced by men, and even members of the clergy, making it hard to draw any conclusions about the sexual experiences of ordinary men, let alone ordinary women. Yet some texts by women may shed light on their sexuality.

Women and sexual pleasure

Writing in the twelfth century, the famous German mystic Hildegard of Bingen described a female orgasm thus: "when a woman makes love with a man, a sort of heat enters her head [...] and all her sexual organs contract." Hildegard was here writing from a medical point of view, focusing on female pleasure which, to her mind, could provoke male orgasm and hence fertilization. At the end of the fifteenth century, Anna Bijns of Antwerp wrote several poems looking back wistfully at her past liaisons. In so doing, she does not conceal that her nocturnal adventures with her lover were "never boring". In a text written by another woman from Antwerp, a widow deplores the death of her husband. She states that she has never felt more voluptuous and wishes to be a "wilder woman", but yet it is hard now

> that she is on her own: "my red lips, my pink cheeks, my taut breasts, my beautiful soft body, I now live freely". These unambiguous terms clearly speak of a wish for sexual pleasure. Better still, a little work printed in 1531 called *Der Vrouwen natuere* [On women's nature], states that, in addition to much food and drink, virgins also need sperm to remain in good health. This text recommends as a medical remedy that sick women, even widows and nuns, sleep with a man. Another appropriate remedy being masturbation ("tickling and scratching").

This ambiguous image is not specific to literature, also transpiring in practice: on the one hand sex was a source of pleasure, on the other it could also lead to scandal. Medieval society's acute sensitivity to honour meant that bodily enjoyment could be shrouded in shame. This condition is clearly illustrated by the following examples, in which the town punished certain insults made against its citizens. In Brussels in 1443, Marie Vandermeulen spread a foul lie about an "honest married woman", claiming that she had not been a virgin on marrying.[5] This insult seriously questioned the victim's chastity and sexual purity, as well as, consequently, her honour and that of her family. A man's image was determined by the behaviour of the women in his entourage just as much as by his own. When one year later Jan Marissys told "an honest man" that his wife "had been with several other men", he insulted the husband by referring to his wife's sexual behaviour and insinuating that he had no control over her. He thereby undermined this honourable man's position within his family, whose head he was meant to be, and, by extension, his standing within society.[6] Yet we may also detect a different reality in the criminal files and records. One only needs think of the remarkable career of Janne Schuts of Antwerp, discussed in chapter 4, who became a wealthy businesswoman thanks to her liaison with her employer, or of the secret affairs and marriages discussed in chapter 2. Certain men and women scorned rules governing relationships and gave in to their sexual desires. Yet living one's sexuality with relative freedom still presupposed complying with a rule or two – namely, being discreet and not jeopardising the honour of the family or the public order.

Rape, consent, and forced sexual relations

As an obverse to the popular vision of medieval society as prudish and conservative, many films and books depict the Middle Ages as a time of brutes when barbaric rapes were the norm and women were constantly subjected to sexual violence. This view is another persistent cliché. The author Christine de Pizan took a firm stand against rape in her *City of Ladies*. She responds to the discourse of some male writers by describing the lives of famous women throughout history. These often misogynist voices held women to be naturally perverse, lustful seductresses, themselves responsible for provoking sexual relations and therefore ineligible to be the victim of any man falling into their trap. Certain historians took up this sensationalistic and misogynistic vision (which certainly existed), giving rise to the idea that rape was not taken seriously in the Middle Ages. From this point of view, women were held to be the victim of dominant men who mistreated them without women being able to enjoy protection or recognition. Yet this stereotypical vision focuses too narrowly on a single group of writers, ignoring other voices, such as that of Christine de Pizan. In the *City of Ladies*, she emphasizes the pain and sorrow of raped women, giving the mythological example of Lucretia, who committed suicide after having been raped by a son of the Etruscan king. She thus argued that the death sentence was a fair punishment for rapists.

Judges were often of this opinion. Rape was definitely deemed a serious offence. The Flemish legal theorist Filips Wielant wrote that decapitation was the fair punishment for anyone who "raped a virgin, a widow, or another honourable woman".[7] Additionally, the authorities were entitled to seize all the goods of those found guilty of rape. Nearly all the legal texts state, in accordance with what Pizan and Wielant wrote, that rape was punishable by death. Several charters even stipulate that rapists were to have their head sawn off using a wooden plank. This horrible means of execution was replaced in the late Middle Ages by decapitation with a sword. In 1489, the Leuven executioner put to death two men for rape: Jermijn Reynier and Jacques Courvosier had brutally raped an honourable woman in Heverlee around St Valentine's Day. The source states that the victim remained sick for a long time after this assault.[8] Yet the execution of rapists such as Jermijn and Jacques was fairly exceptional. Between 1461 and 1504, the Leuven executioner only put seven men to death for rape. Despite the strict legislation, the sources do not record many cases of rapists being sentenced to death.

A key argument in matters of rape was consent to sexual relations. In the Middle Ages, sex was not seen as a two-person act to the extent that it is today. It was rather seen as something that men "did" with women, by penetrating them. According to this way of seeing things, the man was the active partner, with the women playing a subservient role. Certain sources use formulae such as *he had his way with her* (*dede zijn wille*), an expression implying that the man performed the sexual act while the woman underwent it. Such discourse enabled men to easily deny rape: it only had to be argued that the woman had shown no resistance. Thus, evidence against a rapist did not focus on the sexual relations per se, but on the violence inflicted on the victim and on whether she had cried out, thus refusing to submit to her passive role. Women who did not display violent or noisy opposition were not easily recognized as victims of rape. This approach presents interesting parallels with the contemporary debate on "consent" and the low rate of rape convictions. Research shows that even today, external behaviour and the physical consequences of rape are required to prove it conclusively. The present-day quest to establish rape on the basis of measurable consent thus reaches back a very long way.

How did judges establish consent (or the absence thereof)? As for cases of abduction, the victim's calling for help was a key element: as the lawyers argued, "it is clear that force was used if there were cries for help".[9] After the assault, the victim had to go as quickly as possible to the authorities so that her torn clothing and injuries could confirm her testimony. A physical examination by midwives might be used to corroborate the evidence. No doubt all these obstacles often discouraged victims, and offences committed in private thus tended to remain secret. Furthermore, rape could trigger great feelings of shame in the victim, especially if she was a girl. In such cases, rape implied loss of virginity, which, as in cases of abduction, could complicate attempts to find a good match. Hence victims often married their rapists to settle the matter. An example from Ghent may illustrate this phenomenon. In 1462, Berthel Schippers denounced Willem De Wagenaar three years after he had raped her. After raping Berthel, Willem, who was aged 18 at the time, had promised to marry her, according to the source. Berthel, though, was only nine at the time of the events. When Willem married another woman three years later, the brave young Berthel reminded him of his pledge. A serious quarrel ensued in which Willem and Berthel hurled apples, pears, and other things at each other.[10] However perverse it may seem, marriage between victim and assailant could be a legitimate way of settling a rape case.

Does that mean to say that rapists went unpunished? Certainly not. Many women put up fierce resistance or lodged a complaint after being attacked. When Marie Geysers, a young virgin from Leuven, was raped by Roelof Roelofs in 1434, she cried out and subsequently filed a complaint.[11] Roelof was let off with a fine, perhaps because he came from an influential family. Rape was a delicate matter, and attempted rape could result in a conviction. When Geert Den Hase of Leuven entered the bedroom of Lijsken Ausems in Zichem, he was caught in flagrante delicto by the other residents and had to flee. The following day, Lijsken filed a complaint with the bailiff. Geert was summoned before the aldermen and sentenced to a pilgrimage, which he bought off.[12] Aard Coppe committed acts of violence in Lier in 1455, knocking on the door of Lijsken Van Berlaer, who begged him to leave her alone as she was ill. Aard nevertheless entered. "Already naked, and with great force", he seized and raped the girl, *having his way with her*. Lijsken lodged a complaint against Aard, who had fled to Mechelen. He was, however, arrested and taken to Antwerp where he confessed. Though he should have been sentenced to death, his family put forward many arguments to get this condemnation commuted to a fine, which they finally obtained.[13] In another case in 1483, a woman from Antwerp – who, according to the source, was endowed with incredible strength – had put up such resistance that her attacker had not succeeded in his purpose.[14] The case was judged as an attempted rape. All these women did not let their attackers' violent behaviour go unpunished.

In many cases where there was a lack of conclusive proof, rapists paid a *compositie*, a sum used to settle the case. In 1495, Boudewijn Van Stijle followed this route after having been accused of rape by a girl in Antwerp. The bailiff, in justification of this step, mentions the lack of proof. In his line of reasoning, demanding payment of a sum of money meant the culprit was not let off scot-free.[15] Another example is provided by the sexual assault of a servant by her employer, Jan De Witte of Antwerp. On returning home drunk after spending a night in a tavern, Jan had gone through the barn where his servant was gathering hay for the cattle. He had attacked and thrown her to the ground beneath him, using gestures *as if he had wanted to rape her*.[16] The girl had called for help and put up fierce resistance. Jan was not convicted, convincing the bailiff to let him pay a *compositie*. So there was no trial despite the cries for help, perhaps because it was considered an assault, not a rape. Another hypothesis is that it was a case of one word against another, with there being no witness to confirm that the maid had indeed cried for help. Many rapes took place behind closed doors or in remote places, making it a lot more complicated to find witnesses. For example, in Brussels in 1540, a girl was raped in a vineyard, while in another case in Brussels in 1498, a woman was sexually assaulted in a meadow where she was minding cows.[17] These two rapes took place outside without any witnesses, thus also resulting in the payment of a *compositie*.

Although the payment of a sum of money was frequently used to settle such cases, it does not mean that these offences were deemed to be minor. The *compositie* paid by Jan, the man who attacked his servant, was a large sum of money. He was allowed to pay it in two instalments, suggesting he was unable to readily obtain the required sum. Another man from Antwerp also paid a *compositie* after raping a woman around 1500.[18] In this case, there is a remarkable note in the legal document recording the affair. The Brussels Chambers of Account, in charge of overseeing ducal officials, specified in this note that such offences were no longer to be settled via a *compositie* without first consulting the court. This proviso is a clear indication that the central authority did not always agree with how bailiffs handled serious crimes. Not just rapes but also attempted rapes were punished. In the fifteenth century, the records of the Brussels bailiff include 17 such cases, with 21 additional cases of "real" rapes. Furthermore, convictions were not solely for rapists and their accomplices, but also for any witnesses who had not assisted the victim or sought to prevent the crime. In 1412, a Brussels innkeeper thus paid a *compositie* because a rape had taken place in his inn without his intervening for fear of the attacker.[19]

When, in 1455 in Lier, the family of the above-mentioned rapist, Aard Coppe, was busily seeking to prevent his being sentenced to death, one of the arguments they put forward was that his victim, Lijsken, was "a girl whose life was without honour" and that "a man should not waste his body with such a woman". Lijsken was thus a prostitute and, according to the family, raping so dishonourable a woman did not merit the death sentence. The legal theorist Filips Wielant likewise wrote that raping a prostitute should not be punished. It was a widespread line of reasoning. In 1469, two men sought to enter the home of Martine Van Vlaanderen, a prostitute in Leuven. They broke down the door and one of the men raped Martine. The rapist was able to settle the affair by paying a *compositie*, "given that Martine received visitors on her body every day".[20] Martine's work as a prostitute was apparently the reason for settling the case out of court. Although this category of rape could lead to less severe punishments, the case also shows that the attacker had to pay a fine. Furthermore, in half of the recorded cases of rape in Leuven between 1461 and 1504, the victim was a prostitute, indicating that mistreating such women did not go unpunished. As also shown by the example of Griet van Boxelaer and her "smitten monk", prostitutes had rights too. While Wielant advocates for the punishment of men who raped "honourable women," many other legal statutes explicitly state that the rape of any woman is a serious criminal offense. Rape remains a challenging subject for medievalists because records often provide limited information and frequently contain contradictory elements, particularly regarding consent and honour. Ideally, cases of rape were framed in a specific way to increase the likelihood of conviction. Even so, legal practice shows that medieval societies regarded rape as a very serious offence and imposed punishment even in cases that did not conform to the stereotypical narrative.

Prostitution at the heart and on the sidelines of the town community

In the medieval definition, a prostitute was a "woman who submitted to the indecent concupiscence of many men", and who traded in her non-chastity.[21] For moral reasons, prostitutes were marginalized, but at the same time they were at the heart of society. They were caught in the tension between love and repulsion, between latent condemnation and eternal attraction. Prostitution was a sin, not an offence. That is why medieval towns were characterized by a policy of marked tolerance towards it. Paid sex was a distinctive feature of towns. Nevertheless, just like today, prostitution was regulated, and violations were only punished if public order was compromised. Prostitution was treated in much the same way as criminality more generally, with town governors only getting involved should the disturbance become troublesome or citizens' rights be fundamentally infringed. In what follows, we shall look, first, at regulations and a few examples of criminal cases, then we shall depict a red-light district: where did such districts lie, what did the inside of a brothel look like, and who might one meet there? Towns were home to many different types of brothel and of prostitution, but in all cases this world was one of female sex workers. There are hardly any traces of male prostitution or of women offering their services to other women. Prostitution was women's business, as well as a world of men. Women offered their services against payment, and men used them. Consent was important here: sexual relations without consent was a crime. Even if prostitutes were held to be "impure", men could not act towards them with impunity. After surveying the world of prostitution, we shall close our study with a few cases in which things nevertheless turned out very badly.

What was authorized? As with many situations in the Middle Ages, there was no strict legal framework for prostitution. That does not mean that there were no rules: custom, ordinances issued by the authorities, and moral precepts fixed the limits of the permissible. One of the rare charters issued by the dukes of Brabant to mention prostitution is a text forbidding begging, gambling, and dealing in women. In 1459, Philip the Good decreed that nobody in Brabant would henceforth be allowed to "hold" "easy women" (*vrouwen van lichten leven* in Dutch, literally "women with light lives"), nor to receive money from them.[22] In medieval French, these women were often referred to pejoratively as *femmes de vies légères, femme folle, fille de joie, femme commune, fillette, femme de vie sans honneur, fille de l'amoureuse vie* or *de mauvaise vie*, and *baisselette* or *putain*. In Dutch there were also many words reflecting the scorn in which the profession was held, for these women represented "unnatural" sexual relations unjustified by reproduction.[23] A word such as *papenwiven* was more indirect: a "priest's wife" referred especially to disobedience by those meant to live a celibate life, but was also used for prostitutes in general. Yet let us return to Philip the Good's ordinance. It is striking that he did not forbid prostitution, just hoped that nobody would get wealthy at prostitutes' expense. (Single) women were thus allowed to offer their services on their own initiative. What was forbidden was other people pocketing the profit. In other words, the objective was to tackle procuring. Philip the Good established a sentence of ten years for men or women who "held" other women, as his ordinance puts it. The presence of such provisions in an ordinance on begging and gambling shows that the most disturbing aspect of procuring was the social disruption it caused.

Philip the Good thus tolerated the existence of brothels, which were quite simply part of daily life. Yet prostitutes could not act as they pleased. To illustrate this, let us look at the regulations that applied in Maastricht, which are representative of how sex work was managed. Fornication was authorized but subject to control. In 1414, the town forbade soliciting on the streets, for example. Prostitutes caught proposing their services on the street had to "move into *stoven*". In theory a *stove* (literally, a "stove", sometimes referred to in English as a stew) was a place where townspeople came to wash, but some had become brothels because women offered their bodies there. However, they were not allowed to attract clients in public. The punishment consisted in a fine of one mark, a fairly small sum of money, to be paid to the town executioner.[24] These women were not exiled or imprisoned and got off relatively lightly. Or was it in fact a tax? In Bruges, for example, brothels had to pay fines to carry out their business. A similar policy seems to have applied in Maastricht.

> **Executioners and sex workers**
>
> In many towns the executioner was allowed to supplement his meagre income by prosecuting minor offences and receiving the associated fines. Prosecuting prostitutes who did not respect the town rules was one such source of income. The two "professions" were both shrouded in the same negative atmosphere: whereas a prostitute sold her body, the executioner mutilated the human body created by God. In addition to the remuneration the executioner received for carrying out tasks for the town, such as public humiliations and executions, he could thus earn a little extra by hunting down streetwalkers. The Leuven executioner received a considerable sum to supplement his income by controlling prostitution. In 1492, he had asked the town for such compensation, for he deemed he had done enough to control prostitutes. In 1530, the mayor of Antwerp decided to grant the executioner an annual "replacement income" to allow him to cease monitoring "loose women" (*ledige wive*). In other towns, such as Mons, there was a specific official, called the "King of Maidens", in charge of ensuring that the rules governing prostitution were respected.

Two other measures illustrate the Maastricht policy of tolerance towards prostitution. First, in 1389, the town council decided that all women who "united themselves with someone for money" should henceforth wear a clearly visible piece of yellow fabric on their headscarf.[25] This stipulation was to make it possible to distinguish between prostitutes and "honourable women". Once again, it was a widespread practice found in many towns, such as Mons or Namur (where it was a piece of green fabric). People in towns thus immediately knew who they were dealing with. This measure also served to protect "honourable women", for they were sometimes harassed by men looking for prostitutes. The fact that the Maastricht aldermen specified in the same decree that prostitutes were not authorized to make a deal with the executioner, if he came to check whether they were wearing the required identification, suggests that he had hitherto been relatively indulgent towards public prostitution.

Second, in 1381, the town stipulated that prostitutes were no longer authorized to walk the streets, except in the district around the Onze-Lieve-Vrouwekerk (Church of Our Lady). This area was home to two bathing establishments renowned for also housing a brothel. "Outside whores", as the legislation referred to prostitutes from outside the town, together with procurers, were to leave the town immediately, but those working in brothels were free to carry on with their business. In 1406, the applicable rules were amended: prostitutes in the two *stoven* on the square in front of the church were to confine themselves to a circumscribed area around their establishments and were no longer allowed to take up the entire street. In short, as in many European towns in the late Middle Ages, prostitution was authorized within a specific circumscribed area, but it was strictly monitored everywhere else. It would be inaccurate to say the prostitutes were marginalized, for the church square was in the heart of the town, and each inhabitant knew where to go to employ their services. The wearing of a distinctive sign and confining of their activities to a specific neighbourhood were habitual measures to keep prostitution under control. This "spatial policy" and "zoning" still exists in towns of the Low Countries to this day: Amsterdam's (in)famous red-light district, for instance, lies adjacent to its oldest extant church. Given that prostitution is sometimes accompanied by criminality, town authorities still wish to confine any disturbances to a specific area.

Each town had its own red-light district: in Mechelen, there were two *stoven* on Tichelrij, near the butter market. As in Brussels, Stoofstraat ("Stew Street") took its name from these. It is not by chance that the *Manneken Pis* is found on this street. Already in the second half of the fifteenth century, a fountain with this name supplied the neighbourhood with water. The inhabitants of Brussels looking for paid sexual relations could also go to the area next to the church by the fish market. In 1438, an ordinance sought to move prostitutes away from what were known as the *stadheymelicheit*, an open-air sewer of waste and excrement. This place (also referred to as the *communes cloacae* – the public sewers – in a fourteenth-century Latin source) lay next to a Franciscan monastery alongside the River Senne, which had not yet been covered over.[26] It was common to find prostitutes in such districts, for they often worked near rivers and public fountains. Remarkably, prostitution was also very present around churches and monasteries, peopled by single men who had taken a vow of chastity. In Antwerp, men looking for a sexual consort could go to the area around the Franciscan church, to that around the Sint-Jakobskerk, or else to the old ramparts near the Clarisse convent. The districts of Guldenberg and Kauwenberg were also reputed as such.[27] Town ramparts were another popular place for prostitutes. In Antwerp, Brussels, and Leuven, prostitution was authorized there. In 1495, the Leuven aldermen decreed that prostitutes were henceforth to offer their services only outside the old ramparts, on Ravenstraat and Vlamingenstraat, both of which had lain outside the town ramparts in the twelfth century but were within its precinct by the fourteenth century. This location suggests that prostitution had been pushed outside the town ramparts in the twelfth century, before urban spread caught up with it two centuries later. It was here that the chapel of St Catherine stood, dedicated to the patron saint of girls of marriageable age.

The presence of prostitution in the middle of town was obviously not to everybody's liking. One indication of this situation is protest by local residents and even nuns. In 1444, Leuven issued an ordinance that refers to complaints by inhabitants about the disturbance caused by prostitutes in various places in town. Women who "kept company in public" were thus obliged to move to places assigned to them near the town ramparts. This initiative did not issue from the town council but from inhabitants, who thus managed to get the town to reduce disruption. Another well-known brothel in Leuven (whose interior we shall describe later) lay on Halvestraat, a road giving onto the Dyle by the ramparts to the east of the town. It, too, became a source of growing discontent. In 1426, the town forbade prostitutes from soliciting, for they were bothering sisters of the "11,000 virgins" day in day out. This convent, whose – in this context, ironic – name referred to the legend of the virgins who accompanied St Ursula, was home to unmarried religious women who found the business of "women without honour" unbearable. In 1459 the town ended up compelling the brothel to shut its doors, justifying this decision by stating that the presence of prostitutes on Halvestraat was a "bad example". Furthermore, the level of harassment was such that it prevented the nuns from giving themselves fully to their "devotion".[28] The brothel was to close its doors within three days. This example clearly shows that the town council only intervened after receiving complaints from local inhabitants, particularly from ecclesiastics. It stepped in after receiving reports of disturbances.

The situation was the same in Antwerp, where in 1471 the aldermen forbade the opening of new brothels on the Rechtestraat, along which the annual procession paraded. "Women or girls of sin" were no longer allowed to acquire houses or land there for their shameful activities, or to organize "gatherings of men, women or girls". Apparently, though, the ordinance remained ineffective for it had to be reissued six years later, then once again in 1516. The town council thus hoped to limit the inconveniences caused by prostitution, particularly at times of religious feast days, but their efforts were in vain. The ban on soliciting in the Onze-Lieve-Vrouwekerk cemetery was one such attempt.[29] Cemeteries used to have a social function and were often used for gatherings or even spectacles and "fairs". Yet in 1449, the town forbade women from spending the night there, a ban that had to be reissued on several occasions. Punishments included the confiscation of "outer clothing". This punishment was common and often converted into a fine, for the outer clothing was the most expensive part of a woman's attire. The provision is significant: morally, prostitution was reprehensible, certainly in a religious setting. However, provided it was not a matter of total decadence, towns tolerated the activities of "sex workers", albeit preferring them to work on the outskirts rather than in the town centre. A final striking aspect is that neither the aldermen nor the higher authorities – not even the Church – sought to regulate prostitution outside the town. Once outside the city walls and in the countryside, prostitutes could act freely. While it is probable that regulations applied in villages, towns, for their part, made do with managing on their own territory the inconveniences caused by prostitution.

A visit to a "stove"

Exactly what went on inside brothels? The southern Low Countries were known for their rich "*stove* culture", as illustrated in a poem by the French troubadour Eustache Deschamps. In the fourteenth century, he sang the praises of the town of Brussels, "where the baths are pretty, and the *stoven*

Interior of a brothel in the Southern Low Countries in the 15th century. Sex workers and their customers eat and drink, bathe and sleep together. This takes place in a common room, but the beds and curtains still create a certain intimacy. (Bibliothèque Nationale de France, Arsénal, Ms 5196 réserve, 372r). https://archivesetmanuscrits.bnf.fr/ark:/12148/cc853851

and girls are pleasant".³⁰ He added that one also found fine bedrooms where Rhine wine flowed freely, with gentle and most willing company. Each town was home to such well-equipped *stoven* offering not just baths, but also food, drink, and other entertainments. A *stove* was not necessarily a brothel, for there were family *stoven*, and others purely for men and women. In 1471, the Mechelen town council decided that men and women were henceforth to be strictly separated in advance, with a sign above the door informing clients which of the two sexes was welcome. Wives were however allowed to accompany their husbands in "male baths".³¹ Yet one category of establishment for men also employed women who, for a supplemental charge, provided services to visitors in bed or in the bath. In such houses, prostitution was wholly legal, even if husbands and churchmen were not meant to share a bed with *"stove* maids" (*stoefmaerten*). Under Antwerp legislation, any married individuals discovered there were to be fined. This restriction applied both to the (adulterous) men and to the women offering their services. Only prenuptial sexual relations were authorized – at least in theory.

> **Stews**
> Public baths and brothels were both called *stoven* in the Middle Ages, often referred to in medieval (and modern) English as "stews". They owed this name to a central stove, sometimes present in several rooms even. These stoves were generally decorated with enamelled mortar tiles and had an opening to allow the heat to radiate. Both systems were fed hot air by a series of pipes linked to a wood or coal fire and leading to a pot or stove in the various rooms – hence the term *haardstoof* ("hearth stove"), sometimes used to refer to public baths. Although hot air was obviously essential in a *stove*, water was needed too. That is why many public baths lay close to a stream, river, well, or spring. Various waterways also passed through port areas where clients could be found.

Brothels were private institutions which, in the southern Low Countries, were only very rarely run by the town. In southern Europe and in the Rhineland, on the other hand, there were public houses of prostitution. Augsburg, for instance, had a *Frauenhaus* whose profits went to the town.

In Florence, the town authorities ran a house of prostitution designed explicitly as an outlet for the many single young men living there. In southern France, brothel owners rented houses belonging to the town. In Strasbourg, the *Bader*, as they were called – that is, the stew managers – formed a distinct guild with a seat on the town council. There were also public establishments in Cologne and Liège run by the town authorities. The bishop of Liège even received a yearly tax of 100 grammes of gold on the *Matrognard* (or *Estuves Matruilhart*), the Liège brothel with a monopoly on prostitution within the city walls. In 1435, residents of the parish of Saint-Étienne complained about the disturbance caused by visitors to a public brothel (*burdeal publicque*). In the wake of this protest, the town council decided that henceforth no "bad hostelry" or "gambling den" (*malvaix hosteit, herbergage ne spellehuys*) was to remain open in this district. Furthermore, prostitution was to be restricted solely to the *Matrognard*.[32] Such public brothels enabled the authorities to keep tabs on events, make a bit of money, or curb citizens' behaviour. There are hardly any traces however of public brothels in towns in Brabant, Flanders, and Hainaut. In 1492, the Breda town council started building works on a public bath on the Visserstraat, near the town ramparts. It paid for the purchase of 92,400 bricks, nine stained glass windows (two for the kitchen, five for the bathroom, and two for the room "where the girls slept"), a heater, and a stove for the establishment.[33] Later on, the town council rented out the establishment to private business owners, but its building was part of a policy to better protect the town against the risk of fire. In 1490, a major fire had burned part of the town down to the ground. The town's investing in a public bath was exceptional. In general, town councils left the building of such establishments to the private sector.

Given that towns tolerated brothels, their archives contain a number of leases for them. In 1456, for example, Jan van Udekem got the Leuven aldermen to certify a lease for a brothel on the Halvestraat. He had been there for many years, but as seen above, the previous leaseholder (Geert Huts) had been incapable of keeping a lid on disturbances. Jan van Udekem had inherited the establishment from a butcher, Jan Paris, and rented it out to Margriete Scrijters of Lubbeek for a weekly rent equivalent to two days' salary for a skilled labourer. The establishment had 13 beds, probably in separate rooms, and a central stove. It was a large operation, as indicated by the fact that Margriete offered five additional beds in a neighbouring house.[34] She promised to maintain it at her own expense and not to sublet it. Though we do not know exactly how she ran her business, it is probable that men could rent a bed there. Food and drink provided another source of income. In Margriete's lease, one clause stipulates that its owner reserves the right to visit the establishment once per week free of charge, and that he could cede this right to a member of his family. Additionally, he could enjoy local wine free of charge during his visits on the four main religious feast days. Eustache Deschamps's lines of poetry quoted earlier thus seem an accurate description. Interestingly, 18 months later, a new lease appears in the aldermen's archives. It would seem that Margriete had terminated her lease, and Jan had found a new manager in the person of Geert Huts. The rent was initially unchanged, but four months later (in December 1458) the terms of the contract were altered, with the weekly rent being reduced by one fifth. That may indicate that the establishment was generating less revenue than expected, and perhaps it is why the first manager had given up. In any case, the *stove* was clearly in its swansong for, as we have seen, one year later Geert Huts had to leave.

Was it unusual for a woman to run a brothel? Not at all. In such cases the woman was probably a prostitute or ex-prostitute who had gone up in the world, but it was also common for a brothel to be run by a man or a couple – for example, if a former prostitute married or cohabited with a man. We do not have precise figures about the male/female proportion of managers, even less about the number of brothels in each town, given that only a few of the leases have been conserved (assuming, that is, that they were even recorded). Yet it would seem that women were very much involved in running brothels. Between 1415 and 1435, the town of Antwerp closed seven brothels on its territory due to illegal practices. Perhaps there were even more enforced closures, but the sources do not always indicate the details of any sanctions taken. Be that as it may, four of the seven establishments were run by a couple and three by women. In 1426, Jan Sloef and his wife were thus sentenced to a pilgrimage to Aachen for having run a "bad inn", and shortly before a woman named Jute was obliged to take a similar trip to Cambrai for the same reason, as well as for her activities as a procuress.[35] For towns in Brabant, it is hard to ascertain the social origin of the brothel keepers, but perhaps, as in Bruges, they were women or couples who had amassed a considerable fortune.

Let us now go inside one of these brothels. Imagine that we have been invited by the tailor Jacob van Stertbeke and his wife Yde who rented a *stove* on the Wieringstraat (a road giving onto the River Dyle) in Leuven, from the clerk Peter Beyaert. There were no fewer than 16 rooms to rent in their *stove*, all named enticingly: the "women's bedroom", "the falcon", "the peacock", the "lily bedroom", or the "hat with roses". Some rooms bore the name of a girl, such as "Ann's bedroom" or "Marion's bedroom", probably referring to the woman providing services there. The names of flowers or birds of course alluded to the pleasures reputed to take place within. In medieval literature, birds and flowers were regularly used as metaphors for the game of love. For example, the popularity of using "rose" as a name came from the *Roman de la Rose*, a fourteenth-century French erotic saga glorifying physical love, in which the rose symbolized the sexual act. "The parrot" (*papegaai* in Dutch) was used as the name for a *stove* in almost every town. This colourful bird was used as a target in a popular game in which archers fired an arrow at a "prey" made from wood or paperboard, thus symbolizing "the virile act". French even borrowed this name from Dutch: in Douai, for example, the *Étuve des Papegais* was a well-known pleasure house for two centuries, and there was even a public bath in Avignon with a bedroom called the *Papegay*.

What did the inside of one of these places look like? In a simple bedroom (such as the one called "The crown") in the above-mentioned *stove* on Leuven's Wieringstraat, the client had a bed and a chair, while more luxurious rooms were more richly furnished. For instance, in the "Duke's bedroom", a name which owed nothing to chance, there were three beds, a chair, a divan, and two small precious wardrobes placed between the beds. In "The parrot", with two beds, the client could also use a separate bath should he so wish. The establishment also had movable tubs and smaller basins, though, at least according to a lease drawn up in 1463 between the owner and managers.[36] It had 42 beds all in all, making it one of the largest known *stoven* in Leuven, even in the southern Low Countries. There are descriptions of brothels with 15, 29, and 37 beds in Bruges, Ghent, and Sluis.[37] It was the owner of the *stove* in Leuven who provided the leaseholders Jacob and Yde with bed linen, pillows (45 in all), drinking pots, and tools for keeping the fire burning. No doubt the linen was rented out to guests, or else the women receiving guests had to pay a small sum of money to use it. The brothel also had a kitchen where the managers provided food and drink.

A lease drawn up in 1489 for "De Nieuwe Stove", an establishment near Sint-Geertrui-abdij (Saint Gertrude's abbey) in Leuven, makes it clear that the owners and managers of a *stove* could be wealthy people. Each week the woman running it, Hadewijch Cornelis from Utrecht, paid its owner, Liesbet van Sint-Truiden, a considerable sum of money (the equivalent of ten days' salary for a skilled labourer). "De Nieuwe Stove" had four single rooms and eleven rooms for several people. In all, it had 20 beds, with bedding, many tubs, crockery, chests, wardrobes, small precious wardrobes, a cooking range, and even a portable latrine, for a total value of 96 Rhenish guilders. The value of all the movable property was thus estimated to be the equivalent of 18 months' salary for a skilled labourer.[38] This sizeable asset meant that its owner was an important woman from the town's wealthy middle class. It was also true of other people and families who owned a *stove*. Visitors to Leuven could otherwise be welcomed at a large public bath on the Steenstraat with 36 beds, belonging to a priest, Jan Ballinc – a chaplain at Sint-Pieterskerk (Saint Peter's Church) – and his sister Liesbet. The 1476 lease lists heaters, nine baths, and eleven basins.[39] Importantly, this document contains a clause stipulating that the establishment "shall not take in guests of dubious repute", for that would damage its owner's reputation. In this case, then, it was a public bath which was simply an inn where people could wash, eat, and sleep.

Reluctant sex workers?

Although we may glean some information about owners and leaseholders of *stoven*, the identity of prostitutes for its part remains shrouded in mystery. A few names spark the imagination, however. In Mechelen, "Fat Marie" (*Dikke Marie*) was convicted twice for prostitution, while "big-breasted Katelijne, servant at a *stove* behind St John's" (*Katelijne metten mammen, stoefwijf achter Sint-Jans*) had to go into exile in 1452. Fine-legged Jeanne, beautiful Marie – the professional names of convicted prostitutes are highly evocative.[40] Although these girls were well known in their circle, we have no information about their origins or lives. This lack suggests that they came from modest backgrounds, for other than the records of their sentences there are hardly any traces of them in the sources. There are very sporadic instances of prostitutes dressed as men. In 1446, Margriete in de Rolle of Antwerp had to go on pilgrimage to Aardenburg for having entered the town dressed as a man. As for Margriete van der Berct, she was sent to Milan in 1484, for having committed "immoralities" while wearing "men's clothing".[41] Were these two women seeking to appeal to men looking for homosexual acts? Other, better documented cases of this type certainly appear in subsequent centuries. In any case, sexual pleasures may take many forms. Given the heavy taboo weighing on homosexuality, women dressed as men perhaps provided an outlet. It is impossible, though, to have any clear picture of who they might have been.

There were surely many "sorts" of prostitutes: young girls who had arrived from the countryside, impoverished workers, maids making a bit of extra money, women with a reputation, and so on. Most of them worked of their own free will, even though we cannot rule out abuses. A medieval song found in Utrecht and dating from around 1400 describes a market scene in which one hears the plaintive cries of a prostitute. While the song describes a crier unambiguously seeking to attract clients into a brothel ("Come in, come in, the stove is warm"), the prostitute speaks far less joyously: "Dear mother, protect me, even if I am young, I would prefer to have a husband than a thousand pounds".[42] The girl thus aspires to true love and hopes for a more honourable life than that of a prostitute. The song thus exposes a delicate aspect: even though women did opt for this paid activity, it does not mean they were happy to do so.

Let us also note that women from the southern Low Countries provided their services in other regions. We cannot, however, be certain why: did they travel as itinerant prostitutes, did their choice stem from temporary poverty, or were they rather seeking to build up a network in their new region? In Southwark (in London) in the late fourteenth century, there were *frows de Flaundres* (Flemish women) running a brothel, just as there was a "Flemish brothel" in Florence one century later where a certain Marguerite of Brabant worked. There were brothels run by women from Cambrai, Arras, Brussels, and Tournai. Were they emigrants looking to start a new life? There were also many prostitutes from the southern Low Countries in eastern England, where they drew on their foreign origins to attract clients. Once again their names were highly evocative: in Boston, you could visit Joan Fairemaners, Gode for Eve, Long Grete, or Flemish Lysbet, all of whom came from the southern Low Countries.[43] Yet the sources tell us little about their lives or why they were in this line of work. The testimony of Trien van Alden of Brabant, sentenced by Cologne town council for procuring in 1595, nevertheless tells us that she was a widow and had two children to feed. Anna, another prostitute in Cologne, declared to the aldermen that she had long worked in Antwerp before returning to Cologne. Yet why did Anna and many other women travel about? As yet there is no clear answer to this question.

We may suppose that women preferred discretion, just like their clients. Nevertheless, accounts indicate that men from all social backgrounds availed themselves of their services. For instance, Jan van Musene was the descendant of a wealthy Mechelen family of canons and aldermen. He took a Bruges prostitute under his wing, wishing to protect her from an actor who wanted to kidnap her. According to the document in French telling us about her adventures, Maria van der Hoeven was a young prostitute (*fille de joye*) from an itinerant theatre troupe directed by an individual named Mathieu Cricke.[44] However, Mathieu had treated her roughly in Diest. Jan van Musene declared to the Leuven bailiff, who had arrested Mathieu, that the latter had kidnapped Marie in Mechelen, resorting to violence. For his part, the actor firmly denied the accusations and was subsequently reprieved by the duke of Brabant in 1476, in exchange for enlisting in the duke's army. It is hard to ascertain who was telling the truth in this story, for it was one word against the other, and the duke's favour implied that no further legal steps were to be taken against Matthieu. Hence the trial never produced any ruling on the facts of the case. Yet Marie's role in this unsavoury episode suggests in any case that we should not have too dualistic a view of prostitution. As a prostitute, she had at some stage opted for a career on the stage and had then found herself in the circle of wealthy Mechelen citizens. Had she been led to prostitution by her poverty, and was she hoping for a better life by linking her lot with an actor, then with a wealthy man? We can but hypothesize about the motives and intentions of prostitutes and their clients.

Still, the boundary between the generally separate worlds of elites and prostitutes was porous. Both lived in the same town, each in their own circle, but men from the wealthy classes and prostitutes often met. An equally surprising though fragmentary story of a priest from Tongerlo shows that commerce in prostitution was both peripheral and central to society. One evening in 1455, this priest, named Filip, met a prostitute in an Antwerp inn where he had come to buy beer.[45] She offered him a drink which he gladly accepted. Additionally, according to the Antwerp bailiff's account, the woman invited Filip to stay with her, asking, "Would you like to keep me company?". The priest's testimony states that he replied, "I will come back to you."[46] After taking his beer back home, the two departed together. The sources do not indicate if they had sexual relations, but nevertheless, shortly afterwards, the woman filed a complaint against the priest. The bailiff thus threw Filip into gaol, but an investigation revealed that there had been fraudulent behaviour (*boevery*). The partner (or procurer?) with whom the woman lived had apparently encouraged her to swindle Filip. After the intervention of the Antwerp margrave and the prelate of the Tongerlo Abbey, the bailiff ended up releasing Filip, who promised to pay a *compositie* of 20 florins. Although the priest was not convicted, the bailiff's records state that the priest paid the sum to avoid the shame of imprisonment. No information is given about the woman's point of view, but she was not convicted either, even though this sentence would have been normal, given her false accusations. Had she made a deal with the bailiff? The only thing that is certain is that the town was an (appreciated?) place where the wealthy met women selling their charms. The two groups were in continual contact, be it tender or violent, flirting with the boundary of the acceptable – and even of the criminal.

When things took a turn for the worse

In accordance with the above-mentioned ducal ordinance, dealing in women and exploiting them sexually was a step too far. Procuring was forbidden in all towns in Brabant. In the Dutch of that time, the word *puttierscap* refers to procuring, the practice of selling women's services. Given that the *puttier* sold the body of another person, he or she was committing a major offence. The distinction with brothel owners was at times hard to establish, though normally consisted in the fact that a brothel owner did not make money from prostitutes' activity, but only from the accommodation on offer. If, despite this condition, the women had to hand over a share of their revenue, then it was quite possibly a "bad inn". In such establishments the managers lived off the prostitutes, in other words, "held women for their own profit" as the Antwerp legislation puts it.[47] Such people were often targeted by the authorities. In 1428, the Maastricht town council decided that an investigation would henceforth be conducted twice yearly in each parish by a committee composed of senior municipal officials in order to lay hands on people "practising procuring". Arrested procurers were to be immediately put on trial.[48] It was an old problem in the town. In 1385, a Maastricht wine barrel transporter named Renske Wyngaard had to solemnly promise the governors of his guild to no longer keep a brothel for as long as he remained a guild member.⁴⁹ In Brussels, a 1383 ordinance urged inhabitants to file complaints against procurers. Yet the practice was very widespread. Records of convictions for procuring give the impression that culprits were prosecuted mainly when they forced women into prostitution for profit.⁵⁰ It was unacceptable to live off obscene women.

The same doubtless applied to employing minors as prostitutes. Forcing one's own daughters to sell their body was the most serious offence in sex work. Under fifteenth-century rules in Antwerp, all the goods belonging to an inhabitant "who prostituted his daughter" were to be confiscated, and the culprit exiled for life, to which was subsequently added a whipping.⁵¹ A legal document dating from April 1491 shows that this legislation was invoked on occasion. The town had it announced far and wide that it had learned of a case in which a procurer or procuress had offered a man the services of a ten-year-old girl, an act which it described as "unchristian, impious, and unnatural".⁵² The aldermen hoped that anyone knowing anything about the affair would come forward with information as rapidly as possible. One year later, the town did indeed punish a woman (Liesbet Bries) who had pushed minors to prostitute themselves, but it has not been formally ascertained whether this case had any link with the 1491 call for information. In 1431, two Brussels inhabitants were also severely punished. The miller Oste De Dekker and Kateline Faes had taken an underage girl and "thrown her into shame" on the road to Leuven.⁵³ Oste and Kateline were doubtless guilty of having prostituted the girl and were sent on a punitive pilgrimage. Even had the girl consented, such a practice was unacceptable. Consent was essential to avoid criminality, but minors were considered incapable of deciding in this domain. The authorities acted against abuses, but it was hard to eradicate such crimes.

Brawling was commonplace in red-light districts where drinking and crime often flourished. That is why clients of brothels in Diest were forbidden from bearing arms. In any case, those contravening the curfew were subject to a fine.⁵⁴ In addition to limiting violence in *stoven*, these measures also sought to protect prostitutes. Sources about criminal law contain many references to acts of violence against prostitutes. Even if such acts did not always result in punishment, which is highly probable, certain things were clearly not permitted. In Mechelen in 1491, Thomas Claes of Tienen was sentenced to exile because he had earned money at the expense of prostitutes, even though he regularly frequented the stews.⁵⁵ In Brussels in 1480, the aldermen sentenced Gillis van Leghem to a pilgrimage to Milan for having mistreated an individual named Juliane in a brothel. Yet Juliane, too, was convicted and had to pay a fine because she had greatly exaggerated her complaint.⁵⁶ Fate was less kind to an Antwerp prostitute named "Paxken", who, according to the bailiff, was as lightheaded as she was loose-moraled. She died in 1459, after a fight with a drunk client who had thrown a pot at her head.⁵⁷ Of course, prostitutes could also get into fights with one another, as in Antwerp in 1416, when Lise van Diest punched Big Marie (*Groote Marie*), one of her colleagues, because she had apparently slept with her companion. Big Marie had punched Lise in turn, drawing blood.⁵⁸ Lastly, clients could also get into fights with one another, such as the boatman Adriaan who, in 1459, beat a drunkard to death, when the two of them were spending the night with prostitutes.⁵⁹ The many examples illustrate the murkiness sometimes surrounding prostitution, and the sexual assaults to which prostitutes were exposed.

This is why towns sometimes closed brothels, as we have seen. "Bad inns" (*onnutte cabarette*, literally "useless cabarets") sometimes housed wanted criminals and dubious individuals. A brothel might also close its doors due to illness, should the hygiene leave something to be desired. In 1439, the town obliged Kateline van de Berghe to close her *stove*, where a prostitute had died of "sudden illness", probably some form of plague. Another practice which Brussels did not tolerate was begging by prostitutes. In 1424, the town forbade *stove* waiting girls from requesting tarts, cakes, or bread from their clients or wealthy citizens.⁶⁰ Other dubious practices involved forms of witchcraft. A few years later, the Antwerp aldermen sent the wife of Jan Dackenans on a pilgrimage to Rome, after finding her guilty of using spices to attract men to women.⁶¹ In 1433, the Brussels bailiff made a deal with two prostitutes who were let off with a modest fine for having buried something beneath the doorstep of a colleague (or rival?) "to make her lose her work".⁶² The reason they got off so lightly was because people had pleaded their cause with the bailiff. Even so, violence, begging, and witchcraft were offences that the town could not tolerate on its territory.

Concerning witchcraft, Willem Neeten and his companion Yde went a lot further when running the "De Roose" brothel in Leuven (for which the lease has already been discussed above). In 1453, the town council had already found Yde guilty of having allowed women to seduce men on the Halvestraat. At the time she had undertaken to transform her building on the Kwade Brug "into a bathing house", "as others do in town".[63] This building became "De Roose". In 1459, though, she was arrested once again. With Philip the Good's ordinance having been recently decreed, the bailiff punished her for having financially exploited other women. Shortly afterwards, their business took a serious turn for the worse. In 1461, the bailiff imprisoned the couple for having given money to the town executioner to get him to give them the hand of an executed thief. They had hung the bones in a bag in the establishment's heater hoping to attract many visitors each day.[64] In short, this sinister practice was a form of superstition to boost their clientele. Such practices were not rare. Thus, in 1412, a woman was arrested in Brussels, who appeared to be in possession of the finger of someone who had been hanged. On being asked what she had intended to do with it, she replied that "she had planned on putting it under her bed, where she often had sexual relations, so that men would come to her rather than to others".[65]

Yde and Willem were thus arrested for their macabre actions. They were thrown into gaol, for not only had they broken the law by stealing the body parts of a hanged man, but they had further endangered their client's health with this unhygienic practice. The town authorities even had to intervene in this case for – given that Willem and Yde were unable to pay the heavy fine – the bailiff had confiscated their building. The case records enable us to hear Yde's words. She admitted having put an "inappropriate substance" in the heater, but hoped she would be treated "with justice". Despite the bailiff's protestations, the aldermen found in Yde's favour: the mayor ordered that she be released and her building returned to her. The hoped-for settlement followed shortly afterwards. Yde offered the bailiff 50 Rhenish guilders, the equivalent of about one year's rent from "De Roose". Was this arrangement connected to the promise Yde made in 1476, to banish prostitution from her *stove*? We cannot be sure. In any case, on 26 June that same year, she appeared before the aldermen's court, this time to solemnly swear that she would no longer take in young women engaged in "dishonourable" practices. Henceforth, she declared, she would run the business "as one does and should do in a good and honourable *stove*".[66] Whatever the facts may have been in this case, it shows that a category of brothels were home to most disreputable practices. In the following centuries, such behaviour would very probably have counted as witchcraft, but in the Middle Ages they were still cloaked in an association with love.

Conclusions

Medieval towns were not a place of tumultuous decadence where sexual violence went unpunished. In emphasizing rape and prostitution, we run the major risk of reducing medieval women to victims in matters of sexuality. However, such a view is unjustified. That shortcoming is shown by the stories of townswomen who won trials against their rapists and by the adventures of prostitutes. Consent was necessary to have free sexual relations outside marriage. Just as in our day, though, there was debate about the permissible limits to sex acts, for both men and women. Maybe a smitten monk was not a problem in itself, but the presence of a prostitute in a monastery caused discontent. A rapist could not get away with it, but a woman who had not clearly opposed a man's advances could expect firm resistance if she subsequently sought to prosecute her partner. Running a brothel was allowed, but any criminality it might cause was severely punished. In brothels, however, men were free to get carried away. The limits to what was permissible and relations between men and women were perennial subjects of discussion. From this point of view, medieval society is not so distant from our own.

Notes

[1] GSAB, CC, 12902, 247v (*onnuticheit*).
[2] Van Boendale, *Der leken spieghel* (ed. de Vries), I, 93-4.
[3] "in bed you must be kind, secretive, not wild, gentle in the work of love, firm, valiant, and loving, not outside but within the law" (*Ghij sult te bedde zijn vriendelijck, secreet, ende niet fumeux, aerdich int werck van minnen dijn, cloeck, vailliant ende amoureux, niet buyten reghele maer entre deux*); Pleij, *Nederlandse literatuur*, 29-30.
[4] Sweetser, "Les *Cent nouvelles nouvelles*", no. 98.
[5] CAB, CA, 16, 97r.
[6] CAB, CA, 16, 95r.
[7] Wielant, *Corte instructie* (ed. Monballyu), 88.
[8] GSAB, CC, 12659, 256v-257r.
[9] Wielant, *Practijcke criminele* (ed. Orts), 129-30.
[10] GSAB, CC, 14116, 242r-v.
[11] GSAB, CC, 12655, 209r.
[12] GSAB, CC, 12654, 251r-v.
[13] GSAB, CC, 12903, 87v-88r.
[14] GSAB, CC, 12904, 53r.
[15] GSAB, CC, 12904, 208v.
[16] GSAB, CC, 12903, 215v.

17   GSAB, CC, 12795, 120v and 12708, 81v.
18   GSAB, CC, 12904, 257r.
19   GSAB, CC, 12700, 222r.
20   GSAB, CC, 12658, 232v.
21   Van der Tanerijen, *Boec*, 278: a whore (*hoer*) is "an available woman willing to satisfy the licentious desires of many men, and whose filth is for sale" (*een hoere es een wijf die dair der oncuyscher begeerten van veele mannen bereet ende te wille is*, and whose *vuylicheyt veyl ende te coope is*).
22   Godding, *Ordonnances de Philippe*, 440.
23   Such as *deerne van oneerlijk leven* ("maiden of dishonest life"), and sometimes even *wereltwijf* ("woman of the world", hence literally a "public woman").
24   Van der Eerden-Vonk, *Raadsverdragen*, 329.
25   Van der Eerden-Vonk, *Raadsverslagen*, 444.
26   Vanhemelryck, *De criminaliteit*, 132; Deligne, *Bruxelles*, 103.
27   Vanhemelryck, *Marginalen*, 227.
28   Laws for Leuven in CAL, 1524, 88v; 1523, 78v, and 273r; 8130, 47r
29   Laws for Antwerp in CAA, PK, 913, 15v, 47r, and 57v.
30   "Les bains sont jolys, les estuves, les fillettes plaisans", Eustache Deschamps, *Œuvres complètes*, IV, 6.
31   *Maer sal wel geoirlooft sijn den gehuwede vrouwen te mogen gaene met hueren getrouwede manne in de mansstoven* (CAM, OB, 2, 126r-v).
32   Marchandisse, "La police", 86-7.
33   Coomans & Geltner, "On the street", 72.
34   CAL, 7749, 170r; 7751, 55r; 7752, 133v.
35   CAA, VS, 234, 28r.
36   CAL, 7357, 61v-62v.
37   Spindler, "Were medieval prostitutes", 264; Dupont, "Middeleeuwse stoven", 151.
38   CAL, 7382, 202r-v.
39   CAL, 7370, 28r.
40   Van Uytven, "De ledige vrouwen", 19.
41   Respectively: CAA, VS, 234, 85v; Maes, *Vijf eeuwen*, 629: *onseden ... in mans abyte*.
42   Koldeweij, Geysen & Tahon, *Liefde en devotie*, 136: *Ghaet in, gaet in, ghereet die stoof is heet; lieve moeder, hoedet my, al ben ic jonc, ik heb veel liever enen man dan dusent pont*.
43   Lambert, "Double disadvantage", 558. See also Haemers, "Women and stews".
44   Prevenier, "Vorstelijke genade", 234.
45   GSAB, CC, 12903, 297v: *vrouken van lichten leven*.
46   *Wildi meer sitten ende houden my geselscap? Ic sal weder by u comen*.
47   De Longé, *Coutumes*, I, 23 and IV, 23.
48   Crahay, *Coutumes*, 173: "pimping" (*putierscap bedriven*).
49   Van der Eerden-Vonk, *Raadsverdragen*, 107-8: he promised to "never again live off loose women" (*nimmermeer mee te leven op ledige wieve*).
50   See Maes, *Vijf eeuwen*, 215-7 and Vanhemelryck, *De criminaliteit*, 145-7 for the following examples.
51   De Longé, *Coutumes*, I, 146 and IV, 24.
52   CAA, PK, 913, 97r (*onkerstelic, ongodlic ende onnatuerlic*), and VS, 234, 161r (for what follows)
53   CAB, CA, 16, 7r.
54   Stallaert, *Het keurboek*, 43-4.
55   Maes, *Vijf eeuwen*, 217.
56   GSAB, CC, 12703, 320v (*deernenhuys*).

57 GSAB, CC, 12903, 345r.
58 GSAB, CC, 12902, 220v.
59 GSAB, CC, 12903, 345v.
60 CAB, CA, 15, 391v.
61 CAA, VS, 234, 54v and 67v; GSAB, CC, 12701, 297v (for what follows).
62 GSAB, CC, 12701, 297v.
63 CAL, 1528, 81r (*also ende in der maten als anderen die in der stad stove tanderen plaetsen hielden*).
64 GSAB, CC, 12656, 533v (*die beenderkins gebonden in een zacksken... groeten loep van volke dagelijcx in den stoven*).
65 Braekman, *Middeleeuwse witte en zwarte magie*, 403: *dat se dien leggen soude onder hair beddestede, dair op dat men se plach te bruden, ende omme dat die gesellen te bat tot hair comen sauden dan elder gaan.*
66 *Alsoe men in goeden eerberen stoven pleecht ende sculdich is te doene* (CAL, 7370, 7v).

CONCLUSIONS

Of "wise women" and "witless men"

> In the land of Brabant, a fair and pleasant region, well provided with pretty girls, who are generally wise, and by men, too, of whom it is – quite rightly – said that they lose their wits as they grow older...

The *Cent nouvelles Nouvelles* [A Hundred New Tales], a collection of stories which circulated in the Burgundian court in the mid-fifteenth century, contains 100 tales drawn from real life, along with certain exaggerations and the odd touch of merriment to delight the court.[1] Before launching into one of these tales, the (anonymous) author observes that Brabant is a fine land full of dull-witted men and clever women. Yet he has no intention of championing women's intelligence. On the contrary, the ensuing story portrays an adulterous woman who tricks and cheats on her husband. Being wholly unsuspecting, the upstanding fellow believes his wife's many lies, who claims she has never done any wrong while seducing several men. This story reflects the popular view of woman as Eve's descendant: a beautiful, voluptuous, and cunning femme fatale, whom it took a sensible man to resist. The story thus conveys age-old stereotypes about relations between the sexes.

"Urban women" shows that discovering the Middle Ages solely through the prism of texts such as these occludes a far richer and more varied reality, one which, furthermore, contains many elements invalidating entrenched clichés. On one point, at least, we agree with the depiction in the *Cent nouvelles nouvelles*: women played the leading role. The common assumption that medieval women lived in men's shadow is sent packing. Despite the inequality between the sexes characterizing society of the time, women were actively involved in public life. They invested, traded, laughed, criticized, litigated, insulted, and rebelled – often alongside men or else supported by their families. While free women's actions could run directly counter to rigid regulations and expectations, others complied with the norms of their day. Brabant women thus provide a rich array of stories fully deserving their place in history books. This position is of course justified first and foremost by historical accuracy. Yet above and

In 1486, Antoine Vérard published an illustrated version of the Cent nouvelles nouvelles in Paris. This woodcut accompanies the story, which takes place in Brabant, where an unfaithful wife confesses to a priest, who later turns out to be her husband in disguise. He discovers his wife's infidelity, but she uses a clever ruse to fool him in spite of everything. She confessed to having slept with a priest, but said that during her confession she recognised her husband disguised as a priest. So she pretended to confess that she had simply slept with her husband. (Bibliothèque Nationale de France, réserve Y2, 174). http://gallica.bnf.fr/ark:/12148/bpt6k22159s/f455.item)

beyond the wish to unearth women's role down through the ages, the stakes also relate to how our present-day society functions. Research has repeatedly shown the extent to which stereotypes and stereotypical accounts – with women reduced to the role of housewives, femmes fatales, or damsels in distress – influence the patterns of role distribution and the expectations projected onto men and women today. That is why it is so important to set about filling in this blind spot in our collective memory and breaking down stereotypes.

Texts written by women portray a sophisticated urban society fashioned by men and women alike. Complex administrative structures and forms of interaction (generally) secured peace in towns, creating opportunities for both sexes. Earlier historians have already worked to correct the once prevalent dark image of medieval towns: urban society, it turns out, was anything but a place of perdition. In this book, we have presented a dynamic community promulgating numerous rules to curb excess, with varying degrees of success. Hygiene regulations tackled waste problems, physical clashes did not go unpunished and often resulted in an amicable settlement, foundlings and the mentally disabled were taken care of, orphans could count on the protection of their extended families and various organizations, and so on and so forth. From this point of view, the preoccupations of medieval townspeople resemble our own, for on countless points their society differed but little from that of today: there were many separated couples, blended families, as well as single men and women in town. Extramarital sexual relations and adultery were commonplace. Calumny and defamation were repressed. Poor administration sparked protests from the population. There was a policy of tolerating prostitution. Heated debates over what constituted "non-consensual sex" dominated public opinion. Examining the Middle Ages from the perspective afforded by towns and how they were managed holds out the promise of being both instructive and interesting.

Any such description needs to bring women into the picture. Admittedly, positions of power were a male preserve. Women's freedom of movement was hindered by manifestly unequal social structures and patriarchal mindsets. Yet women's roles were not thereby reduced to that of housewives shorn of autonomy, capable at best of tending to their households. The countless examples in this book depict enterprising businesswoman fully aware of their rights; seizing or creating their own opportunities; and partaking in the economic, political, and religious life of their town. That did not prevent violence, brutality, and inequality being integral to their lives. Town authorities tended not to get involved in private matters such as violence between partners, not unless the women or their families brought them to the attention of the courts, or unless public order was compromised. In such cases, women capable of defending themselves took things into their own hands and took legal action against aggressive men, though not all had the network or resources to do so. We have seen women denouncing their husband's misconduct, refusing an arranged marriage, or successfully bringing proceedings against their rapist. Though their chances of success varied, once again this shows that medieval society differed little from our own.

One point emerges very clearly: we must not reason in terms of a singular category, "woman", but of "women" in the plural. In this book we have met married and divorced women, wealthy entrepreneurs, beguines, craftswomen, illegitimate daughters, and orphans. Certain women had more opportunities than others thanks to their socio-economic background, their life course, their network, their personality, and many other factors. Our examples clearly show that there were many opportunities, especially for wealthy women from the middling classes, as we termed them in the introduction. They enjoyed relative prosperity, a high level of education, and could work in the family business or even develop their own business. As for less wealthy women, they had greater freedom when it came to choosing their spouse. They were less hemmed in by their family and by strategies to safeguard assets to be handed down to posterity. Yet their lack of means also deprived them of many opportunities. The richest women, from the elite and the nobility, had less freedom when it came to choosing a partner, but they controlled vast landholdings and lived in luxury. Much also depended on the specific situation in which a woman found herself. Thus, as a single mother, Janne Schuts of Antwerp was not dealt the best hand. Yet she lived in a booming trading city, offering great potential to wealthy citizens. Thanks to her entrepreneurial spirit, lucky breaks, and her network, Janne enjoyed relative freedom and considerable wealth. Even so, the growth of Antwerp also led to increasing inequality, pushing many of its residents to society's margins. In short, various interwoven factors and identities determined women's room for manoeuvring, as was also the case for many other townspeople. After all, women were only one of many social groups with a minority status. Discrimination affected not only those in need, but also migrants. Brabant towns attracted people from the countryside who left their family homes to settle in town, but also people from outside the duchy. To date, there has been very little research into this phenomenon for the Middle Ages, and consequently very little is known about the fate of these groups. There is still much fertile ground to be cultivated in this area.

Another question is the extent to which the situation in the southern Low Countries was exceptional. Many of the authors quoted over the course of this book considered that women's lot was better there than elsewhere. The Spanish captain Alfonso Vasquez was particularly surprised by women's economic activity in Brabant towns, while the Italian Lodovico Guicciardini praised their business skills. The latter added that women even tended to be overbearing in running their household.[2] According to him, Brabant women could act freely, in every sense of the word. They were eloquent, conducted business, travelled around the country without having to justify themselves, and so on. Were these travellers surprised because the situation differed from what they knew back home? Society in the southern Low Countries did indeed present a certain number of specific characteristics resulting in a more favourable situation for women. The combination of intense urbanization, a commercial environment, a legal framework that was fairly advantageous on many points, and high levels of literacy created opportunities for women that often did not exist in regions without these characteristics. Nevertheless, Brabant was not unique in this respect. Women in various other towns and regions enjoyed similar rights and conditions. For instance, Barcelona was a commercial city with egalitarian inheritance laws; the beguine movement in Rhineland met with great success; female workers in Valencia often managed to choose their marriage partner; fishermen's wives in Bilbao waged a successful fight for more rights; and in early thirteenth-century Genoa, a quarter of the investors in the lucrative shipping trade were women. So women elsewhere also managed to draw on opportunities to profit from their talents.

The situation differed from one woman to another, one town to another, and one region to another, but also from one era to another. For example, women's economic opportunities progressively diminished from the thirteenth to the sixteenth centuries. Businesswomen encountered increasing difficulties in controlling their goods, and various guilds forbade more and more women from joining their associations. Specialists in early modern literature report that misogynistic texts and illustrations were on the rise in the fifteenth and sixteenth centuries. The outlook was not universally negative, though, and the deterioration in women's status did not relate to all areas of life. Around 1500, women did not lose court cases more frequently than a century earlier, they were still authorized to trade as merchants, and young women still ran away with partners when denied their family's consent.

They were not more severely punished than previously. Additionally, the late Middle Ages was also the period when women, for the first time, produced major literary works in the vernacular, as exemplified by Christine de Pizan and the Antwerp poet Anna Bijns. Furthermore, the life stories of several of the businesswomen presented in this book show that there were few limits to how far women with financial means could go – to be sure, thanks to Brabant inheritance laws, women in the southern Low Countries had unrivalled access to capital. One only has to think of Hadewijch Cornelis from Utrecht in the late fifteenth century, who ran a large bathing establishment in Leuven, for which she paid a sizeable rent to the wealthy Liesbeth van Sint-Truiden. One can find such examples throughout the centuries.

This observation is a valuable indication that history went through alternating periods where women enjoyed more opportunities, and others, on the contrary, when they were pushed back into the private sphere and the margins of society. When times were economically tough and social tension was on the rise, women were subject to pressure, as were other groups with a minority status. If today we live in a society in which men and women enjoy equal rights, it is not at all due to some linear, regular evolution down through the ages. Although there has never been a "battle of the sexes", relations between men and women have constantly evolved. In medieval society, townspeople fought collectively for their rights, and women did not stand idly by. Whatever their role and wherever their town, in the "pleasant and beautiful land" of Brabant, vigilance was required – and this applied just as much to witless men as to wise women.

Notes

1. Translation of the introduction to text 78 (Sweetser, *Les Cent nouvelles nouvelles*, 461): *Au pais de Brabant, qui est bonne marche et plaisante, fournye a droit et bien garnye de belles filles, et bien sages coustumierement et le plus et des hommes on soult dire, et se trouve assez veritable, que tant plus vivent et plus sont sotz...*
2. The quotations are taken from the seventeenth-century Dutch translation of his work: *Beschryvinghe van alle de Nederlanden*, 29.

Primary sources

GSAB: General State Archives of Belgium
We have followed the numbering given in the inventory of the "Chambres des comptes" holdings (CC), see Gachard L.-P., Nelis H. & Pinchart A., *Inventaire des archives des chambres des comptes*, Brussels, 1837-1931, 6 vol. See http://www.arch.be.

SAA: State archives at Anderlecht
We have consulted the *Archives ecclésiastiques du Brabant* (AEB).

SAL: State archives at Liège
We have consulted the archives of the Officiality (the episcopal court) of Liège (AOL).

SALv: State archives at Leuven
We have consulted the archives of the city of Zoutleeuw (SG – *Steden en gemeenten*) and of the *Openbare Onderstand* (OO).

CAA: City Archives, Antwerp (now: *Felixarchief*)
We have followed the numbering given in a certain number of specific inventories and on the website (http://zoeken.felixarchief.be), where the following abbreviations refer to
GA (*Gilden en Ambachten*): Guilds and crafts
PK (*Privilegekamer*): Register of privileges and municipal records
SR (*Schepenregisters*): Aldermen's registers
VS (*Vierschaar*): Court of justice
The numbers following each abbreviation refer to the numbering present in the respective inventory.

CAB: City Archives, Brussels
We have followed the numbering given in a certain number of specific inventories and on the website (http://www.pallas.be), where the abbreviation CA refers to the *"Cartulaires"* series.

CAL: City Archives, Leuven
We have followed the numbering of J. Cuvelier, *Inventaire des archives de la ville de Louvain*, Leuven, 1929-32. The "Aldermen's registers" (*Schepenregisters*) series may be consulted online at http://www.itineranova.be.

CAM: City Archive, Mechelen
We have consulted the archives of the OCMW and those of the city, using a certain number of specific inventories available at (https://stadsarchief.mechelen.be/).
The abbreviation refers to the city archives, namely the *"Correctieboeck"* (no. 1 for the period 1441-1569), PC refers to the *"Privileges en Charters"* series, and OB to the *"Ordonnantieboek"*.

Literature

General works with an emphasis on the southern Low Countries and Brabant

Ariès P. & Duby G. (eds.), *Histoire de la vie privée. II. De l'Europe féodale à la Renaissance*, Paris, 1985.

Arnade P. & Prevenier W., *Honor, vengeance, and social trouble. Pardon letters in the Burgundian Low Countries*, Ithaca, 2015.

Asaert G., *Ook dat was Antwerpen. Een geschiedenis van de kleine man. Over armoede en politieke onmacht*, Tielt, 2010.

Bardyn A., 'Women in the medieval society', in P. Stabel & V. Lambert (eds.), *Golden times. Wealth and status in the Middle Ages in the southern Low Countries*, Tielt, 2016, 283-317.

Becchi E. et al. (eds.), *Histoire de l'enfance en Occident. I. De l'Antiquité au XVIIe siècle*, Paris, 1998.

Beattie C. & Stevens M.F. (eds.), *Married women and the law in premodern Northwest Europe*, Woodbridge, 2013.

Bellavitis A. & Edelman N. (eds.), *Genre, femmes, histoire en Europe (France, Italie, Espagne, Autriche)*, Paris, 2011.

Bellavitis A. & Zucha Micheletto B. (eds.), *Gender, law, and economic well-being in Europe from the fifteenth to the nineteenth century. North versus South?*, London, 2018.

Bennett J., *History matters. Patriarchy and the challenge of feminism*, Philadelphia, 2007.

Bennett J. & Karras R. (eds.), *The Oxford handbook of women and gender in medieval Europe*, Oxford, 2013.

Blondé B., Boone M. & Van Bruaene A.-L. (eds.), *City and society in the Low Countries, 1100-1600*, Cambridge, 2018.

Blockmans W., *Metropolen aan de Noordzee. De geschiedenis van Nederland, 1100-1560*, Amsterdam, 2010.

Blockmans W. & Hoppenbrouwers P., *Eeuwen des onderscheids. Een geschiedenis van middeleeuws Europa*, Amsterdam, 2016.

Blockmans W. & Prevenier W., *The promised lands. The Low Countries under Burgundian rule, 1396-1530*, Philadelphia, 1999.

Boffa S., *Warfare in medieval Brabant, 1356-1406*, Woodbridge, 2004.

Boone M., de Hemptinne T. & Prevenier W., 'Gender and early emancipation in the Low Countries in the late Middle Ages and early modern period', in J. Munns & P. Richards (eds.), *Gender, power and privilege in early modern Europe*, London, 2003, 21-39.

Bot P., *Tussen verering en verachting. De rol van de vrouw in de middeleeuwse samenleving 500-1500*, Kapellen, 1990.

Boucheron P. & Menjot D., *La ville médiévale. Histoire de l'Europe urbaine – 2*, Paris, 2011.

Bousmanne B. & Savini E. (eds.), *The library of the dukes of Burgundy*, Turnhout, 2020.

Bousmar E., 'Du marché aux *bordiaulx*. Hommes, femmes et rapports de sexe ('gender') dans les villes des Pays-Bas au bas moyen âge. État de nos connaissances et perspectives de recherche', in M. Carlier et al. (eds.), *Hart en marge in de laat-middeleeuwse stedelijke maatschappij*, Leuven, 1997, 51-70.

Bührer-Thierry G., Lett D. & Moulinier L., 'Histoire des femmes et histoire du genre dans l'occident médiéval', *Historiens et géographes*, 392 (2005), 135-46.
Carlier M. & Soens T. (eds.), *The household in late medieval cities: Italy and Northwestern Europe compared*, Leuven, 2001.
Danneel M., *Weduwen en wezen in het laat-middeleeuwse Gent*, Apeldoorn & Leiden, 1995.
De Hemptinne T., 'Vrouwengeschiedenis en geschiedenis van de middeleeuwen: Een terugblik en een verkenning', *Verslagen van het RUG-centrum voor genderstudies*, 7 (1998), 3-16.
De Hemptinne T. & Góngora M.E. (eds.), *The voice of silence: Women's literacy in a men's Church*, Turnhout, 2004.
Delsaux O. & Van Hemelryck T. (eds.), *Christine de Pizan. Figures d'auteur, figures d'autorité, figures exemplaires*, Turnhout, 2016.
Demets L., *Vorsten en vorstinnen in het hertogdom Brabant (1106-1248). Naar een consolidatie van macht?*, Ghent, 2014.
De Moor T. & Van Zanden J.L., *Vrouwen en de geboorte van het kapitalisme in West-Europa*, Amsterdam, 2006.
De Pizan C., *Le livre de la Cité des dames*, C. Le Ninan & A. Paupert (eds.), Paris, 2023.
Depreter M. et al. (eds.), *Marie de Bourgogne. Figure, principat et postérité d'une duchesse tardo-médiévale*, Turnhout, 2021.
Dermineur E., Karlsson Sjögren A. & Langum V. (eds.), *Revisiting gender in European history, 1400-1800*, Abingdon, 2017.
Duby G., *Le chevalier, la femme et le prêtre. Le mariage dans la France féodale*, Paris, 1981.
Duby G., *Love and marriage in the Middle Ages*. Translated by J. Dunnett. Chicago, 1994.
Dumont J. et al. (eds.), *Femmes de pouvoir, femmes politiques durant les derniers siècles du Moyen Âge et de la Renaissance*, Brussels, 2012.
Eichberger D., Legaré A.M. & Hüsken W. (eds.), *Women at the Burgundian court: Presence and influence*, Turnhout, 2010.
Ennen E., *Frauen im Mittelalter. Frauenleben von der Spätantike bis zum Beginn der Neuzeit*, Munich, 1984.
Erler M. & Kowaleski M. (eds.), *Women and power in the Middle Ages*, Athens, 1988.
Erler M. & Kowaleski M. (eds.), *Gendering the master narrative. Women and power in the Middle Ages*, Ithaca, 2003.
Farmer S. & Pasternack C. (eds.), *Gender and difference in the Middle Ages*, Minneapolis, 2003.
Gauvard C., *Jeanne d'Arc. Héroïne diffamée et martyre*, Paris, 2022.
Gilissen J., 'Le statut de la femme dans l'ancien droit belge', *Recueils de la société Jean Bodin pour l'histoire comparative des institutions*, 23 (1962), 255-321.
Godding P., *Le droit privé dans les Pays-Bas méridionaux du 12e au 18e siècle*, Brussels, 1987.
Heene K., 'Vrouwelijke auteurs in de middeleeuwen. De complexe relatie tussen gender, genre en (literatuur)geschiedenis', *Queeste*, 13 (2006), 109-29.
Hicks E. & Moreau T., *Le livre de la cité des Dames de Christine de Pizan*, Paris, 1986.
Howell M., *Women, production, and patriarchy in late medieval cities*, Chicago, 1986.
Howell M., *The marriage exchange: Property, social place, and gender in cities of the Low Countries, 1300-1550*, Chicago, 1998.
Howell M., 'The gender of Europe's commercial economy, 1200-1700', *Gender & history*, 20 (2008), 519-38.
Hutton S., *Women and economic activities in late medieval Ghent*, New York, 2011.
Jackson D., *Medieval women*, Chicago, 2015.
Jackson E. & Harrison J., *Medieval women. Voices and visions*, London, 2024.
Janega E., *The once and future sex. Going medieval on women's roles in society*, New York, 2023.

Karras R., *Sexuality in medieval Europe: Doing unto others*, New York, 2005.
Karras R., *Unmarriages: Women, men, and sexual unions in the Middle Ages*, Philadelphia, 2012.
Kittell E. & Suydam M. (eds.), *The texture of society: Medieval women in the southern Low Countries*, Basingstoke, 2004.
Klapisch-Zuber C. (ed.), *A history of women. Silences of the Middle Ages*, Harvard, 1998.
Lambert V. & Stabel P. (eds.), *Golden times. Wealth and status in the Middle Ages in the southern Low Countries*, Tielt, 2016.
Le Goff J. (ed.), *Hommes et femmes du Moyen Âge*, Paris, 2012.
Lett D., *Hommes et femmes au Moyen Âge. Histoire du genre XIIe-XVe siècle*, Paris, 2013.
Lewis K., Menuge N. & Phillips K. (eds.), *Young medieval women*, Stroud, 1999.
Lynch K., *Individuals, families and communities in Europe, 1200-1800: The urban foundations of Western society*, Cambridge, 2003.
Mostert M. (ed.), *Vrouw, familie en macht. Bronnen over vrouwen in de middeleeuwen*, Hilversum, 1990.
Mulder-Bakker A. (ed.), *Seeing and knowing. Women and learning in medieval Europe, 1250-1550*, Turnhout, 2004.
Paupert A., 'La vision de Christine. Traité allégorique en prose écrit par Christine de Pizan en 1405', in D. Régnier-Bohler (ed.), *Voix de femmes au Moyen Âge. Savoir, mystique, poésie, amour, sorcellerie, XIIe-XVe siècle*, Paris, 2006, 407-542.
Pernoud R., *La femme au temps des cathédrales*, Paris, 1980.
Phipps T., *Medieval women and urban justice. Commerce, crime and community in England, 1300-1500*, Manchester, 2020.
Phipps T. & Youngs D. (eds.), *Litigating women. Gender and justice in Europe, c.1300-c.1800*, Abingdon, 2022.
Pleij H., *Het gevleugelde woord. Geschiedenis van de Nederlandse literatuur, 1400-1650*, Amsterdam, 2007.
Power E., *Medieval women*, Cambridge, 1981.
Prevenier W. (ed.), *Prinsen en poorters. Beelden van de laat-middeleeuwse samenleving in de Bourgondische Nederlanden, 1384-1530*, Antwerp, 1998.
Régnier-Bohler D. (ed.), *Voix de femmes au Moyen Âge. Savoir, mystique, poésie, amour, sorcellerie, XIIe-XVe siècle*, Paris, 2006.
Schaus M. (ed.), *Women and gender in medieval Europe. An encyclopedia*, New York, 2006.
Scott J., 'Gender: A useful category of historical analysis', *American Historical Review*, 91 (1986), 1053-75.
Shepard A. & Walker G. (eds.), *Gender and change. Agency, chronology and periodisation*, Chichester, 2009.
Simonton D. (ed.), *The Routledge history handbook of gender and the urban experience*, London, 2017.
Skinner P., *Studying gender in medieval Europe: Historical approaches*, London, 2018.
Skinner P. & Van Houts E., *Medieval writings on secular women*, London, 2011.
Snellaert F., *Nederlandsche gedichten uit de veertiende eeuw van Jan van Boendale, Hein van Aken en anderen*, Brussels, 1869.
Solórzano Telechea J., Arizaga Bolumburu B. & Andrade A. (eds.), *Ser mujer en la ciudad medieval Europea*, Logrono, 2013.
Solórzano Telechea J., Haemers J. & Liddy C. (eds.), *La familia urbana: Matrimonio, parentesco y linaje en la Edad Media*, Logrono, 2021.
Sperling J. & Kelly Wray S. (eds.), *Across the religious divide. Women, property and law in the wider Mediterranean (ca. 1300-1800)*, New York, 2010.
Stuip R. & Vellekoop C., *Middeleeuwers over vrouwen*, Utrecht, 1984-5.
Sweetser F. (ed.), *Les 'Cent nouvelles nouvelles'*, Geneva, 1966.
Van Bavel B., *Manors and markets. Economy and society in the Low Countries, 500-1600*, Oxford, 2010.

Van Gerven J., 'Vrouwen, arbeid en sociale positie. Een voorlopig onderzoek naar de economische rol en maatschappelijke positie van vrouwen in de Brabantse steden in de late middeleeuwen', *Revue belge de philologie et d'histoire*, 73 (1995), 947-66.

Van Hemelryck T., 'La femme et la paix. Un motif pacifique de la littérature française médiévale', *Revue belge de philologie et d'histoire*, 84 (2006), 243-70.

Vanhemelryck F., *De criminaliteit in de ammanie van Brussel van de late middeleeuwen tot het einde van het Ancien Régime (1404-1789)*, Brussels, 1981.

Van Oostrom F., *Wereld in woorden. Geschiedenis van de Nederlandse literatuur, 1300-1400*, Amsterdam, 2013.

Van Uytven R., *Het dagelijks leven in een middeleeuwse stad. Leuven anno 1448*, Leuven, 1998.

Van Uytven R. (ed.), *De gewestelijke en lokale overheidsinstellingen in Brabant en Mechelen tot 1795*, Brussels, 2000.

Van Uytven R. (ed.), *Geschiedenis van Brabant, van het hertogdom tot heden*, Leuven, 2011.

Vrancken V., *De Blijde Inkomsten van de Brabantse hertogen. Macht, opstand en privileges in de vijftiende eeuw*, Brussels, 2018.

Wiesner M., *Women and gender in early modern Europe*, Cambridge, 1993.

Wilson K. & Margolis N. (eds.), *Women in the Middle Ages. An encyclopedia*, Westport, 2004.

1. From girlhood to widowhood

Blockmans W. & Neijzen T., 'Functions of fiction: Fighting spouses around 1500', in W. Blockmans & A. Janse (eds.), *Showing status. Representation of social positions in the late Middle Ages*, Turnhout, 1999, 265-76.

Blockmans W. & Prevenier W., 'Armoede in de Nederlanden van de 14e tot het midden van de 16e eeuw: Bronnen en problemen', *Tijdschrift voor Geschiedenis*, 88 (1975), 501-38.

Blondé B., *De sociale structuren en economische dynamiek van 's Hertogenbosch, 1500-1550*, Tilburg, 1987.

Bousmar E., 'Een historisch-antropologische kijk op gender in de Bourgondische Nederlanden (15de eeuw)', in N. De Bleeckere, M. Demoor & K. Heene (eds.), *Verslagen van het RUG-centrum voor genderstudies*, Ghent, 1999, 35-49.

Carlier M., *Kinderen van den minne. Bastaarden in het vijftiende-eeuwse Vlaanderen*, Brussels, 2001.

Carlier M., 'Paternity in late medieval Flanders', in W. Blockmans, M. Boone & T. de Hemptinne (eds.), *Secretum scriptorum. Liber alumnorum Walter Prevenier*, Leuven, 1999, 235-58.

Craenen I., *Wel wees, maar niet verweesd. De relatie tussen wees en voogd in Leuven in de periode 1450-1461*, Leuven, 2016.

Danneel M., 'Gender and the life course in the late medieval Flemish town', in W. Blockmans, M. Boone & T. de Hemptinne (eds.), *Secretum scriptorum. Liber alumnorum Walter Prevenier*, Leuven, 1999, 225-33.

Danneel M., *Weduwen en wezen in het laat-middeleeuwse Gent*, Leuven, 1995.

Delva A., *Vrouwengeneeskunde in Vlaanderen tijdens de late middeleeuwen, met een uitgave van het Brugse Liber Trotula*, Bruges, 1983.

De Longé G., *Coutumes de la ville d'Anvers*, Brussels, 1870-1874, 4 vols.

De Ruysscher D., 'From usages of merchants to default rules: Practices of trade, ius commune and urban law in early modern Antwerp', *The journal of legal history*, 33 (2012), 3-29.

Dulac L., 'Le Livre des trois Vertus. Traité en prose écrit par Christine de Pizan en 1405', in D. Régnier-Bohler (ed.), *Voix de femmes au Moyen Âge. Savoir, mystique, poésie, amour, sorcellerie, XIIe-XVe siècle*, Paris, 2006, 543-698.

Gilissen J., 'Le statut de la femme dans l'ancien droit belge', *Recueils de la société Jean Bodin pour l'histoire comparative des institutions*, 12 (1962), 255-321.

Godding P., *Ordonnances de Philippe le Bon pour les duchés de Brabant et de Limbourg et les pays d'Outre-Meuse, 1430-1467*, Brussels, 2005.

Godding P., 'L'ordonnance du magistrat bruxellois du 19 juin 1445 sur la tutelle', in *Code et constitution. Mélanges historiques. Liber amicorum John Gilissen*, Antwerp, 1983, 149-74.

Godding P., 'Le droit des gens mariés à Nivelles (14e-15e siècles)', *Revue d'histoire du droit*, 40 (1972), 73-117.

Goedthals F., *Les proverbes anciens flamengs et françois: Correspondants de sentence les uns aux autres*, Antwerp, 1568.

Greilsammer M., *L'envers du tableau. Mariage et maternité en Flandre médiévale*, Paris, 1990.

Kruyskamp C., *De middelnederlandse boerden*, The Hague, 1967.

Lie O., 'Women's medicine in Middle Dutch', in M. Goyens, P. De Leemans & A. Smets (eds.), *Science translated. Latin and vernacular translations of scientific treatises in medieval Europe*, Leuven, 2008, 459-66.

Lie O. & Kuiper W., *The secrets of women in Middle Dutch: A bilingual edition of Der Vrouwen Heimelijcheit in Ms. Ghent, UB. 444*, Hilversum, 2011.

Maes L., *Costumen van de stad Mechelen. II. Ontwerp-costumen van 1527*, Brussels, 1960.

Opitz C., 'Het dagelijks leven van de vrouw in de late middeleeuwen (1250-1500)', in C. Klapisch-Zuber (ed.), *Geschiedenis van de vrouw. Middeleeuwen*, Amsterdam, 1991, 271-325.

Roelens J., 'Visible women: Female sodomy in the late medieval and early modern Southern Netherlands (1400-1550)', *Bijdragen en mededelingen betreffende de geschiedenis der Nederlanden*, 130 (2015), 3-24.

Rutte R. & Vannieuwenhuyze B., *Stedenatlas Jacob van Deventer. 226 Stadsplattegronden uit 1545-1575 – Schakels tussen verleden en heden*, Bussum, 2018.

Slootmans C., *Paas- en Koudemarkten te Bergen-op-Zoom, 1365-1565*, Tilburg, 1985.

Van Aert L., 'Tussen norm en praktijk. Een terreinverkenning over het juridische statuut van vrouwen in het zestiende-eeuwse Antwerpen', *Tijdschrift voor sociale en economische geschiedenis*, 2 (2005), 22-42.

Van Boendale J., *Der Leken spieghel. Leerdicht van den jare 1330*, M. De Vries (ed.), Leiden, 1844-1846.

Van Cauwelaert E., 'Wettigingen van bastaarden in Brabant (1460-1500)', *Eigen Schoon en de Brabander*, 63 (1980), 55-77.

Van Onacker E., *Village elites and social structures in the late medieval Campine region*, Turnhout, 2017.

Vasquez A., 'Los sucesos de Flandes y Francia del tiempo de Alejandro Farnese', in M. Gachard (ed.), *Les bibliothèques de Madrid et de l'Escurial*, Brussels, 1875, 455-79.

Vleeschouwers C. & Van Melkebeek M., *Liber sentenciarum van de officialiteit van Brussel (1448-1459)*, Brussels, 1983.

Vleeschouwers C. & Van Melkebeek M., 'Aspects du lien matrimonial dans le Liber Sentenciarum de Bruxelles (1448-1469)', *Revue d'histoire du droit*, 53 (1985), 43-97.

Vleeschouwers C. & Van Melkebeek M., 'Marital breakdown before the consistory courts of Brussels, Cambrai and Tournai: Judicial separation a mensa et thoro', *Revue d'histoire du droit*, 72 (2004), 81-90.

Wijsman H., *Handschriften voor het hertogdom. De mooiste verluchte manuscripten van de Brabantse hertogen, edellieden, kloosterlingen en stedelingen*, Alphen, 2006.

Willemsen A., *Back to the schoolyard. The daily practice of medieval and renaissance education*, Turnhout, 2008.

2. Women and marriage

Brundage J., *Law, sex and Christian society in medieval Europe*, Chicago, 2009.
Butler S., *The language of abuse: Marital violence in later medieval England*, Leiden, 2007.
Boquet D. & Nagy P., *Sensible Moyen Age. Une histoire des émotions dans l'Occident médiéval*, Paris, 2015.
Bousmar E., 'Des alliances liées à la procréation: Les fonctions du mariage dans les Pays-Bas bourguignons', *Mediaevistik. Internationale Zeitschrift für Interdisziplinäre Mittelalterforschung*, 7 (1994), 11-69.
Charrageat M., *La délinquance matrimoniale. Couples en conflit et justice en Aragon (XVe-XVIe siècles)*, Paris, 2011.
Danneel M., *Weduwen en wezen in het laatmiddeleeuwse Gent*, Leiden, 1995.
Davis I., Müller M. & Rees Jones S. (eds.), *Love, marriage, and family ties in the later Middle Ages*, Turnhout, 2003.
Decaluwé M., 'Recht kennen om het te omzeilen: Gerechtelijke huwelijksstrategieën in de Zuidelijke Nederlanden in de vijftiende eeuw', *Pro memorie*, 8 (2006), 72-81.
Delameillieure C., *Abduction, marriage, and consent in the late medieval Low Countries*, Amsterdam, 2024.
Delameillieure C., 'Dat zij "haers dancks ende moetswillen gegaen es". De schaking als huwelijksstrategie in vijftiende-eeuws Leuven', *Tijdschrift voor sociale en economische geschiedenis*, 13 (2016), 77-100.
Delameillieure C., 'Partly with and partly against her will. Female consent, elopement, and abduction in late medieval Brabant', *Journal of family history*, 42 (2017), 351-68.
Delameillieure C. & Haemers J., 'Recalcitrant brides and grooms. Jurisdiction, marriage, and conflict with parents in late medieval Ghent', in J. Armstrong & E. Frankot (eds.), *Cultures of law in urban Northern Europe. Scotland and its neighbours, c. 1350-c. 1650*, Abingdon, 2020, 154-70.
De Meyer B. & Van den Elzen E., 'Het huwelijk van burgers in de late middeleeuwen', *Tijdschrift voor sociale geschiedenis*, 14 (1988), 1-28.
De Meyer B., *Min en onmin. Mannen en vrouwen over hun samenleven aan het einde van de vijftiende eeuw*, Hilversum, 1989.
Demonty P., 'Documents concernant le mariage et la famille à Liège (15e s.)', *Bulletin de la commission royale d'histoire*, 152 (1986), 115-46.
Duby G., *Love and marriage in the Middle Ages*. Translated by J. Dunnett. Chicago, 1994.
Dumolyn J., 'Patriarchaal patrimonialisme. De vrouw als object in sociale transacties in het laatmiddeleeuwse Vlaanderen: Familiale strategieën en genderposities', in M. Demoor, K. Heene & G. Reymenants (eds.), *Verslagen van het centrum voor genderstudies – nr. 12*, Ghent, 2003, 1-28.
Dunn C., *Stolen women in medieval England: Rape, abduction and adultery 1100-1500*, Cambridge, 2013.
Falzone E., 'Aspects judiciaires de la séparation de corps dans la pratique des officialités de Cambrai et de Bruxelles: La liquidation du régime matrimonial par acte de juridiction gracieuse (XVe-XVIe siècles)', in V. Beaulande-Barraud & M. Charageat (eds.), *Les officialités dans l'Europe médiévale et moderne. Des tribunaux pour une société chrétienne*, Turnhout, 2014, 281-98.
Godding P., 'Le droit des gens mariés à Nivelles (14e-15e siècles)', *Revue d'histoire du droit*, 40 (1972), 73-117.
Greilsammer M., *L'envers du tableau: Mariage et maternité en Flandre médiévale*, Paris, 1990.
Greilsammer M., 'Rapts de séduction et rapts violents en Flandre et en Brabant à la fin du Moyen Âge', *Revue d'histoire du droit*, 49 (1988), 49-84.
Howell M., 'Marriage in medieval Latin Christendom', in C. Lansing & E. English (eds.), *A companion to the medieval world*, Malden, 2009, 130-60.
Joye S., *La femme ravie. Le mariage par le rapt au haut Moyen Age*, Turnhout, 2012.
Kane B., 'Men and women in love: Courtship, marriage and gender in late medieval England', in A. Brooks (ed.), *The Routledge companion to romantic love*, New York, 2022, 36-47.

Karras R., *Sexuality in medieval Europa: Doing unto others*, New York, 2005.
Karras R., *Unmarriages: Women, men, and sexual unions in the Middle Ages*, Philadelphia, 2012.
Mak J., *De gedichten van Anthonis De Roovere naar alle tot dusver bekende handschriften en oude drukken*, Zwolle, 1955.
Margot T., *Siet hier den man! Intermenselijke relaties in Boendales Der leken spieghel*, unpublished master's thesis, KU Leuven, 2015.
Naessens M., 'Sexuality in court: Emotional perpetrators and victims versus a rational judicial system?', in E. Lecuppre-Desjardin & A.L. Van Bruaene (eds.), *Emotions in the heart of the city (14th-16th centuries)*, Turnhout, 2005, 119-56.
Pleij H., *'t Is al vrouwenwerk. Refreinen van Anna Bijns*, Amsterdam, 1994.
Prevenier W., 'Huwelijk en cliëntele als sociale vangnetten: Leuven in de vijftiende eeuw', in J. Coopmans & A. Veen (eds.), *Van blauwe stoep tot citadel: Varia historica brabantica nova Ludovico Pirenne dedicate*, Bois-le-Duc, 1988, 83-91.
Reynolds P., *How marriage became one of the sacraments: The sacramental theology of marriage from its medieval origins to the council of Trent*, Cambridge, 2016.
Santinelli E. (ed.), *Séparation, divorce, répudiation dans l'Occident médiéval*, Valenciennes, 2006.
Titone F., 'The right to consent and disciplined dissent: betrothals and marriages in the diocese of Catania in the later medieval period', in F. Titone (ed.), *Disciplined dissent. Strategies of non-confrontational protest in Europe from the twelfth to the early sixteenth century*, Rome, 2016, 139-68.
Van Boendale J., *Der leken spieghel*, J. Mak & H. Lambermont (eds.), Antwerp, 1998.
Vleeschouwers C. & Van Melkebeek M., *Liber sentenciarum van de officialiteit van Brussel (1448-1459)*, Brussels, 1983.
Vleeschouwers C. & Van Melkebeek M., *Registres de sentences de l'officialité de Cambrai (1438-1453)*, Brussels, 1998.
Vleeschouwers C. & Van Melkebeek M., 'Classical canon law on marriage: The making and breaking of households', in M. Carlier & T. Soens (eds.), *The household in late medieval cities: Italy and Northwestern Europe compared*, Leuven, 2001, 15-24.
Vleeschouwers C. & Van Melkebeek M., 'Een middeleeuws middel tot "zelf-echtscheiding": Het clandestiene huwelijk in de Zuidelijke Nederlanden', *Handelingen van de Koninklijke Zuidnederlandse maatschappij voor taal- en letterkunde en geschiedenis*, 52 (1999), 319-26.
Vleeschouwers C. & Van Melkebeek M., 'Mortificata est: Het onterven of doodmaken van het geschaakte meisje in het laatmiddeleeuwse Gent', *Bulletin de la commission royale pour la publication des anciennes lois et ordonnances de Belgique*, 51-52 (2011), 357-435.

3. Industrious women

Bardyn A., 'Vermogende vrouwen. Het vastgoedbezit van vrouwen in laatmiddeleeuws Brussel op basis van de cijnsregisters (1356-1460)', *Stadsgeschiedenis*, 9 (2014), 1-24.
Bardyn A., 'The 'egalitarian trend' in practice: Female participation in capital markets in late medieval Leuven', in A. Bellavitis & B. Zucha Micheletto (eds.), *Gender, law, and economic well-being in Europe from the fifteenth to the nineteenth century. North versus South?*, London, 2018, 167-82.
Bardyn A., *Women's fortunes. Female agency, property and investment in late medieval Brabant*, unpublished PhD thesis, KU Leuven, 2018.
Bardyn A., 'The gender distribution of immovable property ownership in late medieval Brussels (1356-1460)', *Continuity and change*, 33 (2018), 29-57.

Beattie C. & Stevens M. (eds.), *Married women and the law in premodern Northwest Europe*, Woodbridge, 2013.
Cappelle K., '"In de macht, plicht en momboorije van heuren man." De rechtspositie van de getrouwde vrouw in Antwerpen en Leuven (16de eeuw)', *Pro memorie*, 18 (2016), 48-68.
Casier C., *Coutumes du pays et duché de Brabant. Quartiers de Louvain et de Tirlemont*, Brussels, 1874.
De Cuyper A., *Coutumes du pays et duché de Brabant. Quartier de Bruxelles*, Brussels, 1869.
De Ruysscher D., *Handel en recht in de Antwerpse rechtbank (1585-1713)*, Unpublished PhD thesis, KU Leuven, 2009.
De Ruysscher D., 'The capacity of married women to engage in contracts. Emancipation through ius commune in the Southern Low Countries (12th-18th centuries)', in G. Jacosen (ed.) *East meets West: A gendered view of legal tradition*, Kiel, 2014, 185-95.
Dulac L., 'Le Livre des trois Vertus. Traité en prose écrit par Christine de Pizan en 1405', in D. Régnier-Bohler (ed.), *Voix de femmes au Moyen Âge. Savoir, mystique, poésie, amour, sorcellerie, XIIe-XVe siècle*, Paris, 2006, 543-698.
Guicciardini L., *Beschrijvinghe van alle de Nederlanden*, P. Montanus (ed.), Haarlem, 1979 (facsimile van uitgave 1612).
Hanus J., *Tussen stad en eigen gewin. Stadsfinanciën, renteniers en kredietmarkten in 's-Hertogenbosch (begin zestiende eeuw)*, Amsterdam, 2007.
Howell M., 'The gender of Europe's commercial economy, 1200-1700', *Gender & history*, 20 (2008), 519-38.
Howell M., *Commerce before capitalism in Europe, 1300-1600*, Cambridge, 2010.
Hutton S., *Women and economic activities in late medieval Ghent*, New York, 2011.
Jansen H., *Landbouwpacht in Brabant in de 14e en 15e eeuw*, Assen, 1955.
Meijers E., *Het West-Brabantsche erfrecht*, Haarlem, 1929.
Reyerson K., *Women's networks in Medieval France. Gender and community in Montpellier, 1300-1350*, Basingstoke, 2016.
Slootmans C., *Paas- en koudemarkten te Bergen-op-Zoom, 1365-1565*, Tilburg, 1985, 3 vol.
Stabel P., 'Women at the market: Gender and retail in the towns of medieval Flanders', in W. Blockmans, T. de Hemptinne & M. Boone (eds.), *Secretum scriptorum. Liber alumnorum Walter Prevenier*, Leuven, 1999, 259-76.
Pleij H., 'Taakverdeling in het huwelijk. Over literatuur en sociale werkelijkheid in de late middeleeuwen', *Literatuur. Tijdschrift over Nederlandse letterkunde*, 3 (1986), 66-76.
Van Aert L., 'The legal possibilities of Antwerp widows in the late sixteenth century', *The history of the family*, 12 (2007), 282-95.
Van Uytven R., *Stadsfinanciën en stadsekonomie te Leuven van de XIIe tot het einde der XVIe eeuw*, Brussels, 1961.
Vázquez A., 'Los sucesos de Flandes y Francia del tiempo de Alejandro Farnese', in M. Gachard (ed.), *Les bibliothèques de Madrid et de l'Escurial*, Brussels, 1875, 455-79.
Vervaet L., 'Women and leasehold in rural Flanders, c. 1290 to c. 1570', *Rural History*, 30 (2019), 1-15.

4. Pious women

De Hemptinne T., 'Reading, writing, and devotional practices: Lay and religious women and the written word in the Low Countries (1350-1550)', in T. de Hemptinne & M.E. Gongora (eds.), *The voice of silence. Women's literacy in a men's Church*, Turnhout, 2004, 111-26.

De Ridder F., 'De oorsprong van het Mechelse begijnhof en van de parochies in de volkswijk van de stad tijdens de 13de-15de eeuw', *Handelingen van de Koninklijke maatschappij voor oudheidkunde, letteren en kunsten van Mechelen*, 35 (1930) 56-84; 'De oudste statuten van het Mechelse begijnhof', *HKMOLK*, 39 (1934), 18-29; 'Mechelen's groot begijnhof binnen de stad (het ontstaan)', *HKMOLK*, 40 (1935), 15-43.

De Moor T., 'Single, safe, and sorry? Explaining the early modern beguine movement in the Low Countries', *Journal of family history*, 39 (2014), 3-21.

Gigliotti O., *Over de begijnen die niet van de hemelse dauw leefden. Vermogende begijnen in laatmiddeleeuws Leuven*, unpublished master's thesis, KU Leuven, 2017.

Goetschalckx P., 'Het begijnhof van Lier', *Bijdragen tot de geschiedenis bijzonderlijk van het aloude hertogdom Brabant*, 3 (1904), 36-51.

Grijp L. & Willaert F., 'Brabantse begijnen tussen Atrechtse trouvères en een Maaslandse minnezanger', in L. Grijp (ed.), *Een muziekgeschiedenis der Nederlanden*, Amsterdam, 2001, 23-30.

Gysseling M., 'De herkomst van het woord begijn', *Heemkundig nieuws*, 13 (1985), 9-12.

Helvétius A.M., 'Les béguines. Des femmes dans la ville aux XIIIe et XIVe siècles', in E. Gubin & J.P. Nandrin (eds.), *La ville et les femmes en Belgique: Histoire et sociologie*, Brussels, 1993, 17-40.

Hoebanx J., *L'abbaye de Nivelles des origines au XIVe siècle*, Brussels, 1952.

Koch E., *De kloosterpoort als sluitpost? Adellijke vrouwen langs Maas en Rijn tussen huwelijk en convent, 1200-1600*, Leeuwarden, 1994.

Lawrence C., *Kloosterleven in de middeleeuwen in West-Europa en de Lage Landen*, Amsterdam, 2004.

Majérus P., *Ces femmes qu'ont dit béguines. Guide des béguinages de Belgique. Bibliographie et sources d'archives*, Brussels, 1997, 2 vols.

Mannaerts P. (ed.), *Beghinae in cantu instructae. Musical patrimony from Flemish beguinages (Middle Ages – Late 18th century)*, Turnhout, 2009.

McDonnell E., *The beguines and beghards in medieval culture, with special emphasis on the Belgian scene*, New Brunswick, 1954.

Meijns B. & Carnier M. (eds.), *De canonicis qui seculares dicuntur: Treize siècles de chapitres séculiers dans les anciens Pays-Bas*, Turnhout, 2018.

Moulaert P., 'Quatre testaments de béguines du XIVe et du XVe siècle', *Analectes pour servir à l'histoire ecclésiastique de Belgique*, 13 (1876), 339-48.

Overlaet K., 'Replacing the family? Beguinages in early modern Western European cities: An analysis of the family networks of beguines living in Mechelen (1532-91)', *Continuity and change*, 29 (2014), 325-47.

Overlaet K., 'To be or not to be a beguine in an early modern town: Piety or pragmatism? The great beguinage of St Catherine in sixteenth-century Mechelen', in J. De Groot, I. Devos & A. Schmidt (eds.), *Single life and the city, 1200-1900*, Leuven, 2015, 148-68.

Peeters Y., *De tafel van de Heilige geest van het Leuvens Groot-Begijnhof (1395-1446)*, unpublished master's thesis, KU Leuven, 1969.

Pirenne H., 'Note sur un cartulaire de Bruxelles conservé à la bibliothèque de Berne', *Bulletin de la commission royale d'histoire*, 59 (1894), 43-67.

Pleij H., *Meer zuurs dan zoets: Refreinen en rondelen van Anna Bijns*, Amsterdam, 2013.

Simons W., '"Staining the speech of things divine": The uses of literacy in medieval beguine communities', in T. de Hemptinne & M.E. Gongora (eds.), *The voice of silence. Women's literacy in a men's Church*, Turnhout, 2004, 85-110.

Simons W., 'Geletterdheid en boekengebruik bij de vroegste begijnen', *Handelingen der Koninklijke Zuidnederlandse maatschappij voor taal- en letterkunde en geschiedenis*, 53 (1999), 167-80.

Simons W., *Cities of ladies: Beguine communities in the medieval Low Countries, 1200-1565*, Philadelphia, 2001.

Simons W., 'Beginnings: Naming beguines in the Southern Low Countries, 1200-50', in L. Böhringer, H. Van Engen & J.K. Deane (eds.), *Labels and libels. Naming beguines in Northern medieval Europe*, Turnhout, 2014, 9-52.

Tits-Dieuaide M., 'L'assistance aux pauvres à Louvain au XVe siècle', in G. Despy et al. (eds.), *Hommage au Professeur Paul Bonenfant (1899-1965), études d'histoire médiévale dédiées à sa mémoire par les anciens élèves de son séminaire à l'université libre de Bruxelles*, Wetteren, 1965, 421-39.

Trio P., 'Moordende concurrentie op de memoriemarkt. Een eerste verkenning van het fenomeen jaargetijde in de Lage Landen in de late middeleeuwen (ca. 1250 tot 1550)', in J. Deploige, B. Meijns & R. Nip (eds.), *Herinnering in geschrift en praktijk in religieuze gemeenschappen uit de Lage landen, 1000-1500*, Brussels, 2009, 141-56.

Uytterhoeven R., *The groot begijnhof of Leuven*, Leuven, 2000.

Vanderputten S., *Dark Age nunneries. The ambiguous identity of female monasticism, 800-1050*, Ithaca, 2018.

Van Gelder H.A., *Correspondance française de Marguerite d'Autriche*, Utrecht, 1925-1942.

Van Nederveen Meerkerk E. & Vermeesch G., 'Reforming outdoor relief. Changes in urban provisions for the poor in the Northern and Southern Low Countries (c. 1500-1800)', in M. Van der Heijden et al. (eds.), *Serving the urban community: The rise of public facilities in the Low Countries*, Amsterdam, 2009, 135-54.

Verellen J., 'De oudste, breed-uitgewerkte begijnenregel. De statuten van het begijnhof van Herentals, 1461-1489', *Bijdragen tot de geschiedenis*, 32 (1949), 198-222.

5. Working women

Adam R., 'Living and printing in Antwerp in the late fifteenth and early sixteenth centuries. A social enquiry', in E. Kavaler & A.-L. Van Bruaene (eds.), *Netherlandish culture of the sixteenth century. Urban perspectives*, Turnhout, 2017, 83-97.

Aerts E., *Het bier van Lier: De economische ontwikkeling van de bierindustrie in een middelgrote Brabantse stad (eind 14de – begin 19de eeuw)*, Brussels, 1996.

Bailey M., Colwell T. & Hotchin J. (eds.), *Women and work in premodern Europe. Experiences, relationships and cultural representation, c. 1100-1800*, London, 2018.

Barron C., 'The "golden age" of women in medieval London', *Reading medieval studies*, 15 (1989), 35-58.

Beattie C., 'The problem of women's work identities in post black death England', in J. Bothwell, J. Goldberg & M. Ormrod (eds.), *The problem of labour in fourteenth-century England*, York, 2000, 1-19.

Bennett J., 'Medieval women, modern women: Across the great divide', in D. Aers (ed.), *Culture and history 1350-1600: Essays on English communities, identities and writing*, Detroit, 1992, 147-75.

Billen C., 'Le marché urbain un espace de liberté pour les femmes rurales?', in E. Gubin & J.P. Nandrin (eds.), *La ville et les femmes en Belgique: Histoire et sociologie*, Brussels, 1993, 41-56.

Bisschops L., 'Het 2de Oudt Register, in 't perkament gebonden, 1438-1459', *Antwerpsch Archievenblad*, (1): 29 (1892), 226-472; (2): 30 (1893), 1-471.

Born T., *De meesters in wording. Een studie omtrent de toetredingen binnen het Mechelse ambachtswezen in de vijftiende en zestiende eeuw*, unpublished master's thesis, KU Leuven, 2017.

Broomhall S., 'Women, work, and power in the female guilds of Rouen', in M. Cassidy-Welch & P. Sherlock (eds.), *Practices of gender in late medieval and early modern Europe*, Turnhout, 2008, 199-213.

Coomans J., 'Policing female food vendors in the late medieval Netherlands', *Yearbook of women's history*, 36 (2017), 97-113.
Crombie L., *Archery and crossbow guilds in medieval Flanders, 1300-1500*, Woodbridge, 2016.
Crowston C., 'Women, gender, and guilds in early modern Europe: An overview of recent research', *International review of social history*, 53 (2008), 19-44.
Danneel M., 'Weduwen en sociale mobiliteit. Het juridisch statuut van de weduwen in Vlaanderen in de 14e-15e eeuw, in het bijzonder te Brugge', in J. De Belder, W. Prevenier & C. Vandenbroeke (eds.), *Sociale mobiliteit en sociale structuren in Vlaanderen en Brabant van de late middeleeuwen tot de 20e eeuw*, Ghent, 1983, 9-21.
De Groot J., 'Zorgen voor later? De betekenis van de dienstperiode voor jonge vrouwen in het laatmiddeleeuwse Gent herbekeken', *Stadsgeschiedenis*, 6 (2011), 1-15.
De Munck B., *Guilds, labour and the urban body politic. Fabricating community in the southern Netherlands, 1300-1800*, London, 2018.
De Munck B. & Haemers J., 'Het politiek zelfbewustzijn van ambachten in Brabant: Een lange-termijnperspectief (13de-18de eeuw)', *Noordbrabants historisch jaarboek*, 35 (2018), 23-49.
De Moor T. & Van Zanden J.L., *Vrouwen en de geboorte van het kapitalisme in West-Europa*, Amsterdam, 2006.
Delva A., *Vrouwengeneeskunde in Vlaanderen tijdens de late middeleeuwen, met uitgave van het Brugse Liber Trotula*, Bruges, 1983.
Des Marez G., *L'organisation du travail à Bruxelles au XVe siècle*, Brussels, 1904.
Ewing D., 'Marketing art in Antwerp, 1460-1560: Our Lady's Pand', *The art bulletin*, 72 (1990), 558-84.
Farmer S., *The silk industries of medieval Paris: Artisanal migration, technological innovation, and gendered experience*, Philadelphia, 2016.
Favresse F., 'Règlements inédits sur la vente des laines et des draps et sur la draperie bruxelloise (1363-1394): Édition critique', *Bulletin de la commission royale d'histoire*, 111 (1946), 167-234.
Génard P., 'Het "Register vanden dachvaerden"', *Antwerpsch Archievenblad*, (1): 19 (1882), 1-472; (2): 20 (1883), 1-472; (3): 21 (1884), 1-247.
Gil M., 'Les femmes dans les métiers d'art des Pays-Bas bourguignons au XVe siècle', *Clio. Femmes, genre, histoire*, 34 (2011), 231-54.
Goldberg J., *Women, work, and life cycle in a medieval economy. Women in York and Yorkshire c. 1300-1520*, Oxford, 1992.
Haemers J., 'Ambachtslieden in de middeleeuwse stad', in V. Lambert & P. Stabel (eds.), *Gouden tijden. Rijkdom en status in de middeleeuwen*, Tielt, 2016, 209-39.
Haemers J., 'Révolte et requête. Les gens de métiers et les conflits sociaux dans les villes de Flandre (XIIIe-XVe siècle)', *Revue historique*, 677 (2016), 27-56.
Hanawalt B., *The wealth of wives. Women, law, and economy in late medieval London*, Oxford, 2007.
Herlihy D., *Opera Muliebria. Women and work in medieval Europe*, New York, 1990.
Howell M., 'Gender in the transition to merchant capitalism', in J. Bennett & R. Karras (eds.), *The Oxford handbook of women and gender in medieval Europe*, Oxford, 2013, 561-76.
Hutton S., 'Women, men, and markets: The gendering of market space in late medieval Ghent', in A. Classen (ed.), *Urban space in the Middle Ages and Early Modern Age*, Berlin, 2009, 409-32.
Hutton S., 'Organizing specialized production: Gender in the medieval Flemish wool cloth industry (c. 1250-1384)', *Urban history*, 45 (2018), 382-403.
Kittel E. & Queller K., '"Whether man or woman ...": Gender inclusivity in the town ordinances of medieval Douai', *Journal of medieval and early modern studies*, 30 (2000), 63-100.
Kloek E., 'Vrouwenarbeid aan banden gelegd? De arbeidsdeling naar sekse volgens de keurboeken van de oude draperie, ca. 1380-1580', *Tijdschrift voor sociale geschiedenis*, 13 (1987), 373-402.

Kowaleski M. & Bennett J., 'Crafts, gilds, and women in the Middle Ages: Fifty years after Marian K. Dale', *Signs: Journal of women in culture and society*, 14 (1989), 474-501.

Lambert B., 'Merchants on the margins: Fifteenth-century Bruges and the informal market', *Journal of medieval history*, 42 (2016), 226-53.

Lampo J., *Het Vleeshuis. Slagerspaleis van Antwerpen*, Leuven, 2004.

Lis C. & Soly H., *Werken volgens de regels: Ambachten in Brabant en Vlaanderen 1500-1800*, Brussels, 1994.

Lis C. & Soly H., *Worthy efforts. Attitudes to work and workers in pre-industrial Europe*, Leiden, 2012.

Maseure H., '"Eerlycke huijsarmen" of "ledichgangers"? Armenzorg en gemeenschapsvorming in Brussel, 1300-1640', *Stadsgeschiedenis*, 7 (2012), 1-21.

McIntosh M., *Working women in English society, 1300-1650*, Cambridge, 2005.

Meulemans A., 'Leuvense ambachten, de beenhouwers', *Eigen schoon en de Brabander*, 42 (1959), 92-107, 212-30 and 294-303.

Michaud F., *Earning dignity. Labour conditions and relations during the century of the black death in Marseille*, Turnhout, 2016.

Peeters J.P., *Bloei en verval van de middeleeuwse stadsvrijheid Vilvoorde*, Tielt, 1975.

Prak M. et al., *Craft guilds in the early modern Low Countries. Work, power, and representation*, Aldershot, 2006.

Quast J., 'Vrouwen in gilden in Den Bosch, Utrecht en Leiden, van de 14de tot en met de 16de eeuw', in W. Fritschy (ed.), *Fragmenten vrouwengeschiedenis. I. Chronologisch*, The Hague, 1980, 26-37.

Reyerson K., *Women's networks in medieval France. Gender and community in Montpellier, 1300-1350*, New York, 2016.

Rivière F., 'Women in craft organisations in Rouen (14th-15th century)', in E. Jullien & M. Pauly (eds.), *Guilds and craftsmen in the medieval and early modern periods*, Stuttgart, 2016, 93-124.

Scholliers P., *Loonarbeid en honger. De levensstandaard in de XVe en XVIe eeuw te Antwerpen*, Antwerp, 1960.

Stabel P., 'Guilds in late medieval Flanders: Myths and realities of guild life in an export-oriented environment', *Journal of medieval history*, 30 (2004), 187-212.

Stabel P., 'Working alone? Single women in the urban economy of late medieval Flanders (thirteenth-early fifteenth centuries)', in J. de Groot, I. Devos & A. Schmidt (eds.), *Single life and the city, 1200-1900*, Leuven, 2015, 27-49.

Van Bruaene A.L., 'Brotherhood and sisterhood in the chambers of rhetoric in the Southern Low Countries', *The sixteenth century journal*, 36 (2005), 11-35.

Van den Branden J., 'Clementynboeck (1288-1414)', *Antwerpsch Archievenblad*, 25 (1888), 101-465.

Van den Branden J., 'Oudt Register, mette Berderen, 1336-1439', *Antwerpsch Archievenblad*, (1): 26 (1889), 414-472; (2): 27 (1890), 1-472; (3): 28 (1891), 1-472; (4): 29 (1892), 1-261.

Van den Heuvel D., 'Partners in marriage and business? Guilds and the family economy in urban food markets in the Dutch Republic', *Continuity and change*, 23 (2008), 217-36.

Van den Heuvel N., *De ambachtsgilden van 's-Hertogenbosch vóór 1629. Rechtsbronnen van het bedrijfsleven en het gildewezen*, Utrecht, 1946.

Van der Stighelen K., *Vrouwenstreken: Vrouwelijke schilders in de Nederlanden (1550-nu)*, Amsterdam, 2010.

Van der Wee H. (ed.), *The rise and decline of urban industries in Italy and in the Low Countries (late Middle Ages – early modern times)*, Leuven, 1988.

Vandeweerdt N., 'Van den vleeschouweren oft pensvrouwen. De economische mogelijkheden voor vrouwen in het Leuvense vleeshouwersambacht in de vijftiende en zestiende eeuw', *Tijdschrift voor sociale en economische geschiedenis*, 15 (2018), 5-30.

Vandeweerdt N., 'Women, town councils, and the organization of work in Bilbao and Antwerp: A north-south comparison (1400-1560), *Continuity and Change*, 36 (2021), 61-87.
Vannérus J., 'De keure der wollewevers van Diest van 1333', *Verslagen en mededeelingen der Koninklijke Vlaamsche academie voor taal- en letterkunde*, 1906, 5-30.
Van Uytven R., *Leuven, de beste stad van Brabant. I. De geschiedenis van het stadsgewest Leuven tot omstreeks 1600*, Leuven, 1980.
Vázquez A., 'Los sucesos de Flandes y Francia del tiempo de Alejandro Farnese', in M. Gachard (ed.), *Les bibliothèques de Madrid et de l'Escurial*, Brussels, 1875, 455-79.
Verhavert J., *Het ambachtswezen te Leuven*, Leuven, 1940.
Vermeylen F., *Painting for the market. Commercialization of art in Antwerp's Golden Age*, Turnhout, 2003.
Wyffels C., *De oorsprong der ambachten in Vlaanderen en Brabant*, Brussels, 1951.

6. 'Bad women'

Aernouts B., *Dwijf es van naturen loes. Vrouwen en criminaliteit in laatmiddeleeuws Mechelen en Lier*, unpublished master's thesis, KU Leuven, 2015.
Bertrijn G., *Chronijck der stadt Antwerpen*, G. van Havre (ed.), Antwerp, 1879.
Bezemer W., *Oude rechtsbronnen der stad Breda*, The Hague, 1892.
Bourguignon M.A. & Dauven B., 'Une justice au féminin. Femmes victimes et coupables dans les Pays-Bas bourguignons au XVe siècle', *Clio. Histoire, femmes et sociétés*, 35 (2012), 215-38.
Bousmar E., 'Neither equality nor radical oppression: The elasticity of women's roles in the late medieval Low Countries', in E. Kittell & M. Suydam (eds.), *The texture of society. Medieval women in the Southern Low Countries*, New York, 2004, 109-27.
Ceunen M., *Middeleeuwse strafbedevaarten vanuit Leuven*, Leuven, 2013.
Cohn S., 'Women in revolt in medieval and early modern Europe', in J. Firnhaber-Baker & D. Schoenaers (eds.), *The routledge history handbook of medieval revolt*, London & New York, 2017, 208-19.
Cohn S., *Women in the streets. Essays on sex and power in Renaissance Italy*, Baltimore, 1996.
Crouzet-Pavan E. & Maire Vigueur J.-C., *Décapitées. Trois femmes de l'Italie de la Renaissance*, Paris, 2018.
Dean T., *Misdaad in de middeleeuwen*, Amsterdam, 2004.
Degroote G. (ed.), *Jan van den Dale. Gekende werken met inleiding, bronnenstudie, aanteekeningen en glossarium*, Antwerp, 1944.
De Wilder L., *Boete of zoen. Een onderzoek naar strafbedevaarten opgelegd vanuit de Leuvense schepenbank vanuit een analyse van het Dbedevaertboeck, 1398-1422*, unpublished master's thesis, KU Leuven, 2014.
Dits die Excellente Chronijcke van Vlaenderen, W. Vorsterman (ed.), Antwerp, 1531.
Dekker R., 'Women in Revolt: Popular protest and its social basis in Holland in the seventeenth and eighteenth centuries', *Theory and society*, 16 (1987), 337-62.
Demets L., 'Spies, instigators and troublemakers. Gendered perceptions on rebellious women in late medieval Flemish chronicles', *Journal of Women's History*, 33 (2021), 12-34.
De Win P., *De schandstraffen in het wereldlijk strafrecht in de Zuidelijke Nederlanden van de Middeleeuwen tot de Franse Tijd, bestudeerd in Europees perspectief*, Brussels, 1991.
Dumolyn J. & Haemers J., '"A bad chicken was brooding": Subversive speech in late medieval Flanders', *Past and present*, 214 (2012), 45-86.

Dumolyn J. & Haemers J., 'We will ask for a new Artevelde. Names, sites, and the social memory of revolt in the later medieval Low Countries', in A. Merle & S. Jettot (eds.), *La mémoire des révoltes en Europe à l'époque moderne*, Paris, 2018, 231-49.

Farge A., 'Évidentes émeutières', in N. Zemon Davis & A. Farge (eds.), *Histoire des femmes en Occident. III. XVIe-XVIIIe siècles*, Paris, 1991, 481-97.

Franssen P., 'Dat Bedroch der Vrouwen, een onderzoek naar de functie van een 16e eeuwse verhalenbundel', *Spektator. Tijdschrift voor Neerlandistiek*, 12 (1982-1983), 270-89 and 13 (1983-1984), 167-81.

Génard P., 'Het "Register vanden dachvaerden"', *Antwerpsch Archievenblad*, (1): 19 (1882), 1-472; (2): 20 (1883), 1-472; (3): 21 (1884), 1-247.

Glaudemans C., *Om die wrake wille. Eigenrichting, veten en verzoening in laat-middeleeuws Holland en Zeeland*, Hilversum, 2004.

Haemers J., 'Commotie in Mechelen. Over sociale conflicten en politiek protest van mannen én vrouwen in de laatmiddeleeuwse stad', *Handelingen van de Koninklijke kring voor oudheidkunde, letteren en kunst van Mechelen*, 120 (2016), 81-96.

Haemers J., 'Women and war. Female spies and messengers in the late medieval Low Countries', *Journal of Women's History*, 36 (2024), 10-29.

Haemers J. & Delameillieure C., 'Women and contentious speech in fifteenth-century Brabant', *Continuity and change*, 32 (2017), 323-47.

Haemers J. & Vrancken V., 'Libels in the city. Bill casting in fifteenth-century Flanders and Brabant', *The medieval Low Countries*, 4 (2017), 165-87.

Howell M., 'Citizenship and gender. Women's political status in northern medieval cities', in M. Erler & M. Kowaleski (eds.), *Women and power in the Middle Ages*, London, 1988, 37-60.

Joossen R., 'Recueil de documents relatifs à l'histoire de l'industrie drapière à Malines (des origines à 1384)', *Bulletin de la commission royale d'histoire*, 101 (1935), 365-572.

Kittell E., 'Flemish female misdeeds. A speculation', in K. Glente & L. Winther-Jensen (eds.), *Female power in the Middle Ages*, Copenhagen, 1989, 105-28.

Kittell E., 'Reconciliation or punishment. Women, community, and malefaction in the medieval county of Flanders', in E. Kittell & M. Suydam (eds.), *The texture of society. Medieval women in the southern Low Countries*, New York, 2004, 3-30.

Lintermans R., *Ter beternisse te doen enen wech. Een onderzoek naar strafbedevaarten opgelegd door de schepenbank van Diest in de periode 1426-1503*, unpublished master's thesis, KU Leuven, 2015.

Maes L., *Vijf eeuwen stedelijk strafrecht: Bijdrage tot de rechts- en cultuurgeschiedenis der Nederlanden*, Antwerp, 1947.

Mémoires de Pontus Payen, avec notices et annotations, A. Henne (ed.), Brussels, 1861.

Peeters R., 'De keuren van Turnhout (1550)', *Taxandria*, 29 (1957), 61-122.

Pleij H., *Anna Bijns, van Antwerpen*, Amsterdam, 2011.

Plovie F. & Haemers J., "Ghij en waert noeyt goed voor de stede van Ghent!' Verbaal geweld, scheldwoorden en politiek verzet in Gent (1477-1506)', *Revue belge de philologie et d'histoire*, 98 (2020), 23-48.

Regina C., *La violence des femmes: Histoire d'un tabou social*, Paris, 2011.

Rousseaux X., 'Religion, économie et société: Le pèlerinage judiciaire dans les Pays-Bas (Nivelles, du XVe au XVIIe s.)', in M.A. Bourguignon, B. Dauven & X. Rousseaux (eds.), *Amender, sanctionner et punir. Histoire de la peine du Moyen Age au XXe siècle*, Louvain-la-Neuve, 2012, 61-85.

Rummel E., *Erasmus on women*, Toronto, 1996.

Schmidt A., *Prosecuting women. A comparative perspective on crime and gender before the Dutch criminal courts, c. 1600-1800*, Leiden, 2020.

Stockmans J., *Het correctieboek der stad Lier, 1401-1484*, Antwerp, 1906.

Van Bael L., *Het bestraffen van kwetsend gedrag door de schepenbank van laatmiddeleeuws Leuven. Onderzoek naar de vijftiende-eeuwse stadsordonnanties*, unpublished master's thesis, KU Leuven, 2014.

Van Bael T., *Op peisbreke ende zoenbreke: Een comparatief onderzoek naar Antwerpse en Leuvense vredes en verzoeningen aan het einde van de vijftiende eeuw*, unpublished master's thesis, KU Leuven, 2016.

Van den Branden J., 'Clementynboeck (1288-1414)', *Antwerpsch Archievenblad*, 25 (1888), 101-465.

Van den Branden J., 'Oudt Register, mette Berderen, 1336-1439', *Antwerpsch Archievenblad*, (1): 26 (1889), 414-472; (2): 27 (1890), 1-472; (3): 28 (1891), 1-472; (4): 29 (1892), 1-261.

Van der Heijden M., *Women and crime in early modern Holland*, Leiden, 2016.

Van der Heijden M. & Schmidt A., 'Theorizing crime and gender in long-term perspective', in E. Dermineur, A. Sjögren & V. Langum (eds.), *Revisiting gender in European history, 1400-1800*, London, 2018, 52-77.

Van Dijck M., 'De stad als onafhankelijke variabele en centrum van moderniteit. Langetermijntrends in stedelijke en rurale criminaliteitspatronen in de Nederlanden', *Stadsgeschiedenis*, 1 (2006), 7-26.

Vangompel M., *Dat sy onvrede veroersaekte tussen man en wyf. Overspel in vijftiende-eeuws Antwerpen*, unpublished master's thesis, KU Leuven, 2017.

Vanhemelryck F., *De criminaliteit in de ammanie van Brussel van de late middeleeuwen tot het einde van het Ancien Régime (1404-1789)*, Brussels, 1981.

Vanhemelryck F., *Het gevecht met de duivel. Heksen in Vlaanderen*, Leuven, 1999.

Van Herwaarden J., *Opgelegde bedevaarten. Een studie over de praktijk van het opleggen van bedevaarten (met name in de stedelijke rechtspraak) in de Nederlanden gedurende de late middeleeuwen (ca. 1300 – ca. 1550)*, Assen, 1978.

Van Rompaey J., 'Rechtsbronnen van de stad Bergen op Zoom', *Verslagen en Mededelingen der Vereniging tot uitgave der bronnen van het oude vaderlandsche recht*, 13 (1967-71), 195-318.

Veldhuizen M., *De ongetemde tong. Opvattingen over zondige, onvertogen en misdadige woorden in het Middelnederlands (1300 – 1550)*, Hilversum, 2014.

Weiler A., 'Desiderius Erasmus of Rotterdam on marriage and divorce', *Dutch Review of Church History*, 84 (2004), 149-97.

7. Eros and women

Beres M., '"Spontaneous" sexual consent: An analysis of sexual consent literature', *Feminism & psychology*, 17 (2007), 93-108.

Braekman W., *Middeleeuwse witte en zwarte magie in het Nederlandse taalgebied. Gecommentarieerd compendium van incantamenta tot einde 16de eeuw*, Ghent, 1997.

Brundage J., *Sex, law and marriage in the Middle Ages*, Aldershot, 1993.

Bullough V. & Brundage J. (eds.), *Handbook of medieval sexuality*, New York, 1996.

Buntinx J., 'Verkrachting en hulpgeroep in het Oud-Vlaamse recht', *Handelingen der Zuidnederlandse maatschappij voor taal- en letterkunde en geschiedenis*, 9 (1955), 15-21.

Bourguignon M.-A., 'Bans de police et comptes urbains à Mons: Regards croisés sur l'ordre public et la moralité', in D. Heirbaut, X. Rousseaux & A. Wijffels (eds.), *Histoire du droit et de la justice: Une nouvelle génération de recherches*, Louvain-la-Neuve, 2009, 257-74.

Coomans J. & Geltner G., 'On the street and in the bathhouse: Medieval galenism in action?', *Anuario de estudios medievales*, 43 (2013), 53-82.

Crahay L., *Coutumes de la ville de Maastricht*, Brussels, 1876.

Dekker R. & Van den Pol L., *Vrouwen in mannenkleren. De geschiedenis van een tegendraadse traditie. Europa, 1500-1800*, Amsterdam, 1989.

De Longé G. (ed.), *Coutumes de la ville d'Antwerp*, Brussels, 1870-1874, 4 vols.

Delport C., *Misdadigheid in Leuven (1461-1504). Een onderzoek gesteund op de rekeningen van de meier Lodewijck Pynnock*, unpublished master's thesis, KU Leuven, 1986.

Deligne C., *Bruxelles et sa rivière. Genèse d'un territoire urbain (12e-18e siècle)*, Turnhout, 2002.

Delmaire B., 'Les étuves du Nord de la France du XIVe siècle au début du XVIe siècle', *Bulletin de la commission historique du Nord*, 58 (2018-19), 11-27.

Den Hartog M., 'Women on top: Coital positions and gender hierarchies in renaissance Italy', *Renaissance Studies*, 35 (2021), 638-57.

Deschamps E., *Oeuvres complètes*, M. de Queux de Saint-Hilaire (ed.), Paris, 1878-1903, 6 vols.

Dronke P., *Women writers of the Middle Ages: A critical study of texts from Perpetua, 203, to Marguerite Porete, 1310*, Cambridge, 1984.

Dubuis R., *Les cent nouvelles Nouvelles*, Lyon, 1991.

Dunn C., *Stolen women in medieval England: Rape, abduction and adultery 1100-1500*, Cambridge, 2013.

Dupont G., *Maagdenverleidsters, hoeren en speculanten. Prostitutie in Brugge tijdens de Bourgondische periode (1385-1515)*, Bruges, 1996.

Dupont G., 'Middeleeuwse stoven aan Gentse wateren', in Vermeiren G., Bru M.A. & Ervynck A. (eds.), *De Krook. Een leerrijk boek*, Ghent, 2018, 134-57.

Dupont W., Hofman E. & Roelens J. (eds.), *Verzwegen verlangen. Een geschiedenis van homoseksualiteit in België*, Antwerp, 2017.

Evans R. (ed.), *A cultural history of sexuality in the Middle Ages*, Oxford, 2011.

Godding P., *Ordonnances de Philippe le Bon pour les duchés de Brabant et de Limbourg et les pays d'Outre-Meuse, 1430-1467*, Brussels, 2005.

Haemers J., 'Étuves, bordels et maisons de bains à Louvain au XVe siècle: Une édition des contrats de location des *stoven* trouvés dans les registres échevinaux de la ville', *Bulletin de la commission royale d'histoire*, 185 (2019), 75-120.

Haemers J., 'Women and stews. The social and material history of prostitution in the late medieval Southern Low Countries', *History Workshop Journal*, 92 (2021), 29-50.

Haemers J., 'Guilty pleasure (1200-1550)', in E. Hofman, M. Rodriguez Garcia & P. Vanhees (eds.), *The business of pleasure. A history of paid sex in the heart of Europe*, Leuven, 2024, 21-40.

Hardwick, J., *Sex in an old regime city. Young workers and intimacy in France, 1660-1789*, Oxford, 2020.

Harvey K., *The fires of lust. Sex in the Middle Ages*, London, 2021.

Irsigler F. & Lassotta A., *Bettler und Gaukler. Dirnen und Henkler. Randgruppen und Außenseiter in Köln, 1300-1600*, Cologne, 1984.

Karras R., 'The regulation of brothels in later medieval England', *Signs: Journal of Women in Culture and Society*, 14 (1989), 399-433.

Karras R., *Sexuality in medieval Europe: Doing unto others*, New York, 2005.

Koldeweij J., Geysen I. & Tahon E., *Liefde en devotie. Het Gruuthusehandschrift: Kunst en cultuur omstreeks 1400*, Bruges, 2013.

Kruiskamp C. (ed.), *De refreinenbundel van Jan van Doesborch*, Leiden, 1940.

Lambert B., 'Double disadvantage or golden age? Immigration, gender and economic opportunity in later medieval England', *Gender & History*, 31 (2019), 545-64.

Lansing C., 'Opportunities to charge rape in thirteenth-century Bologna', in L. Zanetti Domingues, L. Caravaggi & G. Paoletti (eds.), *Women and violence in the late medieval Mediterranean, ca. 1100-1500*, London, 2021, 83-100.

Maes L., *Vijf eeuwen stedelijk strafrecht: Bijdrage tot de rechts- en cultuurgeschiedenis der Nederlanden*, Antwerp, 1947.

Marchandisse A., 'La police du vice. Contrôle et répression de la prostitution dans la principauté de Liège à la fin du Moyen Age', *Bulletin de la commission royale pour la publication des anciennes lois et ordonnances de Belgique*, 43 (2002), 75-93.

McDougall S., 'Judging sexy women in late medieval France', *Postmedieval. A Journal of medieval cultural studies*, 13 (2022), 81-104.

Monballyu J. (ed.), *Filips Wielant. Verzameld werk. I. Corte instructie in materie criminele*, Brussels, 1995.

Naessens M., 'Wat bordeelmadammen ons kunnen leren over het métier. Enkele opmerkingen over de bronnen voor de studie van de laatmiddeleeuwse Gentse prostitutie', *Handelingen van de maatschappij voor geschiedenis en oudheidkunde te Gent*, 58 (2004), 147-62.

Pleij H., *Nederlandse literatuur van de late middeleeuwen*, Utrecht, 1990.

Pleij H., *Oefeningen in genot. Liefde en lust in de late middeleeuwen*, Amsterdam, 2020.

Prevenier W., 'Vorstelijke genade in de praktijk. Remissiebrief voor Matthieu Cricke en diens mede-acteurs voor vermeende vrouwenroof in oktober 1476', *Bulletin de la commission royale d'histoire*, 175 (2009), 225-58.

Roby A., *La prostitution au Moyen Âge. Le commerce charnel en Midi toulousain du XIIIe au XVIe siècle*, Villemur-sur-Tarn, 2021.

Rodriguez Garcia M., Heerma Van Voss L. & Van Nederveen Meerkerk E. (eds.), *Selling sex in the city: A global history of prostitution, 1600s-2000s*, Leiden, 2017.

Rossiaud J., *Amours vénales. La prostitution en Occident, XIIe-XVIe siècle*, Paris, 2010.

Schoorens L., *Ledige vrouwen en quade herberghe. Prostitutie in Antwerpen en Leuven in de vijftiende eeuw*, unpublished master's thesis, KU Leuven, 2018.

Schuster P., *Das Frauenhaus. Städtische Bordelle in Deutschland, 1350 bis 1600*, Paderborn, 1992.

Spindler E., 'Were medieval prostitutes marginals? Evidence from Sluis, 1387-1440', *Revue belge de philologie et d'histoire*, 87 (2009), 239-72.

Stallaert K., *Het keurboek der stad Diest*, Ghent, 1885.

Trexler R., 'La prostitution florentine au XVe siècle: Patronages et clientèles', *Annales ESC*, 36 (1981), 983-1015.

Van der Eerden-Vonk M., *Raadsverdragen van Maastricht, 1367-1428*, The Hague, 1992.

Van der Made R., 'La prostitution dans l'ancien droit belge', *Revue du droit pénal et de criminologie*, 29 (1948-49), 763-73.

Van der Tanerijen W., *Boec der loopender practijken der raidtcameren van Brabant*, E. Strubbe (ed.), Brussels, 1952.

Van Gerven J., 'Marginaliteit en sociale segregatie in de Brabantse steden tijdens de late middeleeuwen', *Bijdragen tot de geschiedenis*, 79 (1996), 3-25.

Vanhemelryck F., *Marginalen in de geschiedenis: Over beulen, joden, zigeuners en andere zondebokken*, Leuven, 2004.

Van Uytven R., 'De ledige vrouwen van de middeleeuwen', in L. De Mecheleer (ed.), *Van badhuis tot eroscentrum: Prostitutie en vrouwenhandel van de middeleeuwen tot heden*, Brussels, 1995, 11-21.

Van Uytven R., *De papegaai van de paus. Mens en dier in de middeleeuwen*, Leuven, 2000.

Verwerft B., *De beul in het Markizaat van Antwerpen tijdens de Bourgondische en Habsburgse periode (1405-1550)*, unpublished master's thesis, Ghent University, 2007.

About the authors

Andrea Bardyn (°1991) is a research fellow at KU Leuven. She studies the social and gender history of Low Country towns in the late Middle Ages, particularly inequalities between men and women in the economy, division of labour, and marital power relationships.

Chanelle Delameillieure (°1992) is a lecturer in medieval history at KU Leuven – KULAK (Kortrijk). Her research examines marital conflicts and choice of partner in the Low Countries in the late Middle Ages. Her interests include family history, legal history, and the history of women and of gender.

Jelle Haemers (°1980) is a professor at KU Leuven. He studies the social and political history of medieval towns in the southern Low Countries. His research includes work on the Burgundian period, gender history, and the history of democracy.

Kim Overlaet (°1987) is a postdoctoral researcher at the University of Antwerp. She studies the importance of family support for elderly men and women needing care in Leiden and Mechelen at the beginning of the modern period. She is particularly interested in the evolution of family structures and social networks.

Nena Vandeweerdt (°1993) is a postdoctoral researcher at the University of the Basque Country (in Vittoria). She is conducting a comparative study of employment opportunities for women in Brabant and in Biscay (in the Basque Country) in the fifteenth and sixteenth centuries. She focuses on women's positions in guilds and in the informal market system.

www.ingramcontent.com/pod-product-compliance
Lightning Source LLC
Chambersburg PA
CBHW051116230426
43667CB00014B/2601